métro

pour l'Écosse

Rouge

Teacher's Guide

Claire Bleasdale

Christine Ross

Heinemann

Heinemann Educational Publishers, Halley Court, Jordan Hill,
Oxford OX2 8EJ.

A division of Reed Educational & Professional Publishing Limited.

Heinemann is a registered trademark of Reed Educational &
Professional Publishing Limited.

OXFORD MELBOURNE AUCKLAND IBADAN
BLANTYRE JOHANNESBURG GABORONE
PORTSMOUTH (NH) USA CHICAGO

First published 2002

07 06 05 04 03 02
10 9 8 7 6 5 4 3 2 1

A catalogue record is available for this book from the
British Library on request.

ISBN 0 435 38133 4

Produced by Ken Vail Graphic Design, Cambridge.

Cover photograph by Paul Raferty

Printed and bound in Great Britain by Athenaeum Press Ltd.

The authors and publisher would like to thank Julie Green for her
help in writing this guide.

Contents

Introduction

Métro pour l'Écosse Vert and **Rouge** have been written specifically for the Scottish exam system and provide material to cover the whole of S3 and S4. The Student's Books are differentiated to cater for different levels of ability. Broadly speaking, **Métro pour l'Écosse Vert** is suitable for students working towards Foundation/General level at Standard Grade and Intermediate 1. **Métro pour l'Écosse Rouge** is suitable for students working towards General/Credit level at Standard Grade and Intermediate 2.

Métro pour l'Écosse is suitable for students who have followed different courses in S1 and S2 but it can also follow on from earlier stages of **Métro** (**1**, **2** and **3**). It can be used after either **Métro 2** or **Métro 3**, depending on time available. However, in most cases, teachers should allow two sessions to cover **Métro pour l'Écosse Vert** or **Rouge**.

All stages of **Métro** offer a lively, communicative approach, underpinned by clear grammatical progression.

The components

Métro pour l'Écosse Rouge consists of:
Student's Book
Cassettes
Teacher's Guide
Cahier d'exercices
Assessment Pack (Standard Grade and Intermediate)

Student's Book
The Student's Book is designed to last for two years and contains all the language required for the preparation for the Scottish exams. There are ten modules, and it is expected that the first six will be completed in the first year of the course and four in the second, allowing more time in the second year for exam preparation.

Each module begins with a **Déjà vu** section, which revises 5–14 level language. This is followed by the core teaching spreads. At the end of each module, there is a summary of the vocabulary covered, arranged into subject groups. These pages (**Mots**) will also serve as a valuable revision tool.

At the end of each module, there is also a double-page spread entitled **Entraînez-vous**. These pages are designed to help students prepare for the speaking component of the examination and for extended writing. Speaking pages (**À l'oral**) come after Modules 2, 4, 6, 8 and 10 and writing pages (**À l'écrit**) come after Modules 1, 3, 5, 7, and 9.

At the back of the Student's Book there are four further sections of practice and reference material: the **À toi!** section, the **Grammaire** section, and two vocabulary lists (**Vocabulaire**).

The **À toi!** section provides self-access reading and writing material. There are two differentiated **À toi!** pages for each module: **À toi! A** for reinforcement and **À toi! B** for extension. The **Grammaire** section explains and practises the grammar points introduced in **Métro pour l'Écosse Rouge** – see separate section of this introduction for further information. Finally, there is a comprehensive French–English word list and a shorter English–French word list.

Cassettes
There are three cassettes for **Métro pour l'Écosse Rouge**, containing listening material for both presentation and practice. The material includes passages, dialogues and interviews recorded by native speakers.

Workbooks
There are two parallel workbooks to accompany **Métro pour l'Écosse Vert** and **Rouge: Cahier d'exercices Vert** for Foundation/General and Intermediate 1 and **Cahier d'exercices Rouge** for General/Credit and Intermediate 2. The workbooks provide self-access reading and writing tasks and are ideal for homework. At the end of each module, there is a page of grammar revision and a **Bilan** page which allows students to test themselves on what language they should know from each module. References to corresponding Student's Book pages in the workbook make it clear which is the best point for each activity to be used. All workbook pages are referred to at the appropriate point in the Teacher's Guide, with a miniature version of the pages and solutions to the activities.

Teacher's Guide
The Teacher's Guide contains:
– overview grids for each module
– clear teaching notes for all activities
– solutions Student's Book activities
– solutions to Workbook activities
– full transcripts of recorded material
– matching charts for Standard Grade and
  Intermediate syllabuses

Assessment
A separate **Assessment Pack** is available to accompany **Métro pour l'Écosse Vert** and **Rouge**. Written by Douglas Angus, an experienced examiner, the design and types of question included in the pack follow the examinations' own papers and provide much-needed regular practice in developing examination skills.

Each pack contains assessment materials at three levels, making it suitable for use with **Métro pour l'Écosse Vert** and **Rouge**:
● Foundation/Intermediate 1 level
● General/Intermediate 1 & 2 level
● Credit/Intermediate 2 level

Each of the main assessment blocks represents two modules. It is suggested that one assessment block be used at the end of each term of a two-year course. In addition, there is an end-of-S3 assessment and an end-of-course assessment as a pre-examination test.

The **Métro pour l'Écosse Assessment Pack** includes the following important features:

- Assessment tasks in all four skills, suitable for Standard Grade and Intermediate 1 and 2.
- Assessment tasks which reflect the task types used in Standard Grade and Intermediate, familiarising students with examination questions from the beginning of the course.
- Assessments with clear, concise marking schemes.

Features of the Student's Book

À l'oral
There is an **À l'oral** spread after Modules 2, 4, 6, 8, and 10 which provides speaking activities based on the previous two modules. These spreads give regular practice in the three types of speaking activity required for the internally assessed speaking elements of the Standard Grade and Intermediate courses: conversations, transactions and prepared talks.

The activities on the speaking pages are designed to allow students to improve their speaking skills while working with a partner independently of teacher support. These pages also include handy hints on how students can improve their speaking grades.

À l'écrit
The **À l'écrit** spreads come after Modules 1, 3, 5, 7, and 9. They give regular, guided practice in preparing for the writing sections of Standard Grade and Intermediate examinations. Each double-page spread always starts with a model text, which acts as a stimulus to give students ideas for their own piece of work. Structured reading activities encourage students to look at the detail of the text. Students are then guided to produce accurate French sentences and build them into an extended piece of writing. The *Au Secours!* column is a feature on all of the **À l'écrit** spreads. It gives students examples of language and structures they can include in their writing, and reminds them of general points that will enable them to get a better grade.

Reading/Writing pages (*À toi!*)
The **À toi!** pages are designed to give students extra practice in independent reading and writing. There are two differentiated pages for each module: **À toi! A** offers reinforcement and **À toi! B** offers extension activities. Sometimes, the texts relate closely to the relevant modules of the book and sometimes the link is more general.

You may feel that it is useful to work with the class on the **À toi!** activities, but it should also be possible for most students to work independently, using dictionaries where appropriate.

Grammar (*Le détective*)
The key structures introduced in a spread are presented in a grammar box (*Le détective*) on the

Student's Book page, providing support for the speaking and writing activities. Structures that have already been met in **Métro pour l'Écosse Rouge** are highlighted in a *Rappel* box. *Le détective* boxes contain page references to the comprehensive grammar section at the end of the Student's Book, where grammar points are explained more fully. The **Grammaire** section also includes grammar practice activities, and there is further grammar practice on the **Grammaire** pages of the workbook.

Skills and strategies
Many of the pages of **Métro pour l'Écosse Rouge** have boxes giving students tips to improve their language-learning skills or suggesting strategies that will enhance their performance in the forthcoming examination. These are highlighted within a pin board panel to make them easily recognisable.

Skills and strategies taught in the core spreads are listed in the planning summary at the beginning of each module in the Teacher's Guide.

Use of dictionaries
Activities in the Student's Book containing vocabulary that may be unfamiliar to some students are suitable for practising dictionary skills and are highlighted using a dictionary symbol.

Creating a CV
In Modules 1–5 there are opportunities for students to create their own CV, adding more information in each module. The CV activities can be completed by all students, but are particularly relevant for students following the Intermediate 1 course.

Progression
The **Déjà vu** spreads at the start of each module are mostly devoted to language that will already be familiar to students. The remaining spreads may revise material already covered, but most will introduce new material. The spreads generally increase in difficulty as the module progresses, with the final spread of each module often containing more difficult concepts and structures. Additional activities, which teachers could use as a follow-up to material in the Student's Book, are indicated in the Teacher's Guide by ✚.

As well as the clear progression within each module, language is recycled through all the modules in a systematic spiral of revision and extension. Clear objectives are given in the Teacher's Guide, in the planning summary at the beginning of each module, to help teachers plan a programme of work appropriate for the ability groups that they teach.

Incorporating ICT

Appropriate use of ICT to support Modern Foreign Language learning is an entitlement for all students. Activities in **Métro pour l'Écosse Rouge** with an ICT component are highlighted within a computer screen in the Student's Book

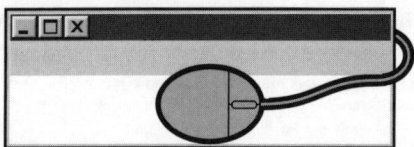

and by █ in this guide.

Word-processing and desktop publishing skills will be particularly useful for all students who are preparing external writing assignments. Students will be motivated by a steadily increasing number of completed and accurate pieces of work. Ensure that your students have a French work folder on your intranet, into which you can copy texts for adaptation or texts with gaps for students to complete.

Students should also be encouraged to e-mail contemporaries in French-speaking countries and to research authentic French on the internet. A selection of useful websites is provided on the Heinemann website (www.heinemann.co.uk/secondary/modlang/) for the most up-to-date information.

Standard Grade topic coverage in *Métro pour l'Écosse Rouge*

Main themes	Coverage in *Métro pour l'Écosse Rouge*
Relationships	Module 1: attitudes and opinions about school, polite modes of address; Module 2: members of the family, their description, interpersonal issues
Living and working with others	Module 3: leisure time; Module 4: work; Module 7: holidays
Culture and society	Module 5: towns in France and other French-speaking countries; Module 6: shopping and money; Module 8: visiting a French-speaking country
Contemporary issues	Module 5: the environment; Module 8: films and music; Module 9: healthy eating, smoking and drugs; Module 10: transport and the environment
Emotions – hopes and fears	Modules 1 & 4: hopes and fears for the future (emotions, attitudes and opinions are dealt with throughout the course)

Basic topics	Standard Grade topic development
Personal information:	
name, age, spelling: Module 2, pp. 22–23	polite language: Module 1, p. 6
nationality: Module 7, p. 110	phone language: Module 4, pp. 64–65
domicile, cardinal points: Module 5, p. 76	
Family:	
members of the family: Module 2, pp. 24–29	character description: Module 2, pp. 28–31
physical description: Module 2, pp. 26–27	interpersonal problems: Module 2, pp. 28–35
parts of the body: Module 9, p. 154	illness and accidents: Module 9, pp. 154–155; Module 10, pp. 172, 174–175
	making appointments: Module 9, p. 155
Home:	
own house and rooms: Module 8, pp. 128–133	comparison of routine: Module 8, pp. 128–131; Module 9, pp. 146–149
routine: Module 9, pp. 146	helping at home: Module 2, pp. 32–33
birthdays, days, dates: Module 2, p. 24	past events in routine: Module 3, pp. 52–53
	future events: Module 1, pp. 16–17, Module 4, pp. 66–67
School:	
school subjects: Module 1, pp. 10–11	comparison of education systems: Module 1. pp. 7–9
time: Module 1, p. 7	
Leisure:	
sports and leisure activities: Module 3, pp. 40–45	healthy eating: Module 9, pp. 150–151, pp. 158–159
	exercise: Module 3, pp. 40–45
	drugs: Module 9, pp. 148–149
	TV and films: Module 8, pp. 138–141

MÉTRO

Basic topics	Standard Grade topic development
Food:	
food and drink: Module 8, p. 146	restaurants and menus: Module 8, pp. 134–137
snack food: Module 8, pp. 150–151	making arrangements: Module 3, pp. 48–51
Towns:	
simple directions: Module 10, pp. 164–165	simple directions: Module 10, pp. 164–165
buildings: Module 5, pp. 76–77	buildings: Module 5, pp. 76–77
	directions to adults: Module 10, pp. 164–167
	tourist information: Module 5, pp. 76–81, 86–87; Module 7, pp. 116–117
	comparison of town/country: Module 5, pp. 82–83
	helping the environment: Module 5, pp. 84–85; Module 10, p. 173
Money:	
pocket money: Module 6, pp. 101–102	changing money: Module 6, pp. 102–103
simple transactions (buying gifts, food & clothes): Module 6, pp. 92–100	transactional problems: Modules 6, 8, 9 & 10
booking accommodation: Module 7, pp. 118–121	jobs: Module 4, pp. 58–59
buying snacks: Module 8, pp. 104–105	relative merits of jobs: Module 4, pp. 68–69
	work experience: Module 4, pp. 60–65
	future employment: Module 1, pp. 16–19; Module 4, pp. 66–69
Transport:	
simple transactions: Module 10, pp. 170–171	simple transactions: Module 10, pp. 170–171
	relative merits of transport: Module 10, p. 168–169
	travel information: Module 10, pp. 170–171
Holidays:	
countries and places: Module 7, p. 110	comparison of countries: Module 5, pp. 86–87
weather: Module 7, pp. 111–113	holidays: Module 7, pp. 110–123
	past and future holidays: Module 7, pp. 114–115
	ideal holidays: Module 7, pp. 122–123

Intermediate 2 topic coverage in *Métro pour l'Écosse Rouge*

Intermediate 2 themes	Module in *Métro pour l'Écosse Rouge*	Topics covered
Lifestyles	Module 2: Chez moi	Talking about self, members of the family, descriptions of people, interpersonal issues
	Module 3: Temps libre	Free time, hobbies, invitations
	Module 5: Ma ville	Home area
	Module 6: Aux magasins	Shopping
	Module 8: Bienvenue en France!	Books and films
	Module 9: En bonne forme	Keeping fit, healthy eating, health issues facing young people
Education and work	Module 1: Études	School, attitudes and opinions about school
	Module 4: Au boulot	Part-time jobs, the world of work
	Module 9: En bonne forme	Daily routine
The wider world	Module 7: En vacances	Different holiday destinations, problems on holiday
	Module 8: Bienvenue en France!	Visiting France for business or pleasure
	Module 10: Le transport	Different types of transport, problems with transport

Topics: coverage in *Métro pour l'Écosse Rouge*	Intermediate 2 topic development: coverage in *Métro pour l'Écosse Rouge*
Personal language and communication	
Lifestyles	
Family and friends: Module 2	Description of family, friends and relationships: Module 2, all
Leisure: Module 3	Leisure interests and leisure facilities: Module 3, all; Module 8, pp. 138–141
	Financing leisure: Module 6, pp. 100–101
	Personal achievements to date: Module 3, pp. 45, 52–53
Education and work	
School/College: Module 1	Daily routine: Module 1, p. 7
	Reasons for subject choice: Module 1, pp. 8–11
	Personal achievement to date: Module 1, pp. 8–11; Module 4, pp. 60–65
	Facts about school/college: Module 1, pp. 12–15
	Information about schools/colleges in France: Module 1, p. 9

Topics: coverage in *Métro pour l'Écosse Rouge*	Intermediate 2 topic development: coverage in *Métro pour l'Écosse Rouge*
The wider world	
Holidays and travel: Modules 7, 8 & 10	Making holiday/travel plans: Module 7, pp. 116–119; Module 10, pp. 168–169
	Past holidays, trips, journeys: Module 7, pp. 114–115
Tourism: Module 5	Descriptions of local area as tourist centre: Module 5, pp. 76–80, 88–89
Language in work	
Negotiating services orally	Accommodation: Module 7, pp. 118–121
	Travel: Module 10, pp. 168–171
	Shopping: Module 6, pp. 92–99
	Restaurants: Module 8, pp. 134–137
Responding to correspondence	Accommodation: Module 7, pp. 118–121
	Job interviews: Module 4, pp. 62–65

Answers to Grammaire exercises (Student's Book pp.200–221)

2.3 Articles: the partitive article 'some' (p.201)

1 pain
2 tarte
3 stylos
4 maisons
5 coca

3.1 Verbs: the infinitive (p.202)

1 attendre/*You must wait here.*
2 fumer/*It is forbidden to smoke.*
3 jouer/*I love playing football.*
4 visiter/*You can visit the castle.*
5 laver/*I help to wash the car.*

1 Il faut changer? *Must you change?*
2 Je dois partir. *I must go.*
3 Je peux vous aider? *May I help you?*
4 Pouvez-vous me donner deux kilos de carottes? *Can you give me two kilos of carrots?*
5 Je dois faire mes devoirs. *I must do my homework.*
6 Je voudrais être pilote. *I would like to be a pilot.*
7 Je veux aller à l'université. *I want to go to university.*
8 Il refuse de partir. *He refuses to leave.*
9 Je travaille bien pour avoir de bons résultats. *I work hard to have good results.*
10 Il est interdit d'entrer. *It is forbidden to enter.*

3.2 Verbs: the present tense: irregular verbs (p.203)

1 je commence *I begin, I am beginning*
2 tu aimes *you like*
3 ils finissent *they finish, they are finishing*
4 nous aidons *we help, we are helping*
5 on descend *we go down, we are going down*

1 je vais
2 tu as/vous avez
3 il fait
4 elle est
5 nous prenons

1 J'étudie l'espagnol. *I study/am studying Spanish.*
2 Elle parle allemand. *She speaks/is speaking German.*
3 L'école finit à quatre heures. *School finishes at 4 o'clock.*

4 Vous aimez le français? *Do you like French?*
5 Nous détestons l'informatique. *We hate IT.*
6 Ils font de l'équitation. *They go/are going horseriding.*
7 Tu prends le déjeuner à quelle heure? *At what time do you have/are you having lunch?*
8 Il a les cheveux noirs. *He has black hair.*
9 Je suis très impatient. *I am very impatient.*
10 Nous allons au lycée en autobus. *We go/are going to school by bus.*

3.2 Verbs: the present tense: reflexive verbs (p.204)

1 Je me douche. *I have a shower.*
2 Tu t'amuses. *You are having fun.*
3 Ils s'amusent. *They are having fun.*
4 Vous vous habillez. *You get dressed.*
5 On se lave. *We wash.*

1 Elle se réveille.
2 Je m'habille.
3 Il se couche.
4 Ils s'appellent Harry et Jenny.
5 Nous nous lavons./On se lave.

3.3 Verbs: the perfect tense (p.205)

1 J'ai joué *I played, I have played*
2 Tu as aidé *You helped, You have helped*
3 Il a fini *He finished, He has finished*
4 Elle a attendu *She waited, She has waited*
5 On a bu *We drank, We have drunk*

1 Je suis allé *I went*
2 Il est tombé *He fell*
3 Vous êtes nés *You were born*
4 Elle est venue *She came*
5 Je suis resté *I stayed*

1 Elle a vu
2 Nous avons aidé
3 Ils ont fait
4 Vous avez été/Tu as été
5 J'ai pris
6 Elle est partie
7 Ils sont arrivés
8 Je suis sorti(e)

9 Il est mort
10 Je suis né

3.4 Verbs: the perfect infinitive (p.206)

1 regardé *After having watched TV, we had dinner.*
2 acheté *After having bought the sweater, I saw some jeans I liked very much.*
3 parlé *After having talked to my father, I went out.*
4 rentrée *After having come home at midnight, she started doing her homework.*
5 couché *After having gone to bed, he watched TV.*

3.5 Verbs: the imperfect tense (p.206)

1 I was washing the car.
2 I was doing my homework.
3 I was watching a video.
4 I was playing cards with friends.
5 I was walking the dog.
6 I was sleeping.
7 I was eating a hamburger at MacDonalds.
8 I was talking on the telephone.
9 I was having a shower.
10 I was at the cinema.

1 Il pleuvait. *It was raining.*
2 Ils allaient à la pâtisserie. *They were going to the cake shop.*
3 J'étudiais l'allemand. *I was studying German.*
4 Il regardait le spectacle. *He was watching the show.*
5 J'avais souvent mal à la tête. *I often used to have a headache.*

1 L'hôtel était extra.
2 Elle avait les cheveux roux.
3 Tu étais/vous étiez fatigué(e)/(es)/(s).
4 Nous étions en France.
5 Il faisait beau.

3.6 The near future tense (p.207)

1 Je vais regarder la télévision.
2 Il va lire un livre.
3 Nous allons jouer au foot./On va jouer au foot.
4 Ils/Elles vont préparer le déjeuner.
5 Tu vas acheter une voiture./Vous allez acheter une voiture.

3.7 Verbs: the near future tense (p.207)

1 You will work in Africa.
2 You will play football for Scotland.
3 You will buy a Ferrari.
4 You will get married at the age of 30.
5 You will fall in love with a famous person.

1 Vous vous marierez … *You will get married at the age of 26.*
2 J'oublierai … *I will forget everything.*
3 Je travaillerai … *I will work very hard so that I can retire young.*
4 Vous vivrez … *You will live until you are eighty.*
5 Il rencontrera … *He will meet a very beautiful woman.*

3.8 Verbs: conditional tense (p.208)

Students give their own answers.
1 J'aimerais …/Ce serait …
I would like to work outdoors. I think it would be less boring.
2 Je préférerais …/Ce serait …
I would prefer to be an air-hostess. It would be more fun.
3 Je voudrais …/Ce serait …
I would like to be a company director. It would be exciting.
4 Il aimerait …/Il gagnerait …
He would like to be a footballer. He would earn a lot of money.
5 Elle voudrait … *She would like to travel around the world to get some experience.*

3.9 Verbs: the pluperfect tense (p.208)

1 We had noticed the driver.
2 She had said 'goodbye' for the last time.
3 He had put the sugar in his cup.
4 I had forgotten to buy the newspaper.
5 She asked us if we had already visited Germany.
6 You had already gone.
7 I had gone out before my mother.
8 She had got up early.
9 Had you got lost?
10 He had gone to bed late.

3.10 The imperative (p.208)

1 Stay in bed!
2 Take these tablets.
3 Drink this syrup.
4 Don't forget your exercise book.
5 Open the window.

3.11 Verbs: the passive voice (p.209)

1 The sea is polluted.
2 The oceans are contaminated.
3 The forest is laid waste.
4 Rare species are threatened.
5 The air is poisoned.
6 The lakes are polluted.
7 My bicycle is broken.
8 You are irritated.
9 We are destroyed.
10 She is tired.

3.12 Verbs: the present participle (p.209)

1 écoutant
2 faisant
3 rentrant
4 sortant
5 prenant

3.13 Verbs: depuis (p.209)

1 I have been a member of the club for five months.
2 I have been learning French for four years.
3 I have been living here for ten months.
4 I have been playing the piano for seven years.
5 I have been going out with Tom for four weeks.

4.1 Questions: question words (p.210)

(Examples)
1 Où est-ce que tu travailles?
2 À quelle heure est-ce que tu arrives?
3 Tu pars quand?
4 Qu'est-ce que tu préfères manger?
5 Pourquoi vas-tu à Paris?

(Examples)
1 Vous avez une serviette?
2 As-tu vu 'Superman'?
3 Tu peux m'aider?
4 Aime-t-il le café?
5 Est-ce que nous allons attendre?

4.3 Questions: quel (p.211)

1 Quelle
2 Quel
3 Quels
4 Quelles
5 Quelle

5.1 Negatives: ne … pas (p. 211)

1 Je ne loge pas dans un hôtel.
2 Je ne partage pas ma chambre.
3 Je n'ai pas de chaîne stéréo dans ma chambre.
4 Je ne m'entends pas bien avec mes parents.
5 Les boîtes ne sont pas recyclées.

5.2 Negatives: other negatives (p.211)

1 Je n'habite plus ici.
2 Je n'ai rien bu.
3 Il n'y a ni cinéma ni piscine en ville.
4 Je ne vais jamais chez le dentiste.
5 Je n'ai que €10.

5.4 Negatives: more than one negative (p.212)

1 There is no longer anyone there.
2 I don't have anything any more.
3 There is never anything in this shop.
4 I have never seen anyone in this night-club.
5 No more turns.

6.3 Adjectives: Beau, nouveau, vieux (p.213)

1 le beau garçon
2 la nouvelle maison
3 les vieux livres
4 les beaux arbres
5 le vieil arbre

6.4 Adjectives: position of adjectives (p.213)

1 un stylo rouge
2 une nouvelle règle
3 de beaux garçons
4 des filles intelligentes
5 un autre ballon

6.5 Adjectives: comparative and superlative (p.214)

1 Philippe is taller than Paul.
2 Thérèse is just as tall as Marie.
3 Marie is less tall than Paul.
4 Philippe is the tallest.
5 I am cooler than Paul.

1 He is the best football player.
2 The uniform was the worst thing.
3 It/She is the best of the two.
4 Best wishes.
5 I am in better health.

6.6 Adjectives: demonstrative adjectives (p.214)

1	ce	4	cet
2	ces	5	ces
3	cette		

6.7 Adjectives: possessive adjectives (p.214)

1	ma sœur	4	tes parents
2	leurs parents	5	sa sœur
3	notre père	6	mon collège/ mon école

6.9 Adjectives: adverbs (p.214)

1 She was listening attentively.
2 Unfortunately, he missed the train.
3 We can get there very quickly by plane.
4 Speak more slowly, please.
5 She left as quickly as possible.
6 That pleased me enormously.
7 She was seriously injured.
8 She had understood vaguely.
9 We all concentrated very well.
10 I am usually at home in the evening.

(p.215)

1 I play better basketball than volleyball.
2 She likes French better than history.
3 The best thing would be to go on holiday.
4 Everything is for the best.
5 He is better today.

7.2 Pronouns: direct object pronouns (p.215)

1 Do you like Celine Dion? – No, I hate her.
2 Do you have your homework? – No, I left it at home.
3 Where is your jacket? – I have lost it.
4 Do you get on well with your mother? – Yes, I love her very much.
5 Have you seen my purse? – Yes, you put it in the kitchen on the fridge.

7.3 Pronouns: indirect object pronouns (p.216)

1 Have you spoken to the teacher? – Yes, I have spoken to him.
2 Do they have any money? – Yes, I have given them €30.

3 Have you discussed it with your mum? – Yes, I spoke to her earlier.
4 I told them to come at eight o'clock.
5 She asked him if he wanted to go out with her.

1 Je lui donne son argent de poche.
2 Elle leur donne les billets.
3 Je lui ai dit la vérité.
4 Elle leur a donné un cadeau.
5 Tu lui as donné le livre?

7.6 Pronouns: negatives (p.216)

1 He has not bought them.
2 I have never seen her.
3 She had never met him.
4 I never eat it.
5 You will not see them any more.
6 There was neither any sunshine, nor a swimming pool there.
7 I had not noticed him.
8 They never call me.
9 I cannot give him a present.
10 Didn't you want to visit them?

7.8 Pronouns: emphatic pronouns (p.217)

1 avec lui
2 chez toi/vous
3 avec elle
4 chez moi
5 avec eux
6 pour vous

7.9 Pronouns: relative pronouns qui and que (p.217)

1	que	6	qui
2	qui	7	que
3	qui	8	qui
4	qui	9	qui
5	qu'	10	que

7.10 Pronouns: demonstrative pronouns (p.218)

- Et les gants? Tu aimes **ceux-ci**?
- Ah non, je préfère **ceux-là**.
- Regarde-moi **ces** bottes! J'adore **celles-ci**.
- Non, **celles-là** sont plus jolies.
- **Ce** pullover est bien.
- J'aime mieux **celui-ci**.
- Et **cette** jupe? Tu ne vas pas l'aimer. **Celle-là** est sûrement plus à la mode, à ton avis, non?
- Au contraire, j'aime bien **celle-ci**, je vais l'acheter.

8.2 Prepositions: to or in with names of places (p.219)

1	en	4	à
2	en	5	à
3	au		

Études

(Student's Book pages 6–23)

Topic area	Key language	Grammar	Skills/Strategies
Déjà vu (pp. 6–9) Using French in the classroom Talking about the school day Talking about school subjects	*Je ne comprends pas. Je ne sais pas. Je m'excuse ... Qu'est-ce que ça veut dire? Pouvez-vous nous aider? Je peux vous aider? Pouvez-vous répéter? Comment ça se dit en français? J'ai oublié ... Tu peux me prêter ...? Tu as ...? Je n'ai pas de ... Je peux avoir ...? un bic/cahier/crayon/livre/stylo une gomme/règle Mon lycée s'appelle .... Le lycée commence à ... et finit à ... Il y a une récréation à ... La pause de midi est à ... On a (cinq) cours le matin et (quatre) cours l'après-midi. Un cours dure (40) minutes. On va au lycée tous les jours sauf (le mercredi). Comme matières, j'ai ... [+ subjects] C'est facile/intéressant/difficile/ennuyeux/utile/nul/super/barbant/stupide/ affreux/génial. Ça m'intéresse/me passionne. On s'amuse. Ça ne m'intéresse pas. Je suis fort(e)/faible en (anglais). Le prof est sévère/sympa. J'ai trop de devoirs. Moi, j'aime/je déteste ... Moi aussi ... Je suis d'accord. Je ne suis pas d'accord.*	*Je n'ai pas de ...* Question words *à* + time Adjectives don't agree after *c'est ...* Regular present tense *–er* verbs *depuis* + present tense	Using French in the classroom Agreeing and disagreeing
1 Emploi du temps (pp. 10–11) Talking about your timetable	*Je suis sportif/sportive. Je suis fort(e) en sport. Le prof est compréhensif/méchant/sévère/sympa. C'est compliqué/nul/pénible/facile/inutile/passionnant/utile/simple. On a trop de devoirs. On n'a pas assez de devoirs. Le prof va trop vite. Le prof est trop lent. Je suis faible en EPS. Je suis paresseux/euse.*		Using *car* and *parce que* Using phrases to express opinions and qualifying opinions
2 Mon lycée (pp. 12–13) Describing your school/ college	*Le collège se trouve près du centre-ville/en banlieue/à la campagne/dans un petit village. C'est un collège mixte. Il y a une très grande bibliothèque/un gymnase/une cantine. C'est très moderne. C'est un vieux bâtiment gris à ... étages. On a des courts de tennis. C'est animé/calme/démodé/moderne. C'est un vieux/grand/petit bâtiment à (3) étages. Il y a 500 élèves, 56 professeurs. Je fais partie d'un club/Je vais au club de photographie/informatique/ échecs/escalade/danse/gymnastique/musique/théâtre. Je fais partie de l'orchestre/de l'équipe de foot/volley/hockey. Je ne fais pas partie d'un club.*	*Je fais partie de ...* Irregular verbs: *aller, faire*	Using time indicators

Topic area	Key language	Grammar	Skills/Strategies
3 Le règlement (pp. 14–15) Talking about rules and regulations	*On ne doit pas fumer. Il ne faut pas porter le maquillage. On ne doit pas utiliser les portables. On ne doit pas porter les bijoux. On doit apporter tout son équipement.* *On doit respecter les autres. Il faut arriver à l'heure. Il ne faut pas manger en classe.* *Chez nous … C'est juste/Ce n'est pas juste. On doit avoir le droit de …* *C'est une bonne/mauvaise idée. C'est une idée bizarre.* *C'est pratique/bête/ridicule/pas cher/cher/démodé.* *On sait toujours quoi mettre. Ça supprime l'individualité.* *Il y a moins de différences entre les classes sociales. Tout le monde se ressemble.* *L'individualité est importante.*	Using *on* *Il faut/On doit* + infinitive	Using set expressions in discussions Talking about advantages and disadvantages
4 Après le collège (pp. 16–17) Talking about plans for the future	*D'abord …/Après …/Ensuite … L'année prochaine …* *Je vais gagner un peu d'argent/voyager/travailler/passer mes examens/quitter le collège/faire un apprentissage/continuer mes études/passer mon bac/aller au lycée/à l'université/faire un stage/perfectionner mon français/faire une formation générale/professionnelle.* *Si possible je vais …*	The immediate future tense Using *si* + immediate future	Using time indicators
5 Les problèmes (pp. 18–19) Discussing difficulties at school and for the future	Language from the whole of Module 1	Expressions of quantity Determiners	Being familiar with small but important words Recording new words and phrases
Entraînez-vous: À l'écrit (pp. 20–21) Les études	Language from Module 1		Extended writing Writing an e-mail Using linking words
À toi! A and B (pp. 180–181)	Language from Module 1		Reading and writing skills

The vocabulary and structures taught in Module 1 are summarised on the **Mots** pages of the Student's Book, pages 22–23.
Further speaking practice on the language of the module is provided on **À l'oral**, page 36.
Assessment tasks for Modules 1 and 2 combined are provided in the separate Assessment Pack.

Déjà vu

(Student's Book pages 6–9)

Main topics and objectives

- Using French in the classroom
- Talking about the school day
- Talking about school subjects

Key language

Je ne comprends pas. Je ne sais pas.
Je m'excuse … Qu'est-ce que ça veut dire?
Pouvez-vous nous aider? Je peux vous aider?
Pouvez-vous répéter?
Comment ça se dit en français?
J'ai oublié … Tu peux me prêter … ?
Tu as … ? Je n'ai pas de …
Je peux avoir … ?
   un bic/cahier/crayon/livre/stylo
   une gomme/règle
Mon lycée s'appelle …
Le lycée commence à … et finit à …
Il y a une récréation à … La pause de midi est à …
On a (cinq) cours le matin et (quatre) cours l'après-midi.
Un cours dure (40) minutes.
On va au lycée tous les jours sauf (le mercredi).
Comme matières, j'ai …
C'est facile/intéressant/difficile/ennuyeux/utile/nul/
super/barbant/stupide/affreux/génial.
Ça m'intéresse/me passionne.
Ça ne m'intéresse pas.
On s'amuse.
Je suis fort(e)/faible en (anglais).
Le prof est sévère/sympa.
J'ai trop de devoirs.

Grammar

- *Je n'ai pas de …*
- Question words
- *à* + time
- Adjectives following *c'est* (no agreement)
- Regular *–er* verbs in the present tense
- *depuis* + present tense

Skills/Strategies

- Using French in the classroom
- Agreeing and disagreeing

Resources

Cassette A, side 1
Cahier d'exercices, pages 2–4

The aim of this section is to ensure that students are up to speed with core vocabulary areas, without boring them. Use the **Déjà vu** pages for quick whole-class revision, for self-access or homework material, as appropriate.

Get students to brainstorm all the classroom language they know. This is an excellent opportunity to revise asking questions.

1a Listen. Which speech bubble is used in each dialogue?

Listening (1–8). Classroom language. Students match the sentences they hear to the correct speech bubble.

Tapescript

1 – *Oh là là, j'ai un problème … Ça, qu'est-ce que c'est?*
   – *Je m'excuse, je ne sais pas.*
2 – *Excusez-moi, monsieur, qu'est-ce que ça veut dire?*
   – *Eh bien, ça, c'est difficile à expliquer!*
3 – *J'ai oublié le mot pour 'help' en français.*
   – *On dit 'au secours'.*
4 – *'Ruler', comment ça se dit en français?*
   – *C'est une règle.*
5 – *Alors, je peux vous aider?*
   – *Est-ce que je peux avoir un stylo?*
6 – *Tu peux me prêter une gomme?*
   – *Je suis désolé, je ne comprends pas.*
7 – *Pouvez-vous nous aider?*
   – *J'arrive.*

8 – *J'adore les maths.*
   – *Pouvez-vous répéter, s'il vous plaît?*
   – *J'ai dit 'j'adore les maths'.*

Answers

| 1 c | 2 a | 3 g | 4 h | 5 e | 6 b | 7 d | 8 f |

Tip box

Encourage your students to use as much French as they possibly can in the classroom. Students could create a grid to record every time they use a classroom phrase in the correct context.

1b Match the English sentences to the right speech bubbles.

Reading (1–8). Students match the speech bubbles from **1a** to the correct English sentences.

Answers

| 1 g | 2 e | 3 f | 4 b | 5 d | 6 a | 7 h | 8 c |

2a Listen and identify the right picture.

Listening (1–7). Students match each sentence to the correct picture.

Tapescript

1 *Madame, j'ai oublié ma gomme.*
2 *Monsieur, je n'ai pas de stylo.*
3 *J'ai oublié mon cahier de français.*
4 *Tu peux me prêter un crayon, s'il te plaît?*

5 Je n'ai pas de règle, mademoiselle.
6 Madame, je n'ai pas de livre.
7 Je peux avoir un bic, s'il vous plaît, monsieur?

Answers

1 e	2 a	3 d	4 b	5 g	6 f	7 c

2b In pairs. Use the key language box and the pictures in **2a**. Take turns to say a sentence and reply.

Speaking. Students work in pairs to practise *un/une*, *mon/ma* and *je n'ai pas de* in the context of requesting classroom objects. Stress from the outset that they should swap roles as soon as one exchange is completed.

Tip box

Revise the structure *je n'ai pas de …* by revisiting language students are very familiar with, e.g. *je n'ai pas d'animal, je n'ai pas de frère/de sœur*.

3a Copy and complete Flore's statements about school.

Reading (1–8). Students write the complete sentences, using information from Flore's timetable. Make an electronic version of these gapped sentences available to your students, or ask the students to copy-type them. The same framework can then be used for **3b** and **3d**.

Answers

> 1 Mon lycée s'appelle le Lycée Jules Verne.
> 2 Normalement, le lycée commence à 8 heures et finit à 17 heures (one hour after the start of the final lesson).
> 3 Il y a une récréation à 10 heures.
> 4 La pause de midi est à midi et quart.
> 5 D'habitude, on a 4 cours le matin et 3 cours l'après-midi.
> 6 Un cours dure 60 minutes.
> 7 On va au lycée tous les jours sauf le mercredi et le dimanche.
> 8 Comme matières, j'ai chimie, espagnol, biologie, maths, français, histoire-géo, anglais, musique, physique, dessin, technologie et EPS.

3b Listen to the interview about a new school in France. Complete the 8 statements from **3a** with the new information.

Listening (1–8). Students listen and make notes in French, then type in the relevant details.

Tapescript

– Eh bien Anne-Claire, comment s'appelle ton lycée?
– Mon lycée s'appelle le Lycée Victor Hugo,
  V… I… C… T… O… R… H… U… G… O.
– Et le lycée commence et finit à quelle heure?
– On commence à huit heures et quart, et on finit à quatre heures et demie normalement.

– Il y a une récréation à quelle heure?
– La récré est à dix heures et quart.
– La pause de midi est à quelle heure?
– On déjeune à midi et demie.
– Tu as combien de cours par jour?
– Il y a six cours par jour dans notre lycée, quatre cours le matin et deux cours l'après-midi.
– Et les cours durent combien de temps?
– Les cours durent une heure.
– Quels jours vas-tu au lycée?
– Chez nous, on va au lycée tous les jours sauf le samedi et le dimanche. On a changé pour donner un week-end complet aux élèves et aux profs.
– Quelles sont tes matières?
– Mes matières obligatoires sont le français, les maths, l'histoire, la géographie, l'anglais et le sport. Je fais aussi de la musique et de l'EMT.
– Qu'est-ce que c'est exactement, l'EMT?
– C'est la technologie.

Answers

> 1 Mon lycée s'appelle le Lycée Victor Hugo.
> 2 Normalement, le lycée commence à 8h15 et finit à 4h30.
> 3 Il y a une récréation à 10h15.
> 4 La pause de midi est à midi et demie.
> 5 D'habitude, on a 4 cours le matin et 2 cours l'après-midi.
> 6 Un cours dure une heure.
> 7 On va au lycée tous les jours sauf le samedi et le dimanche.
> 8 Comme matières, j'ai français, maths, histoire, géographie, anglais, sport, musique, et EMT.

Tip box

Revise the use of question words by linking each one to a familiar question (avoiding *comment t'appelles-tu?*!).

Le détective

at + time. Practise asking and answering questions about 'at what time' by using the starting times of well-known TV programmes and events as well as school times: EastEnders, the news, football matches, etc.

3c In pairs. Take turns to ask and answer these questions, using the key language box.

Speaking. Point out to students that they already have most of the answers to these questions in the framework they have used in **3a** and **3b**.

3d Write 8 statements about your school/college, using your answers from **3c**.

Writing. Consolidation exercise to formalise language used in **3c**.

➕ As a follow-up to work on this page, students could e-mail their partner school or a school with a web-site and e-mail address, asking the same questions.

Student's Book, pages 8-9

Introduce work on this spread by revising the school subjects. Put them into gender groups to help students remember whether subjects are masculine or feminine (or plural). Point out that most subjects are feminine, apart from the languages, sport and drawing (which are activities occurring outside the classroom as well). Then, in groups, play a version of 'My grandmother went shopping'. Student A: *Moi, le lundi, j'ai maths.* Student B: *Moi, le lundi, j'ai maths et géographie,* etc.

4a Listen to the interviews. Which subjects do they like and dislike, and why?

Listening (1–8). Students listen for subjects, likes and dislikes and reasons. If necessary, they could listen several times, concentrating on one piece of information at a time.

Tapescript

1 J'aime l'anglais et le dessin, mais je n'aime pas la technologie, c'est ennuyeux.
2 J'adore les maths, mais je n'aime pas le français, je trouve ça stupide.
3 Je déteste la musique parce que c'est ennuyeux, mais j'aime les sciences et le sport. Je trouve ça bien.
4 J'adore le français, mais je déteste l'allemand, c'est nul.
5 Je n'aime pas tellement l'histoire, je trouve ça un peu ennuyeux. Par contre, j'aime beaucoup la géographie, c'est super.
6 J'aime l'informatique, c'est génial, mais je n'aime pas les maths, c'est barbant.
7 Ce que je déteste, c'est les sciences et la technologie. J'adore les langues, surtout l'anglais et l'allemand: ça me passionne.
8 J'adore l'éducation physique: on s'amuse et c'est bon pour la santé. Je n'aime pas l'histoire, ça ne m'intéresse pas du tout, et je déteste le dessin. Je trouve ça affreux.

Answers

	:)	reason(s)	:(	reason(s)
1	English, art	–	technology	boring
2	maths	–	French	stupid
3	sciences, sport	good	music	boring
4	French	–	German	rubbish
5	geography	great	history	boring
6	ICT	good	maths	boring
7	languages (English, German)	interest him	sciences	–
			technology	–
8	sport	fun, good for health	history	no interest
			art	terrible

Tip box

After *c'est*, adjectives don't agree. Draw your students' attention to this handy, error-saving fact.

4b Match the pictures to the reasons in the key language box.

Reading (1–10). Students demonstrate understanding by writing a phrase from the key language box to match each picture.

Answers

a Le prof est sympa.
b C'est ennuyeux.
c Je suis fort(e) en maths.
d Le prof est sévère.
e C'est facile.
f C'est utile.
g C'est intéressant.
h Je suis faible en maths.
i J'ai trop de devoirs.
j C'est difficile.

Before going on to **4c**, look at the key language box accompanying it. At General/Credit and Intermediate 2 levels, students should readily be able to express agreement and disagreement. Feed expressions of agreement/disagreement to students gradually. In groups, use a pile of subject cards and a randomly ordered pile of smiley/frowny face cards face down to practise first *Moi aussi, j'aime/Ah non, moi je déteste,* then *Je (ne) suis (pas) d'accord,* then both.

4c In pairs. Take turns to ask if your partner likes the same subjects as you. Use the key language box to help you.

Speaking. Students now use the language they have practised to express their own opinions, as well as agreement and disagreement.

Le détective

depuis. Draw students' attention to the use of the present tense: 'I have been learning, and still am.'

5a Listen. Note the languages and how long these people have been learning them.

Listening (1–5). Students hear the *depuis* structure and each time note the language and the length of time.

Tapescript

1 J'apprends l'anglais depuis 5 ans.
2 J'apprends l'italien depuis 4 ans.
3 J'apprends l'espagnol depuis 6 ans.
4 J'apprends le latin depuis 2 ans.
5 J'apprends le français depuis 3 mois.

Answers

1 English – 5 years
2 Italian – 4 years
3 Spanish – 6 years
4 Latin – 2 years
5 French – 3 months

5b Write how long you have been learning these subjects for.

Writing (1–4). Students now use *depuis* actively to write sentences based on the pictures.

Answers

1 J'apprends le français depuis 4 ans.
2 J'apprends l'anglais depuis 6 ans.
3 J'apprends la musique depuis 1 an.
4 J'apprends les maths depuis 8 ans.

Before moving on to exercise **6**, find out how much students know already about the school, college and university systems in France. You may need to explain the differences between a *collège* and a *lycée*, and the function of a *lycée technique* (the nearest equivalent in Scotland being FE college). Use the diagram on page 9 to help you explain the system.

6 Look at the structure of the French education system. Find the French equivalent for:

Reading (1–6). Students find equivalent expressions in French for elements of the Scottish school and FE systems. These are all terms which they will find useful when comparing systems.

Answers

1 École primaire	**2** Lycée technique	**3** Baccalauréat
4 Formation	**5** Apprentissage	**6** Brevet

7a Read this e-mail and choose the correct phrase to complete each sentence.

Reading (1–6). Students use dictionaries and the diagram to complete this very structured comprehension task.

Answers

1 c	**2** c	**3** b	**4** c	**5** b	**6** c

7b Use what Julien has written in the first paragraph to write 75 words about your school/college. Make sure what you write is very accurate by only changing the words in red.

Writing. Encourage your students to write French they know will be accurate in the first instance.

Le détective

-er verbs. Point out to students that the only really irregular *-er* verb is *aller*, so they can be sure their French will be accurate as long as they choose an *-er* verb from the dictionary! Draw your students' attention to *parler* and *écouter* in the margins of each speaking and listening exercise.

7c **CV** Choose at least 5 statements about your school and combine them in a paragraph under the title *École* on disc. Call the document CV.doc. You will be adding further data in Modules 2–5.

This activity is very motivating for students. Firstly, it has concrete relevance to potential future work experience abroad. Secondly, students will see their CV taking shape as the course progresses. They should be encouraged to incorporate their most impressive writing into their CV.

Further practice of the language and vocabulary of these spreads is provided as follows:

Cahier d'exercices, pages 2–4

1 Emploi du temps

MODULE 1 ÉTUDES

(Student's Book pages 10–11)

Main topics and objectives

● Talking about your timetable

Key language

Je suis sportif/sportive. Je suis fort(e) en sport.
Le prof est compréhensif.
C'est compliqué. C'est nul/pénible.
Le prof est méchant/sévère/sympa.
C'est facile/inutile/passionnant/utile/simple.
On a trop de devoirs. On n'a pas assez de devoirs.
Le prof va trop vite. Le prof est trop lent.
Je suis faible en EPS.
Je suis paresseux/euse.

Skills/Strategies

● Using *car* and *parce que*
● Using phrases to express opinions and qualifying opinions

Resources

Cassette A side 1
À l'oral, page 36: Conversation 1

Introduce the spread by helping students, in pairs or small groups, to generate more sophisticated reasons for liking and disliking subjects. They could either do this from scratch, or you could give them a list of *-er* verbs they may find useful e.g. *expliquer, aider, trouver que, penser que, travailler, étudier, améliorer,* etc. Draw their attention to the tip box at the top of page 11.

1 Look at the sentences in the key language box. Find the sentence with the opposite meaning.

Reading. This activity helps make students more aware of opposites, in order to be able to express agreement and disagreement more readily later on.

Answers

je suis sportif/sportive : je suis paresseux/euse
le prof est compréhensif : le prof est sévère
c'est simple : c'est compliqué
le prof est sympa : le prof est méchant
c'est facile : c'est pénible
on a trop de devoirs : on n'a pas assez de devoirs
c'est passionnant : c'est nul
c'est utile : c'est inutile
le prof va trop vite : le prof est trop lent
je suis fort(e) en sport : je suis faible en EPS

2a Listen to Flore talking about her subjects. Copy the grid and complete it in English.

Listening (1–5). Students listen and use the key language from **1** to complete the grid.

Tapescript

1 *Au collège, ma matière préférée, c'est le dessin. J'aime le dessin parce que le professeur est très sympa et les cours sont intéressants.*
2 *J'aime aussi l'EPS. Je suis sportive et j'adore le rugby et le basket.*

3 *Je n'aime pas tellement les sciences, surtout la physique. Je trouve ça très difficile, et en plus je suis plutôt faible en sciences.*
4 *Quant à l'histoire-géo, c'est assez intéressant mais on a souvent trop de devoirs: 2 ou 3 heures par semaine, c'est fatigant.*
5 *L'anglais est très bien. Notre professeur est très bizarre et j'adore écouter des cassettes et parler anglais en classe. L'anglais, c'est extra!*

Answers

	subject	opinion	reasons
1	art	☺	teacher is nice it's interesting
2	sport	☺	likes rugby and basketball, she's sporty
3	sciences	☹	difficult + not good at it
4	history/geography	😐	too much homework, tiring, but quite interesting
5	English	☺	strange teacher, likes the cassette and speaking English in class

Tip box

Draw your students attention to the words *car* and *parce que* and how they can be used. Encourage students to give reasons every time they give an opinion!

2b Write these sentences in French.

Writing (1–6). Students practise using *car* and *parce que* by giving reasons for each opinion, using the picture prompts.

20

ÉTUDES • MODULE

Answers

> 1 J'aime les maths car le prof est sympa et c'est
>   intéressant.
> 2 J'aime les sciences parce que je suis fort en sciences/
>   c'est facile.
> 3 Je n'aime pas la musique car c'est ennuyeux et c'est
>   difficile.
> 4 Je n'aime pas l'anglais parce que je suis faible en
>   anglais et j'ai trop de devoirs.
> 5 J'aime le français car c'est facile et utile.
> 6 Je n'aime pas le sport parce que le prof est trop sévère.

Before going on to activity **3a**, go over the sentences with students, to make this an exercise in recognition and not in reading and listening comprehension combined.

3a Listen and note which phrases form a complete sentence.

Listening (1–8). Students listen and build sentences from the phrases given.

Tapescript

1 La physique est assez difficile, mais le prof est compréhensif, il nous aide beaucoup.
2 J'aime l'informatique – c'est compliqué mais je pense que c'est très important pour l'avenir.
3 Je n'aime pas du tout la géographie, je trouve ça pénible.
4 Je pense que le dessin est inutile. En plus, le prof est nul.
5 Moi, je n'aime pas les sciences, je trouve ça compliqué – j'ai horreur de ça et aussi le prof me fait peur.
6 L'histoire-géo, le prof va trop vite – je n'aime pas ça.
7 Je trouve le théâtre passionnant. Monter une pièce, c'est sensass.
8 Ma matière préférée, c'est les travaux manuels, le prof est super sympa.

Answers

1 m, d	**2** b, h	**3** i	**4** f	**5** g, e	**6** a	**7** k, l	**8** c, j

➕ Students write out the five sentences most relevant to them, or change details in five sentences to match their own opinions.

Tip box

This reminds students to use one of the useful phrases *À mon avis …* and *Je pense que …* every time they give an opinion and to give a reason to justify an opinion. Ask them to go back to **2b**, swapping the reasons given with the smiley faces for those given with the frowny faces. This generates sentences like *Je n'aime pas les maths, car c'est difficile et un peu ennuyeux.*

3b In pairs. Take turns to ask for and give the opinions in the pictures. Then ask and answer questions of your own.

Speaking. Students give the opinions represented by the pictures, then develop this by asking and answering their own questions.

3c Develop a conversation with your partner about your favourite subjects. Take turns to ask and answer questions.

Speaking. This exercise brings together much of the language and structures covered so far.

4a Read Mario's e-mail and decide whether the statements are true or false.

Reading (1–7). This provides a comprehension check of simple statements of liking and disliking, as well as of more complicated expressions.

Answers

1 true	**2** false	**3** false	**4** false
5 false	**6** false	**7** true	

4b These are Mélanie's opinions. What is she talking about?

Reading (1–5). This provides a further comprehension test on the contents of Mario's e-mail.

Answers

> 1 *le collège* – school
> 2 *les choses scientifiques et techniques* – technical and
>   scientific things
> 3 *le travail pratique* – practical work
> 4 *le sport* – sport

4c Write an e-mail answering Mario's questions.

Writing. Students consolidate all the language of the spread in writing their own e-mail.

> Further practice of the language and vocabulary of this spread is provided as follows:
>
> À l'oral, page 36: Conversation 1

2 Mon lycée

(Student's Book pages 12–13)

Main topics and objectives

● Describing your school/college

Key language

Le collège se trouve …
C'est un collège mixte.
Il y a une très grande bibliothèque.
C'est très moderne. C'est un vieux bâtiment gris à (2) étages.
On a des courts de tennis.
C'est animé/calme/démodé/moderne.
C'est un vieux/grand/petit bâtiment à (3) étages.
Le collège se trouve …
  près du centre-ville/en banlieue/à la campagne/ dans un petit village.
Il y a 500 élèves, 56 professeurs.
un gymnase/une cantine
Je fais partie d'un club. Je vais au club …

de photographie/d'informatique/d'échecs/ d'escalade/de danse/de gymnastique/de musique/ de théâtre.
Je fais partie de l'orchestre/de l'équipe de foot/volley/hockey.
Je ne fais pas partie d'un club.

Grammar

● *Je fais partie de …*
● Irregular verbs: *faire, aller*

Skills/Strategies

● Using time indicators

Resources

Cassette A side 1
Cahier d'exercices, pages 5–6 (exs 6–7b)

Introduce this spread by getting the students to answer questions about their own school or college. You could provide a floor plan of the building (e.g. a fire-drill map), either on OHT or as a paper copy, and ask questions orally or in written form. Ask questions which require answers similar to those in the key language box, e.g. *Où se trouve Kemnay Academy? C'est comment? Il y a combien de professeurs?* This revises comprehension of question words (covered in the **Déjà vu** section on page 7) and presents new vocabulary.

1a Find the right sentence for each picture.

Reading (a–i). Students show understanding by matching each sentence in the key language box to a picture.

Answers

a Il y a environ mille élèves.
b On a des courts de tennis.
c C'est un collège mixte.
d C'est très moderne.
e Le collège se trouve près du centre de Paris.
f Il y a quatre-vingts professeurs.
g C'est un vieux bâtiment gris, à quatre étages.
h Il y a une très grande bibliothèque.
i C'est très animé.

1b Listen to the descriptions and write the correct letter for each one.

Listening (1–3). Students show understanding of the main details in the descriptions of three different schools, by matching them to the pictures.

Tapescript

1 *Dans mon collège on est 500 élèves et je crois qu'il y a trente-cinq profs … je ne sais pas exactement. Le collège est un peu démodé. C'est un bâtiment traditionnel avec une cour. Il se trouve près du centre commercial.*
2 *Mon collège se trouve dans la banlieue de Paris. C'est une construction énorme, puisque nous sommes mille cinq cents élèves. C'est un bâtiment à cinq étages qui est assez moderne. Ce que j'aime bien, c'est qu'il y a beaucoup de verdure.*
3 *On vient de construire notre collège: c'est très, très moderne et je l'aime bien. Le bâtiment est en verre et en métal. C'est cool, on aime bien parce qu'il y a des espaces pour nous aussi où on peut se reposer, jouer au ping-pong ou au baby-foot. C'est très bien fait.*

Answers

| 1 b | 2 a | 3 c |

1c In pairs. Take turns to change the sentences in **1a** with your own details.

Speaking. Students practise the language they were introduced to at the start of the spread, adapting the language to describe their own school.

2a Read the description. Which school is being described?

Reading. Students have plenty of clues to help them identify which school from the two pictured is being described.

Answer

a

2b Describe the other school in **2a**, using the text in **2a** as a model.

Writing. Students now demonstrate greater understanding of the text by changing details in order to describe the other school.

Answer

Possible answer:
Il y a la cantine au premier étage ainsi que les salles de classe. Au rez-de-chaussée on a les bureaux: le secrétariat et la salle des profs. On a aussi la bibliothèque.

Revise free-time activites and time indicators (*souvent, tous les lundis, le mercredi après-midi, deux fois par semaine*) before going on to **3a**. Do this by putting a list of time indicators on the board/OHT and miming a sport/activity. Students say e.g. *Je joue au ping-pong une fois par semaine.*

3a Listen. Note the school activities and, if mentioned, when they take place.

Listening (1–5). Students listen for more than one activity and more than one time indicator each time.

Tapescript

1 Il n'y a pas assez de clubs dans notre collège. Moi, je fais partie du club d'informatique et du club de danse. On fait de la danse le mercredi après-midi et il y a un club d'informatique tous les soirs: on y va quand on veut.

2 Moi, je suis plutôt sportif. Je fais partie de l'équipe de foot: on s'entraîne tous les lundis. Je fais partie aussi de l'équipe de hockey, et j'adore ça. Normalement le hockey, c'est le jeudi.

3 J'ai de la chance, il y a beaucoup de clubs et d'ateliers dans mon collège. Je participe à l'atelier théâtre et je fais partie de l'orchestre aussi: je joue de la clarinette. Sinon, des fois je vais au club de photographie: j'aime bien prendre des photos. Ça a lieu le vendredi après les cours.

4 Je fais partie d'un atelier de théâtre qui a lieu tous les mercredis après-midi. C'est génial. Une fois par an, on monte une pièce. Cette année, c'est 'Alice au pays des merveilles.'

5 Les clubs au bahut, c'est un peu nul. Enfin y a des clubs d'échecs, d'informatique par exemple, mais il n'y pas d'activités, rien de spécial. S'il y avait un club d'escalade, moi j'irais, mais pour l'instant, j'y vais pas. Y a rien d'intéressant.

Answers

	activity	when?
1	dancing	Wednesday afternoon
	ICT	every evening
2	football	every Monday
	hockey	Thursdays
3	theatre	
	orchestra	
	photography	Friday after school
4	theatre	every Wednesday afternoon
5	chess	
	computer	
	climbing	

Le détective

faire and *aller*. Encourage your students to learn irregular verb paradigms off by heart. These two verbs together (in the *je/tu/il* and *nous/vous/ils* parts only) fit a rap rhythm, or can be sung to the tune of 'Here we go Louby-Lou'.

Before going on to **3b**, ask students about their extra-curricular activities. Make sure they can say or construct all the activities they will need in French.

3b Conduct a survey in your group to find out about extra-curricular activities. Ask these questions.

Speaking. Students practise asking and answering questions about clubs.

➕ Students make a bar chart or pie chart from the information they have gathered.

Tip box

This encourages students to use time indicators as much as possible. They can generate their own list: ask them to find as many as possible in groups in a short period of time, e.g. 3 minutes.

3c Write a report of your findings in **3b**.

Writing. Students write up the information they have gathered and made into charts. They may also need vocabulary like: *la plupart des étudiants, la moitié de la classe, deux sur cinq étudiants, presque personne ne …*

Further practice of the language and vocabulary of this spread is provided as follows:

Cahier d'exercices, pages 5–6 (exs 6–7b)

3 Le règlement

(Student's Book pages pages 14–15)

Main topics and objectives

● Talking about rules and regulations

Key language

On ne doit pas fumer.
Il ne faut pas porter le maquillage.
On ne doit pas utiliser les portables.
On ne doit pas porter les bijoux.
On doit apporter tout son équipement.
On doit respecter les autres.
Il faut arriver à l'heure.
Il ne faut pas manger en classe.
Chez nous …
C'est juste … Ce n'est pas juste …
On doit avoir le droit de …
C'est une bonne/mauvaise idée.
C'est une idée bizarre.
C'est pratique/bête/ridicule/pas cher/cher/démodé.
On sait toujours quoi mettre.

Ça supprime l'individualité.
Il y a moins de différences entre les classes sociales.
Tout le monde se ressemble.
L'individualité est importante.

Grammar

● Using *on*
● *Il faut/On doit* + infinitive

Skills/Strategies

● Using set expressions in discussions
● Talking about advantages and disadvantages

Resources

À toi! A, page 180
Cassette A side 1
Cahier d'exercices, page 6 (exs 8a & 8b)

Introduce the spread by a dictionary activity. Put two columns on the board/OHT headed *Il faut …* and *Il ne faut pas …* Explain that these mean 'you have to…' and 'you mustn't'. Give students a time limit (e.g. 5 minutes) to write as many of your school/college rules as they can using these structures + an infinitive. Collate their answers at the end of the 5 minutes.

1a Match the pictures to the phrases in the key language box.

Reading (a–h). Students demonstrate understanding by matching the rules to the pictures.

Answers

a Il ne faut pas porter le maquillage.
b On ne doit pas utiliser les portables.
c On ne doit pas fumer.
d On doit respecter les autres.
e Il ne faut pas manger en classe.
f On ne doit pas porter des bijoux.
g On doit apporter son équipement.
h Il faut arriver à l'heure.

Tip box

Using *on*. Use this box to help your students vary their language by using *on* rather than 'we' or 'you', where appropriate.

Le détective

il faut and *on doit*. Revisit the use of dependent infinitives after a finite verb. Look together at examples of this in the sentences of **1a**. **1b** provides further practice of this point.

1b Write the following in French.

Writing. Students translate the sentences into French. This activity formalizes the activity in **1a** and the initial brainstorming activity.

Answers

1 Il faut arriver à huit heures et demie.
2 Il ne faut pas boire en classe.
3 On ne doit pas porter des boucles d'oreille.
4 On doit écouter les profs.
5 Il faut apporter ses cahiers/livres.

Tip box

Useful expressions. Again, stress to your students the importance of varying their language when they speak or write.

1c Do any of the rules above apply in your school? What do you think of them? Discuss them with your partner.

Speaking. Students discuss the rules in their own school/college, and give their opinion of them in French. You may need to structure this activity for your students. Put rules (or symbols) onto individual prompt cards and put the cards in a pile face down. Make another pile of 'opinion' cards (e.g. *c'est (pas) juste, c'est une bonne/mauvaise idée, c'est une idée pratique/bizarre*). Once students are used to giving a rule + an opinion, get them to justify the opinion!

✚ Students write their own school rules, or invent some more bizarre rules.

2a Listen and note whether these people are for (✔) or against (✗) school uniform.

Listening (1–5). This provides gist listening where students note an overall opinion.

Tapescript

1 L'uniforme, c'est une bonne idée à mon avis. C'est pratique, c'est pas cher et on sait toujours quoi mettre.

2 Je suis pour l'uniforme. J'aimerais bien porter un uniforme, on sait toujours quoi mettre, c'est pratique. L'inconvénient, c'est que des fois on n'a pas le droit de porter de baskets. Je n'aimerais pas ça.

3 Je suis contre l'uniforme. Ça supprime l'individualité, tout le monde se ressemble, c'est démodé. C'est une idée bizarre. La seule bonne chose que je peux voir, c'est que, grâce à l'uniforme, il y a peut-être moins de différences entre les classes sociales, mais je ne suis pas entièrement persuadée.

4 Je n'aime pas l'idée de l'uniforme. Je pense que l'individualité est importante dans la vie. Tout le monde a le droit de s'exprimer. L'uniforme, c'est un peu bête.

5 L'uniforme est bien parce qu'avec un uniforme, il y a très peu de différences entre les classes sociales et c'est important, ça. Malheureusement, l'argent fait tout et il faut décourager ça au collège.

Answers

1 ✔	2 ✔	3 ✗	4 ✗	5 ✔

2b Listen again and note their reasons.

Listening. Students listen to the same texts for more detail this time.

Answers

1 practical, cheap (or not expensive), you always know what to put on
2 you always know what to put on, practical, but you can't wear trainers
3 suppresses individuality, not fashionable/strange idea, but less difference between social classes
4 individuality important, uniform a bit silly
5 less difference between social classes

2c Work with a partner. A agrees with uniform and B disagrees. Use phrases from the key language box.

Speaking. Students discuss the pros and cons of uniform. Prompt cards (see **1c**) would also help them carry out this activity.

3a Read this letter. Are the statements true or false?

Reading (1–5). Encourage students to read the complete text through first for gist before they answer the true/false questions.

Answers

1 false	2 true	3 true	4 true	5 false

➕ Students correct the false statements, demonstrating a higher level of comprehension.

3b In pairs. Prepare your answers to these questions, then take turns to ask and answer them.

Speaking. Students practise these questions and answers which draw together the language of the spread.

3c Use your preparation for **3b** to write an article (75 words) on school uniform and school rules for a magazine. Learn what you have written and make a recording of it!

This activity gives students early practice in preparing a talk and speaking at length from memory. Recording the talk, and subsequent talks, gives students a concrete record of progress throughout the course.

Further practice of the language and vocabulary of this spread is provided as follows:

À toi! A, page 180

Cahier d'exercices, page 6 (exs 8a & 8b)

4 Après le collège

(Student's Book pages pages 16–17)

Main topics and objectives

● Talking about plans for the future

Key language

D'abord …/Après …/Ensuite …
  L'année prochaine …
Je vais …
  gagner un peu d'argent.
  voyager/travailler.
  passer mes examens.
  quitter le collège.
  faire un apprentissage.
  continuer mes études.
  passer mon bac.
  aller au lycée (technique)/à l'université.
  faire un stage.
  perfectionner mon français.
  faire une formation générale/professionnelle.
Si possible je vais …

Grammar

● The immediate future tense
● Using *si* + immediate future

Skills/Strategies

● Using time indicators

Resources

Cassette A side 1
À l'oral page 36: Conversation 2 and prepared talk
Cahier d'exercices, page 7

Introduce this spread by giving students a revision quiz or mini-test on vocabulary connected to the French/Scottish education systems. Remind students that a *lycée* is like a sixth form college or an S5/6 college where you can do Highers and Advanced Highers.

1a Listen. What are these pupils going to do after they leave the collège?

Listening (1–5). Students listen and identify what the five students are going to do. They hear the structure *aller* + infinitive but should focus on the infinitive for their answers. Tell them that it does not matter if they do not understand everything.

Tapescript

1 Je vais faire un apprentissage. Je vais être apprenti dans un garage, j'espère.
2 Je vais aller au lycée pour passer mon bac.
3 Je vais aller au lycée technique.
4 J'espère faire une formation générale pour pouvoir travailler dans une banque plus tard.
5 Je vais faire un BEP secrétariat.

Answers

1 apprenticeship in a garage
2 go to 6th form/S5-6 college to take my bac
3 go to FE college
4 general training to work in a bank
5 do a secretarial qualification

1b Read Sylvie's letter. Fill the gaps with the verbs on the right.

Reading. Students demonstrate comprehension as well as application of the structure by filling in gaps. Warn students that the verbs might fit in more than one gap.

Answers

1 passer 2 quitter 3 continuer 4 étudier 5 passer
6 aller 7 être

1c Using the key language box, prepare to record 2 or 3 sentences about your plans for next year. Join your sentences with: …

Speaking. Students add to their tape of prepared speaking. They should also add these phrases to their list of 'impressive' phrases.

2 What are Marc's plans? Listen and put the pictures in the right order.

Listening (a–g). Students listen to more examples of the immediate future.

Tapescript

D'abord je vais travailler dans un supermarché pour gagner un peu d'argent et ensuite je vais voir mes grands-parents qui habitent au bord de la mer. J'espère qu'on va aller à la plage tous les jours. Je vais me reposer, dormir jusqu'à onze heures. Ensuite, je vais partir en vacances avec des amis: on va faire du camping dans les Pyrénées. On va s'éclater! Vers la fin du mois d'août, je vais recevoir mes résultats. S'ils sont bons, je vais continuer mes études à la fac.

Answers

b, c, a, g, e, d, f

3a Read these e-mails. Note in English each person's future plans under these headings: …

Reading. Students demonstrate understanding, both of plans and of timescales, noting their answers in English.

Answers

> **Alice:**
> After exams: go on holiday with family
> After results: continue studies
> **Elsa:**
> After exams: earn money by working in a small shop in town. Try to perfect her English.
> After results: continue studies at University
> **Alex:**
> After exams: travel around the world, visiting Africa
> After results: do a plumber's apprenticeship

Le détective

The immediate future. Students have already met the structure 'finite verb + infinitive'. Ask students to look up infinitives they will find useful in expressing their own plans, and to write six or seven simple sentences using this structure. The song *Aujourd'hui, c'est lundi* from *Un Kilo de Chansons* by Jaspar Kay uses the near future. Put a list of words that rhyme with *faire* on the OHT and ask students to come up with their own verses.

3b Write about what you are going to do next year. Write about 25 words under each of these headings: …

Writing. Students use the headings given to help structure their first extended piece of writing, using the texts in **3a** as models.

Tip box

Using time indicators and *si*. Students should add these time indicators to their lists from page 13, and try to use a time indicator every time they say something. They should add the phrases using *si* to their store of 'impressive' additional phrases. Encourage them to write, use and revise these phrases and to keep them together for easy reference.

3c Use your written notes to help you speak for about a minute on your future plans.

Speaking. Students use their notes from **3b** to plan a presentation, which they should record onto their Speaking tape.

> Further practice of the language and vocabulary of this spread is provided as follows:
>
> À l'oral, page 36: Conversation 2 and Prepared talk
>
> Cahier d'exercices, page 7

5 Les problèmes

(Student's Book pages 18–19)

Main topics and objectives

● Discussing difficulties at school and for the future

Key language

Language from the whole Module

Grammar

● Expressions of quantity
● Determiners

Skills/Strategies

● Being familiar with small but important words
● Recording new words and phrases

Resources

Cassette A side 1
À toi! B, page 181
Cahier d'exercices, pages 8–10

Start the spread by brainstorming, in English, the problems that students have at school/college.

1a Read and listen to the poem.

Listening. Read and listen to the poem with students. Ask them to add *on ne peut pas …*, *on doit …*, *on a trop de …* and *on n'a pas assez de …* to their list of useful phrases.

Le détective

Expressions of quantity. Encourage your students to see if they can add to the list given here, thinking of as many expressions of quantity as they can.

1b Write a new poem: *Le chant de la liberté*, using the model below.

Writing. Prepare your students for this activity by asking them, in groups, to find at least five possible endings for each phrase they are given, and then collating all the responses. Students then have a wider linguistic resource to work with in writing their own poem.

2 Read this article and answer the questions in English.

Reading (1–4). This is an exam-style reading comprehension. Encourage students to use these two techniques in dictionary use:
– identifying possible occurences in the text (i.e. looking up key English words in the questions)
– identifying key words in a French text to look up.

Answers

1a too busy – too many things to do (1)	**b** too long (1)
c too stressed (1)	**d** too much of it (1)
e important but makes us suffer (2)	
2 people who don't have the bac (1)	
3 leave school, do an apprenticeship or something practical (3)	
4a the breaks (1)	
b he can talk with friends, go to the shops or play football (3)	

Tip box

Determiners. Draw your students' attention to this box. Look back at texts in the module and show your students that all nouns are prefaced by a determiner (unless prefaced by an expression of quantity).

3a Read and listen to these young people's opinion on school and their future. Who thinks: …

Reading (1–9). Students read the three texts on the page and listen to them and answer the questions. This activity provides more practice of the technique of looking up words in English and locating them in the text. To exploit the texts further, ask students to choose one person and to summarise what they say in English.

Answers

1 Mathieu	**2** Yannick	**3** Annie	**4** Mathieu	**5** Annie
6 Yannick	**7** Yannick	**8** Yannick	**9** Annie	

Tip box

Understanding small words. Most students have no difficulty in locating answers in texts. Their problems lie in putting the answers into comprehensible English. Insist, right from the start, on accurate recall of a range of very common verb forms (*est, a, il y a*, etc.), prepositions (*à, de, sans*, etc.), quantities (*trop de, assez de, (un) peu de*, etc.), and other words which are time-consuming or difficult to look up in a dictionary. Set a selection of these as a test on a regular basis.

3b What are your opinions on studying and on the future? Write about 75 words, using the opinions in **3a** and the vocabulary box.

Writing. Students use the language they have learnt in the module to create a piece of extended writing. They may benefit from headings in French (and/or in English) to help them write at this length and to help them structure their writing. Encourage them to learn each piece of drafted and corrected writing, and to reproduce these under controlled conditions.

Tip box

Recording new words. Students already have a section in their jotters/folders/ICT work file of 'impressive' phrases. Encourage them to build their own classified vocabulary, cross-referencing or repeating words which could belong to more than one section.

Further practice of the language and vocabulary of this spread is provided as follows:

À toi! B, page 181

Cahier d'exercices, page 8

All the key vocabulary and structures from this module are listed on the **Mots** pages 22–23. These can be used for revision by covering up either the English or the French. Students can check here to see how much they remember from the module and use them to prepare for the assessments.

Assessment materials for Modules 1 and 2 are available in the separate Assessment Pack.

Further speaking and grammar practice on the whole module is provided on **Cahier d'exercices** pages 9–10.

Writing practice: Les études

The **À l'écrit** spreads give regular, guided practice in preparing for the writing sections of Standard Grade and Intermediate examinations. Each double-page spread always starts with a model text which acts as a stimulus, giving students ideas about what they might want to include in their own writing. Students are encouraged to look at the detail of the text through the structured reading activities, and are guided gradually towards producing their own sentences in French, in preparation for the final task in which they are asked to produce an extended piece of writing. The **Au Secours!** column is a feature on all the **À l'écrit** spreads. It presents language and structures that students can include in their writing, and reminds them of general points that will help them to get a better grade.

To qualify for the writing components at Standard Grade or Intermediate writing N.A.B.s, final versions must be produced under controlled conditions. Students should be encouraged to use the language they understand and are familiar with so as to learn what they have written with a high degree of accuracy. They should be warned about the dangers of copying. At Standard Grade, students should be guided to write over 25 words at Foundation level, 50 words at General level and 100 words at Credit level.

Students should be encouraged to see that they can get Credit marks at Standard Grade and A grades at Intermediate 2 in Writing! Remind them of the following tips to help them get a better grade.

Handy tips for students

1 Structure your writing: a good beginning and ending, and 3 distinct paragraphs!

   Choose formats which structure themselves, e.g. a letter.

2 Focus your writing on one aspect of a module.

3 Choose aspects which give you opportunities to write about your opinions.

4 Choose aspects which allow you to use impressive vocabulary and phrases.

5 Make sure you include examples of different tenses in your writing.

6 It is very important to write accurate French! Make sure the language you choose for your writing is memorable for **you**. Only you can know how much new and impressive French you can learn to write out accurately in exam conditions!

This spread guides students towards producing an extended piece of writing on the topic of **school**.

1 In Thierry's e-mail, what do the 10 phrases in blue mean?

Answers

1 *un jour de libre* – a free day/day off
2 *envoyer* – send
3 *pénible* – hard
4 *la journée* – the day
5 *chacun* – each one
6 *chargés* – overloaded
7 *sauf* – except
8 *argent* – money
9 *une formation* – training
10 *prochain* – next

2a How would Thierry answer these questions? His answers are underlined in the letter. Make sure you answer in whole sentences (change *qui* to *il* or *elle*).

Answers

1 Mon école est un lycée mixte.
2 Mon lycée se trouve dans le centre-ville de Rouen dans le nord de la France.
3 Il est assez grand, avec 1,300 étudiants.
4 Mes matières préférées sont les maths et les sciences, et surtout la physique.
5 Ce que je n'aime pas du tout, c'est l'informatique. Je trouve ça pénible, et en plus le prof est nul. Il me fait même un peu peur!
6 D'habitude les cours commencent à 8 heures du matin. Le lycée finit à 5 heures du soir.
7 On a quatre cours le matin et trois cours l'après-midi.
8 Mon lycée n'est pas mal.
9 On a cours tous les jours sauf le dimanche, le jeudi après-midi et le samedi après-midi.
10 Je vais d'abord gagner un peu d'argent. Après, j'espère faire une formation professionnelle pour devenir ingénieur, ou peut-être que je vais aller à l'université.

2b Now answer the questions with your own information. Adapt Thierry's answers.

3 Write an e-mail to a French student, describing your school/college. Use the *Au secours!* panel to help you.

Au secours!

This section reminds pupils of the following points:
● the importance of writing accurate French
● starting and finishing letters/e-mails
● structure
● linking words
● talking about rules and problems

À toi! A & B

(Student's Book pages 180–181)

Self-access reading and writing at two levels

These pages are designed to give students extra practice in reading and structured writing. There are two differentiated pages relating to each chapter: A and B. Page A is at an easier level and page B more challenging. You may wish students to work on the page most appropriate to their level, or work through both pages. You may feel it is useful to work with students on the activities, but it should be possible for most students to work on them independently. The most appropriate time to use each page is indicated within the relevant teaching notes.

À toi! A, page 180

This page is best used after pages 14–15 of the Student's Book.

1a Read the text. Then copy out this English version and fill in the blanks.

Answers

1 different	**2** school life	**3** pupil	**4** work	**5** earlier
6 homework	**7** Teaching	**8** group	**9** practical	
10 bigger				

1b Here are translations for the phrases in blue in the text, which are useful for comparing things. Note the French phrases with their English translations.

Answers

1 whereas – *tandis que*
2 earlier – *plus tôt*
3 bigger than – *plus grandes que*
4 however – *pourtant*
5 different from – *différente de*
6 only – *ne … que, ne … qu'*
7 the same – *les mêmes*
8 this is known as – *c'est ce qu'on appelle*

2 Write 100 words or more comparing a French student's school life with your own. Use the information below and on pages 14–17 to help you.

À toi! B, page 181

This page is best used after pages 18–19 of the Student's Book.

1a Read this article. Who …

Answers

1 Céline	**2** Annick	**3** Mohamed	**4** Samuel
5 Céline	**6** Mohamed		

1b Choose one text from **1a** and translate it into English.

2 In a group, create an article like the one above. Use all the texts in Module 1 to help you. Write 20–40 words to answer each of the questions below.

Then cut up your answers and swap with classmates so everyone has a variety of different people's opinions on different subjects in their article. Use photographs (of your classmates or of famous people) to make your article more attractive.

Cahier d'exercices, page 2

1a
Answers

| a ✗ | b ✓ | c ✓ | d ✗ | e ✓ | f ✓ | g ✗ | h ✗ | i ✗ | j ✓ |

1b
Answers

a Medhi a une heure d'études le mardi. **d** Il finit à cinq heures le lundi. **g** Il finit à 11.15 le samedi. **h** Il a deux heures d'EPS le vendredi. **i** Il a seulement six cours le mardi.

Cahier d'exercices, page 3

2a
Answers

a J'aime les maths parce que c'est utile.
b Je ne fais pas le dessin parce que c'est ennuyeux.
c Je n'aime pas la géographie car j'ai beaucoup de devoirs.
d J'aime l'histoire car la prof est géniale.
e Je n'aime pas le français parce que c'est difficile.

2b (writing task)

3
Answers

| **1** l'anglais | **2** les maths | **3** l'histoire |
| **4** la géographie | **5** le français | |

Cahier d'exercices, page 4

4
Answers

a *She started IT six years ago.* Elle apprend l'informatique depuis six ans. = *She has been learning IT for six years.*
b *I started Art last year.* J'apprends le dessin depuis un an. = *I have been learning Art for one year.*
c *You started Dance yesterday.* Tu apprends la danse depuis hier. = *You have been learning Dance since yesterday.*
d *We started German in March.* Nous apprenons l'allemand depuis mars. = *We have been learning German since March.*
e *They started Portuguese fourteen years ago.* Elles apprennent le portugais depuis quatorze ans. = *They have been learning Portuguese for fourteen years.*
f *He started Italian two years ago.* Il apprend l'italien depuis deux ans. = *He has been learning Italian for two years.*
g *I started Gymnastics four years ago.* J'apprends la gymnastique depuis quatre ans. = *I have been learning Gymnastics for four years.*

5
Answers

| **a** l' | **b** les, la | **c** le, le | **d** la | **e** le | **f** la |

ÉTUDES

Cahier d'exercices, page 5

6
Answers

| 1 c | 2 a | 3 b |

7a
Answers

5 clubs: *le club de photographie, le club de théâtre, le club de hand-ball, le club d'échecs et le club de poésie*
3 opinions: any 3 from *c'est bien, ennuyeux, passionnant, pas mal, démodé, peu pratique*
2 périodes de vacances: any 2 from *Toussaint, Noël, février, Pâques*

Cahier d'exercices, page 6

7b (writing task)
8a
Answers

1 ✓ 2 ✗ 3 ✗ 4 ✓ 5 ✗ 6 ✗ 7 ✓ 8 ✗ 9 ✓ 10 ✗

8b (writing task)

Cahier d'exercices, page 7

9a
Answers

a Ma matière préférée, c'est le français.
b J'aime beaucoup la grammaire.
c J'ai de la chance d'avoir de bons professeurs.
d Je vais travailler et gagner de l'argent.
e J'espère être prof de français.
f Je vais passer des examens.
g Je vais travailler très dur cette année.
h Je ne sais pas encore ce que je vais faire.
i J'ai déjà pas mal de projets pour mon avenir.
j J'ai l'intention d'aller à l'université.

9b
Answers

I don't yet know what I'll do after school. I have very important exams next year (bac). I'd like to be a teacher of French but before going to university, I'm going to earn money and travel in Europe. I shall work hard this year to have good marks.

9c (writing task)

Cahier d'exercices, page 8

10a
Answers

a tu as vraiment de la chance	b j'en ai marre
c à partir de demain	d je suis trop fatigué
e un salaire important	f j'ai eu tant de devoirs
g seulement une fois	h tu me manques

10b
Answers

1 b   2 c   3 a   4 c

Cahier d'exercices, page 9

1
Answers

a les   b ma, la   c les   d le, les   e mes   f des, la

2
Answers

a Tu vas faire tes devoirs.
b Sophie va regarder dans le dictionnaire.
c Je vais aller à un cours de piano.
d Nous allons gagner un peu d'argent.
e Ils vont aller à la leçon de musique.
f Il va faire un apprentissage.
g Elles vont terminer les études.
h Marc va manger tous les sandwichs.
i Vas-tu continuer tes études?/Tu vas continuer tes études?
j Je vais perfectionner mon français.

3
Answers

a pourquoi   b quelles   c combien   d à quelle heure   e où

Cahiers d'exercices, page 10

Chez moi

(Student's Book pages 24–39)

Topic area	Key language	Grammar	Skills/Strategies
Déjà vu (pp. 24–27) Talking about your family Describing people's appearance Talking about your extended family	Je m'appelle … Il/Elle s'appelle … J'ai/Il a/Elle a (14) ans. Dans ma famille, il y a (5) personnes. J'ai une sœur/un frère. Je suis enfant unique. J'ai un chien/chat/hamster/cochon d'Inde/lapin. Je n'ai pas d'animal. Mon anniversaire, c'est le (7 avril). mon père/frère/oncle/cousin/neveu/grand-père/demi-frère ma mère/sœur/tante/cousine/demi-sœur/nièce/grand-mère J'ai/Tu as Il/Elle a les cheveux courts/longs/noirs/blancs/gris/bruns/noirs/blonds/roux. J'ai les yeux bleus/verts/marron. Il a une barbe. Je porte/Tu portes des lunettes. Je suis … Il/Elle est petit(e)/grand(e)/mince/de taille moyenne/gros(se). J'ai un visage long/oval/carré/rond. J'ai le teint clair/foncé. Je pèse (45) kilos. Il/Elle est divorcé(e)/marié(e)/célibataire/séparé(e).	Possessive adjectives (singular) en avoir/être (present tense)	Making answers as full as possible Giving details when describing someone
1 Comment êtes-vous? (pp. 28–29) Describing personality	Il/Elle est aimable/amusant(e)/bavard(e)/bête/calme/casse-pieds/drôle/equilibré(e)/gentil(le)/idiot(e)/impatient(e)/intelligent(e)/ méchant(e)/paresseux(-euse)/plein(e) de vie/poli(e)/sage/sévère/ sympathique/timide/travailleur(-euse)/cool/sérieux(-euse)/formidable/charmant(e)/ content(e)/dynamique/égoïste/triste. de temps en temps/en général/ne … jamais/toujours assez/très/un peu/trop antisocial(e)/arrogant(e)/bruyant(e)/embêtant(e)/extraverti(e)/ indépendant(e)/ouvert(e) patient(e)/strict(e)/agréable/antipathique/artistique/autoritaire/désagréable/ modeste pénible/rigolo(te)/sensible/sociable/compréhensif(-ive)/ennuyeux(-euse)/ généreux(-euse)/creatif(-ive)/charmant(e)/mûr(e)	Agreement of adjectives	Using qualifiers
2 Les qualités (pp. 30–31) Talking about friends	Il/Elle a le sens de l'humour/beaucoup d'imagination/le sens pratique/mauvais caractère/beaucoup d'initiative. On sort ensemble. On discute. On fait tout ensemble. On rigole. On a beaucoup de choses en commun. Je m'entends bien avec … Je me dispute avec …	Using on Reflexives (present tense)	Using qualifiers
3 Aider à la maison (pp. 32–33) Talking about helping at home	Je passe l'aspirateur. Je range ma chambre. Je mets/débarrasse la table. Je garde mon petit frère. Je nettoie la salle de bains. Je fais la lessive/la cuisine/les courses. Je fais la vaisselle/le ménage. J'étends le linge. Je sors la poubelle. Je travaille dans le jardin. Je vais chercher le lait. Je lave la voiture. ensuite/puis/après/le lendemain/une heure plus tard Je dois/On doit/Nous devons + infinitive	Regular and irregular present tense verbs devoir	Giving as much detail as possible Using adverbs

Topic area	Key language	Grammar	Skills/Strategies
4 Les problèmes en famille (pp. 34–35) Talking about relationships	*Je m'entends bien avec … J'en ai marre de …* *Ma mère m'énerve/me respecte/me critique.* *On discute/se dispute/s'entend bien/mal.* *Je peux sortir/me confier/faire ce que je veux.* *J'ai le droit de sortir/fumer.*	Direct object pronouns: *le/la/les*	Working out unknown words Picking out details from listening
Entraînez-vous: À l'oral (pp. 36–37)	Language from Modules 1 and 2		Practice for the speaking exam Adding details Presentation skills
À toi! A and B (pp. 182–183)	Language from Module 2		Reading and writing skills

The vocabulary and structures taught in Module 2 are summarised on the **Mots** pages of the Student's Book, pages 38–39.

Further writing practice on the language of the module is provided on **À l'écrit**, pages 54–55.

Assessment tasks for Modules 1 and 2 combined are provided in the separate Assessment Pack.

MODULE 2 CHEZ MOI — *Déjà vu*

(Student's Book pages 24–27)

Main topics and objectives

- Talking about your family
- Describing people's appearance
- Talking about your extended family

Key language

Je m'appelle … Il/Elle s'appelle …
J'ai/Il a/Elle a (14) ans.
Dans ma famille, il y a (5) personnes.
J'ai une sœur/un frère.
Je suis enfant unique.
J'ai un chien/chat/hamster/cochon d'Inde/lapin.
Je n'ai pas d'animal.
Mon anniversaire, c'est le (7 avril).
mon père/frère/oncle/cousin/neveu/grand-père/demi-frère
ma mère/sœur/tante/cousine/demi-sœur/nièce/grand-mère
J'ai/Tu as/Il a/Elle a les cheveux … courts/longs/noirs/blancs/gris/bruns/noirs/blonds/roux.
J'ai les yeux bleus/verts/marron.
Il a une barbe.

Je porte/Tu portes des lunettes.
Je suis/Il est/Elle est …
petit(e)/grand(e)/mince/de taille moyenne/gros(se).
J'ai un visage long/oval/carré/rond.
J'ai le teint clair/foncé.
Je pèse (45) kilos.
Il/Elle est divorcé(e)/marié(e)/célibataire/séparé(e).

Grammar

- Possessive adjectives singular
- *en*
- *avoir/être* (present tense)

Skills/Strategies

- Making answers as full as possible
- Giving details when describing someone

Resources

Cassette A side 2
Cahier d'exercices, page 11

Introduce this spread by brainstorming how many family members students can think of and note them on the board/OHP. Revise family members and pets round the class – *tu as des frères et des sœurs*, etc.

1a Read the letter. Copy and complete the form.

Reading. Students read the letter and note details in English on the form.

Answers

Surname: Beregi
First name: Adrien
Brother(s): 1 brother, Manu, 3 months
Sister(s): 2 sisters, Juliette (9) and Elsa (18)
Parent(s): Michel and Édith
Grandparent(s): grandmother lives with them: Marthe
Pets: none

Le détective

Possessive adjectives. Revise possessive adjectives, and encourage students to learn them by heart. Remind them that in French the possessive adjective agrees with the thing owned and not the owner, and that there are no separate words for 'his', 'her' and 'its'. You may wish at this point to teach the whole table rather than the 1st, 2nd and 3rd person singular given here.

1b Write about your family, then use your writing to prepare a short talk. You should include the names and ages of family members and whether you have any pets.

Writing and Speaking. Students prepare a short presentation on their family and then use their notes to give a short talk. Point out that they can use the text in **1a** as a model. Some students may prefer not to discuss their families – remind them that they can make up a family if they wish. Indeed, this may give them an opportunity to use vocabulary they would not otherwise use. They can add this to their speaking tape.

2 Listen. Note the birthday and age of these people.

Listening (1–8). Students listen and note each person's birthday and age.

All the ages are calculated as if the speakers are talking in 2001.

Before embarking on this exercise, you may wish to ask for birthdays and ages round the class. Use this opportunity to pick up on pronunciation errors.

Tapescript

1 – *Quelle est la date de ton anniversaire?*
 – *C'est le cinq janvier. Je suis né en soixante-cinq, j'ai donc trente-six ans.*
2 – *Quelle est la date de ton anniversaire?*
 – *C'est le 12 mai. Je suis né en quatre-vingt-un, alors j'ai vingt ans.*
3 – *Quelle est la date de ton anniversaire?*
 – *C'est le 21 novembre. J'ai seize ans et demi.*
4 – *Quelle est la date de ton anniversaire?*
 – *C'est le premier octobre. Je suis né en quatre-vingt-six. Vous n'avez qu'à calculer!*
5 – *Quelle est la date de ton anniversaire?*

– *C'est le 2 mars. Je suis née en quatre-vingt-neuf. J'ai douze ans.*

6 – *Quelle est la date de ton anniversaire?*
– *C'est le 15 juin. J'ai quinze ans et je suis né en quatre-vingt-six.*

7 – *Quelle est la date de ton anniversaire?*
– *C'est le 4 novembre. J'ai dix-neuf ans.*

8 – *Quelle est la date de ton anniversaire?*
– *C'est le 14 février. Je suis née en quatre-vingt-treize, alors j'ai huit ans.*

Answers

1 5th January; 36
2 12th May; 20
3 21st November; 16½
4 1st October; 15
5 2nd March; 12
6 15th June; 15
7 4th November; 19
8 14th February; 8

Tip box

Giving full answers. Before moving on to **3**, encourage students to try to make their answers as full as possible. Point out that the more detailed their answers are, the better grade they are likely to get.

3 In pairs. Interview each other about your families.

Speaking. Students use the example conversation as a basis for interviewing each other about family members.

Le détective

en. Practise this with students, using examples they may already know, e.g. *As-tu un crayon? Oui, j'en ai un. As-tu une sœur? Oui, j'en ai une.*

✚ Play the treasure hunt game. Find someone in the class who: has a middle name beginning with 'M', has 3 brothers, has a rabbit, has no sisters, etc.

Before going on to **4a**, revise the language for describing people. Hold up a picture (of someone famous perhaps) and describe them. Then start asking questions, e.g. *Est-qu'il a les yeux verts? Est-ce qu'il porte des lunettes?*, etc. Encourage students gradually to start describing other people.

4a Read Vincent's letter and answer the questions which follow.

Reading (1–8). Students read the letter which contains a lot of information about Vincent's family members, and answer the questions. As further exploitation, ask students to pick out from the text the French for English phrases you call out, e.g. She wears glasses.

Answers

1 He's 14, quite tall (1m 67), blue eyes, brown hair, very slim. (3)
2 Vincent looks like him. (1)
3 Sylvie, quite small and slim, 39, blond, short hair and blue eyes. Wears glasses or contact lenses. (3)
4 He lives in Belgium. (1)
5 His stepfather. (1)
6 Quite small (1m 55), a bit fat (87 kilos), short curly hair, green eyes, beard and funny. (3)
7 Her father. (1)
8 His grandfather. (1)

Student's Book pages 26–27

4b Listen. Copy and complete the first 3 columns of the grid. Then listen again to complete the final 2 columns.

Listening (1–4). Students listen and complete the first three columns of the grid. They then listen again to complete the final two columns. Students may need to hear each part three times.

Tapescript

1 *Ma sœur s'appelle Audrey. Ça s'écrit A-u-d-r-e-y. Elle a 13 ans, et son anniversaire est le 4 juin. Elle a les yeux bleus et les cheveux roux. Elle est grande et assez grosse.*
2 *Mon père s'appelle Yves. Yves, ça s'écrit Y-v-e-s. Mon père a 43 ans. Son anniversaire est le 25 décembre, le jour de Noël. Il n'a pas beaucoup de cheveux, mais ceux qu'il a sont gris! Il a les yeux bleus comme ma sœur. Il est grand et il porte des lunettes pour regarder la télé.*
3 *Ma mère est morte. Marthe, c'est ma belle-mère. Marthe, ça s'écrit M-a-r-t-h-e. Elle est plus âgée que mon père, elle a 45 ans. Son anniversaire est le 18 janvier. Elle est petite, aux cheveux marron et aux yeux verts.*
4 *Mon beau-frère s'appelle Boris. Il a les cheveux blonds et les yeux marron. Il est assez grand pour son âge. Il a 16 ans et son anniversaire est le 9 avril. Il adore le rock.*

Answers

	relation	name	age	birthday	other detail(s)
1	sister	Audrey	13	4 June	blue eyes, red hair, tall and quite fat
2	father	Yves	43	25 December	grey hair, not much hair, blue eyes, tall, wears glasses
3	stepmother	Marthe	45	18 January	small, brown hair, green eyes
4	step-brother	Boris	16	9 April	blond hair, brown eyes, quite tall, likes rock

5a Listen. Who's talking?

Listening (1–5). Students listen and identify who is talking from the pictures.

Tapescript

1 Je suis gros, et j'ai les cheveux courts et bruns.
2 J'ai le visage carré, et le teint foncé. J'ai aussi les cheveux longs et noirs. On dit que je suis mignonne.
3 J'ai le visage long, mais je suis assez beau avec de courts cheveux blonds.
4 J'ai le visage ovale et je suis mince. J'ai les cheveux assez courts et noirs. Ma petite amie pense que je suis très beau.
5 Moi, j'ai le visage rond, et les cheveux longs et bruns. J'ai le teint clair.

Answers

1 e	2 c	3 a	4 d	5 b

5b In pairs. Choose a famous person and describe them. Can your partner guess who it is?

Speaking. Using the key language box, students describe a famous person to their partner who should try to guess who it is. They then swap roles.

Le détective

avoir and *être*. Remind students how vitally important it is to know these verbs thoroughly. Remind them of the times we use 'to be' in English where the French use *avoir*, e.g. when giving your age.

6a How old are all the people mentioned? Choose from the ages above the text.

Reading. Students read the text and identify the ages given. Remind them that it is very important to know numbers really well, particularly 13, 14, 15 and 16, which are often tricky numbers to remember.

Answers

Jeanne – 17
Roxane – 16
Arnaud – 19
Pascal – 18

6b Which relative is it? Choose from the key language box.

Reading (1–6). This activity involves identifying relatives from the more extended family. Introduce them first if necessary. Students identify the name of the relative from the descriptions given in French.

Answers

1 ma tante	2 ma sœur	3 mon demi-frère
4 mon oncle	5 mon cousin	6 ma grand-mère

Tip box

Describing people. This reminds students to include lots of details when describing someone.

7 Write a description of two members of your family.

Writing. Students write a description of two members of their family. Remind them it does not need to be true!

8 Read the speech bubbles, then match the people to the sentences in the key language box.

Reading. Students match the name with each speech bubble to the correct sentence. This deals with language which many students may need when talking about their own family.

Answers

Alain: Il est célibataire.
Anne: Elle est divorcée.
Michel: Il est séparé.
Marion: Elle est mariée.

Further practice of the language and vocabulary of these spreads is provided as follows:

Cahier d'exercices, page 11

Main topics and objectives

● Describing personality

Key language

Il/Elle est …
aimable/amusant(e)/bavard(e)
bête/calme/casse-pieds
drôle/équilibré(e)/gentil(le)
idiot(e)/impatient(e)/intelligent(e)
méchant(e)/paresseux(-euse)
plein(e) de vie/poli(e)
sage/sévère/sympathique
timide/travailleur(-euse)
cool/sérieux(-euse)/formidable/charmant(e)
content(e)/dynamique/égoïste/triste
de temps en temps/en général/ne … jamais/toujours
assez/très/un peu/trop
antisocial(e)/arrogant(e)/bruyant(e)/embêtant(e)

extraverti(e)/indépendant(e)/ouvert(e)
patient(e)/strict(e)/agréable/antipathique
artistique/autoritaire/désagréable/modeste
pénible/rigolo(te)/sensible/sociable/compréhensif(-ive)
ennuyeux(-euse)/généreux(-euse)/créatif(-ive)/
charmant(e)/mûr(e)

Grammar

● Agreement of adjectives

Skills/Strategies

● Using qualifiers

Resources

Cassette A side 2
Cahier d'exercices, page 12

Start this spread by putting students into groups of 4 or 5 and challenging them to be the first group to identify correctly (by guessing or looking up) the meanings of all the words in the panel.

1a List the adjectives on the right in 2 groups – positive and negative.

Reading. Students divide the adjectives into two categories – positive and negative. They should be encouraged to use a dictionary.

Answers (open to interpretation!)

> **Positive:** aimable, calme, drôle, équilibré, gentil, poli, plein de vie, sympathique, intelligent, travailleur, cool, sage, bavard, amusant, formidable, charmant, content, dynamique
> **Negative:** bête, casse-pieds, idiot, impatient, timide, méchant, paresseux, sévère, sérieux, égoïste, triste

➕ As a follow-up, ask students to use each of the adjectives in turn, writing a sentence about somebody they know who has that quality, e.g. *Rolf Harris est aimable*. Then ask them to make a spider diagram with *JE SUIS* in the middle and their own personal qualities round the outside. They can use the dictionary to find some new adjectives if they wish.

1b Listen to Nicolas talking about himself and his family. Note in French each person and the adjectives Nicolas uses.

Listening (1–6). Students listen and note in French the person being described and the adjectives used. They may wish to make rough notes while listening and then tidy up their spelling at the end.

Tapescript

1 *Moi, Nicolas, je suis cool et plein de vie, mais aussi paresseux. Je pense que je suis assez amusant.*
2 *Sylvie, ma mère, elle est sympathique, et très gentille.*
3 *Mon beau-père, Christian, est assez sévère, calme et drôle. Il est charmant en fait.*
4 *Magalie, ma demi-sœur, est aimable mais aussi trop bavarde et impatiente. Elle est un peu sérieuse des fois.*
5 *Pierre, le bébé, est casse-pieds!*
6 *Ma grand-mère est formidable. Elle est dynamique pour son âge et pas du tout égoïste. Et elle n'est jamais triste.*

Answers

> 1 moi (Nicolas) – cool, plein de vie, paresseux, amusant
> 2 Sylvie (mère) – sympathique, gentille
> 3 Christian (beau-père) – sévère, calme, drôle, charmant
> 4 Magalie (demi-sœur) – aimable, bavarde, impatiente, sérieuse
> 5 Pierre (bébé) – casse-pieds
> 6 Grand-mère – formidable, dynamique, pas égoïste, jamais triste

1c Look at this picture of the Simpsons. Write a short description of each person and give it to a partner – can they guess who it is?

Writing. Students write a short description of each Simpson character before showing it to their partner to guess who it is. Students may choose to read out their description instead.

2a Listen. Note each characteristic, and whether the speakers think it is good (✓) or bad (✗), or can't agree (?).

Listening. Students listen to the tape, note the characteristics and what each speaker thinks of them.

This introduces more adjectives (see the key language box) which you may want to introduce first.

Tapescript

– Être autoritaire, c'est quelque chose de négatif à mon avis.
– Oui, c'est pas une bonne qualité. C'est négatif.
– Être arrogant aussi.
– Oui, je suis d'accord avec ton point de vue.
– Et si on est indépendant?
– Ça, c'est une bonne chose, c'est plutôt positif.
– Être antisocial, antipathique et désagréable, ce sont des défauts?
– Oui.
– Tandis que si on est généreux, ouvert et modeste, ce sont des qualités, des choses positives?
– Oui. À mon avis, être bruyant, c'est négatif?
– Ah non, je ne suis pas d'accord. Ça peut être très positif. Par exemple, je connais quelqu'un qui est rigolo et extraverti, et qui est très, très bruyant. Mais il est créatif en même temps.
– Si on est ennuyeux et embêtant, c'est négatif.
– Oui, d'accord.
– Et si on est compréhensif et patient?
– Ce sont des caractéristiques positives pour moi.
– Oui.
– Finalement, si on est artistique et sensible.
– Eh bien, ça dépend de la situation.

Answers

autoritaire ✗, arrogant ✗, indépendant ✓, antisocial ✗, antipathique ✗, désagréable ✗, généreux ✓, ouvert ✓, modeste ✓, bruyant ?, ennuyeux ✗, embêtant ✗, compréhensif ✓, patient ✓, artistique ?, sensible ?

Le détective

Agreement of adjectives. You may wish to refer to the grammar notes on page 212 of the Student's Book. Students could brainstorm other adjectives they know and put them in sentences to practise agreements.

2b In groups. Choose one of these people and give your opinion of them.

Speaking. Students give their opinion of one or more of the people listed.

Tip box

Using qualifiers. Remind students that using qualifying words makes their writing more interesting and will help them get a better grade.

2c Copy and complete these statements with adjectives to describe yourself.

Writing. Students complete the sentences to describe themselves, using qualifying words.

3 Read the text and listen to it. Then answer the questions in English.

Reading and Listening. Students read the text and listen to it before answering the questions in English. You may wish to play the recording first before students see the text. Ask them for any facts they have understood. For further exploitation, ask students to find the French expressions in the text for English ones that you call out.

Answers

1 When his mother goes on business trips. (1)
2 He gets on well with her. (1)
3 He is the eldest. (1)
4 Mostly they are good and quite funny but they can be irritating. (3)
5 Small, looks like his mother, curly hair, sweet. (3)
6 Like his mum but charming like his dad! (2)
7 Paternal grandfather is dead; maternal grandfather visits them from time to time; he is calm and intelligent, recounts stories. (5)
8 He is an only child. (1)

4 CV Choose at least 5 statements about your family and combine them in a paragraph under the title *Famille* on disc. Insert the data into your CV document.

Writing. Students will find it useful to add to the CV document they started in Module 1.

Further practice of the language and vocabulary of this spread is provided as follows:

Cahier d'exercices, page 12

2 Les qualités

(Student's Book pages 30–31)

Main topics and objectives

- Talking about friends

Key language

Il/Elle a … le sens de l'humour.
  beaucoup d'imagination
  le sens pratique
  mauvais caractère
  beaucoup d'initiative
On sort ensemble.
On discute.
On fait tout ensemble.
On rigole.
On a beaucoup de choses en commun.
Je m'entends bien avec …
Je me dispute avec …

Grammar

- Reflexive verbs: present tense
- Using expressions with *On …*

Skills/Strategies

- Using qualifiers

Resources

Cassette A side 2
À l'oral, page 37: Prepared talk
Cahier d'exercices, page 13

Introduce the spread by presenting the language in the key language box using either flashcards/pictures or mime.

1a Read the banners and make notes on what you think each one means.

Reading. Students read the banners and note what they think each one means in English, working them out from their similarity to English.

Answers

> 1 My friend Franck has a sense of humour.
> 2 We laugh all the time.
> 3 Julie really has a lot of initiative.
> 4 Sandrine is very practical.
> 5 We do everything together.
> 6 Patrice has a lot of imagination.
> 7 We go out together.
> 8 I don't like Sophie. She has a bad personality.
> 9 We talk about everything.
> 10 We have a lot of things in common.

1b Listen. Note 2 qualities for each person.

Listening (1–4). Students listen and note two qualities in English for each person.

Tapescript

1 *Mon meilleur ami s'appelle Jérémy. Il est super sympa. Il est drôle, il ne se prend pas trop au sérieux, il a le sens de l'humour. En fait, on a le même sens de l'humour. On rigole la plupart du temps. Mais on discute ensemble aussi. On se dispute rarement.*
2 *Ma meilleure copine s'appelle Chloé. Elle est mignonne comme tout. On fait tout ensemble. Elle a beaucoup d'imagination, on est tout le temps en train d'inventer des choses. On a beaucoup de choses en commun.*
3 *Ma meilleure amie s'appelle Aline. Elle est très mûre pour son âge. Elle est un peu plus jeune que moi. Elle a le sens*

pratique, ce que j'aime chez les gens, et elle a beaucoup d'initiative. On sort ensemble, on discute, c'est sympa.
4 *Il y a un garçon que je connais que je n'aime pas du tout. Il a mauvais caractère, il peut être très désagréable. Il n'a pas d'amis. Il est toujours seul et … des fois il me fait pitié.*

Answers

> 1 Jérémy – really nice, funny, sense of humour, we laugh, talk, rarely argue.
> 2 Chloé – sweet, do everything together, has a lot of imagination and is always inventing things. We have a lot of things in common.
> 3 Aline – very mature for her age, younger than me, very practical and has initiative. We go out together and talk.
> 4 Le garçon – bad personality, very unpleasant, no friends.

1c Listen again and note which of the expressions on the right are mentioned for each person.

Listening (1–4). Students listen to the same recording again and note which of the expressions in the key language box are mentioned for each person.

Answers

> 1 Il a le sens de l'humour. On rigole. On discute.
> 2 On fait tout ensemble. Elle a beaucoup d'imagination. On a beaucoup de choses en commun.
> 3 Elle a le sens pratique. Elle a beaucoup d'initiative. On sort ensemble. On discute.
> 4 Il a mauvais caractère.

2a Read the text and look up the words in red.

Reading. Students read the text and find out the meaning of the words in red. This is a pre-reading activity, providing dictionary practice and giving students an understanding of some key words before they read in more detail.

Answers

Je m'entends bien – I get on well
se disputer – to argue with
critiquent – criticise
souvent – often
vraiment – really, truly
toujours – always
j'ai besoin – I need
se marre – have a laugh

2b Re-read the text. Choose the correct answers.

Reading. Students read the text in more detail and identify the correct answers by choosing from the three given.

Remind students that they should not try to laboriously translate every word of a text – it is not necessary for the understanding of it nor for answering any questions.

Answers

1 b	**2** c	**3** a	**4** a

Tip box

Qualifiers. Give students some basic sentences and ask them to add qualifiers in the appropriate places.

3 Respond to this magazine article.

Writing. Students read the text and respond using the prompts as a guide. Brainstorm some ideas as a class first if necessary.

Le détective

Reflexive verbs. You may wish to extend this to give the full paradigm of the verbs. Which other reflexive verbs do they know, or can they guess the meaning of?

Point out to students that many reflexive verbs in French mean either 'to do something to oneself' (e.g. *se laver*), 'to be …ed' (e.g. *s'inquiéter*) or 'to get …ed' (e.g. *se marier*).

> Further practice of the language and vocabulary of this spread is provided as follows:
>
> À l'oral, page 37: Prepared talk
>
> Cahier d'exercices, page 13

3 Aider à la maison

(Student's Book pages 32–33)

Main topics and objectives

● Talking about helping at home

Key language

Je passe l'aspirateur.
Je range ma chambre.
Je mets/débarrasse la table.
Je garde mon petit frère.
Je nettoie la salle de bains.
Je fais la lessive/la cuisine/les courses.
Je fais la vaisselle/le ménage.
J'étends le linge.
Je sors la poubelle.
Je travaille dans le jardin.
Je vais chercher le lait.
Je lave la voiture.

ensuite/puis//après/le lendemain/une heure plus tard
Je dois/On doit/Nous devons + infinitive

Grammar

● Regular and irregular present tense verbs
● *devoir*

Skills/Strategies

● Giving as much detail as possible
● Using adverbs

Resources

Cassette A side 2
À l'oral, page 37: Conversations 1 and 2
Cahier d'exercices, pages 14–15

To introduce this spread, give an initial presentation of household job vocabulary. Let students see it written and hear how it is said. Brainstorm the different chores: How many can they work out? How many can they guess? Delegate dictionary looker-uppers (perhaps racing one another) to check and find the others.

1a Choose and write a sentence from the key language box for each picture.

Writing. Students choose a sentence from the key language box to describe each picture.

Answers

a Je fais le ménage.   **b** Je travaille dans le jardin.
c Je nettoie la salle de bains.   **d** Je fais la lessive.
e Je lave la voiture.   **f** Je passe l'aspirateur.
g Je range ma chambre.   **h** Je mets la table.
i Je fais la vaisselle.   **j** Je garde mon petit frère.
k Je fais les courses.   **l** Je fais la cuisine.
m Je vais chercher le lait.   **n** Je sors la poubelle.
o Je débarrasse la table.   **p** J'étends le linge.

1b Listen and look at the pictures in **1a**. Which household jobs does each person mention?

Listening (1–6). Students listen to the recording and identify the jobs each person mentions.

Tapescript

1 Alors, moi, je passe l'aspirateur une fois par semaine dans toute la maison. Je dois ranger ma chambre, et je mets la table et je débarrasse la table aussi tous les jours. On me paie, quoi. Je gagne de l'argent si je fais ça, mais si j'oublie, on ne me paie pas!

2 Moi, je fais la vaisselle, ça ne me gêne pas, et je garde mon petit frère aussi. En fait j'aime bien faire ça et en plus, je reçois €15 par semaine!

3 Moi, j'adore l'eau, et j'aime bien que tout soit propre. Tout ce qui est nettoyage, c'est pour moi! Je nettoie la salle de bains, je fais la lessive et j'aime bien étendre le linge quand il y a du vent! Et aussi je lave la voiture de ma mère toutes les quinzaines. Je ne reçois pas d'argent, mais ça m'amuse.

4 Moi, je vais chercher le lait et le pain tous les matins avant le collège. Je sors la poubelle aussi. Ma mère me donne €7.50 par semaine pour mon aide.

5 Je fais beaucoup de choses pour aider à la maison puisque maman travaille. Je dois faire les courses, et je fais la cuisine pour toute la famille tous les jours. J'aime bien aider ma mère et elle me donne volontiers mon argent de poche.

6 Moi, je fais beaucoup de ménage et je fais aussi le jardinage. Je sais que beaucoup de jeunes n'aiment pas ça, mais moi, j'adore travailler dans le jardin. C'est peut-être parce que j'aime la biologie. Oh, et on me donne de l'argent aussi, €23 par semaine.

Answers

1 f, g, h, o	**2** i, j	**3** c, d, p, e	**4** m, n	**5** k, l	**6** a, b

1c Listen again. Who says what? Choose a speech bubble for each speaker.

Listening. Students listen to the same recording again and put the speech bubbles in the right order. This concentrates on particular phrases in the listening. Look at the speech bubbles and work out their meaning before playing the recording.

Answers

1 c	**2** e	**3** d	**4** f	**5** b	**6** a

Tip box

Giving detailed answers. This reminds students that they need to extend their answers as much as possible – without necessarily telling the truth! You could put some basic sentences on the board and brainstorm how you might extend them.

Rappel

Regular and irregular verbs. Before doing the speaking activity, remind students that not all of the verbs they will use are regular and draw their attention to the verb reference tables on pages 120–121.

2 In pairs. What do you do to help at home?

Speaking. Students describe what they do to help at home, giving as much detail as possible.

3 Listen. Note what this au pair has to do each day.

Listening. Students listen to the recording and note the jobs for each day.

Tapescript

Julie Mann est anglaise. Elle travaille comme jeune fille au pair à Toulouse en France. Elle s'occupe d'un petit garçon de 4 ans.
Le lundi, elle fait le ménage dans toute la maison.
Le mardi, elle doit aller en ville pour faire les courses au supermarché.
Le jeudi, elle fait la cuisine, parce que les parents rentrent tard ce jour-ci.
Tous les jours, Julie a beaucoup à faire. Elle fait les lits et elle passe l'aspirateur. Elle doit aussi ranger la chambre du petit garçon.
Heureusement, le week-end, elle a du temps libre, et elle va au cinéma ou chez McDonald pour manger un hamburger.
Julie aime bien être jeune fille au pair, mais le travail est assez difficile, et très fatigant.

Answers

1 Monday: housework
2 Tuesday: do the shopping at the supermarket
3 Thursday: cooking
4 Everyday: make the beds and vacuum. Tidy the little boy's bedroom.
5 At the weekend: cinema and McDonalds.

4 Read the text. Who … ?

Reading. Students read the text and note who does what. You can further exploit the text by asking

students to find the French phrases from some English ones you give them, or by asking questions in French.

Answers

a Martine	**b** Michel	**c** Nina	**d** Antoine

5 You are staying with your penfriend and want to help out as much as possible. In pairs. One partner asks a question, the other says which picture it is.

Speaking. Students use the example as a basis for asking other questions starting with *Est-ce que je peux … ?*

Rappel

devoir + infinitive. You may wish to teach the whole paradigm of *devoir* here.

6 You have had a party – the house is a mess! What do you have to do to tidy up?

Writing. Students follow the example to write about what will have to be done to tidy the house, using *je dois* + infinitive.

Tip box

Using adverbs. Ask students to write a sentence for each adverb given. They can then use the adverbs in activity 7.

7 Prepare a short presentation on what you do to help at home. You may have to use your imagination!

Speaking. Students prepare a presentation on what they do to help at home, using the speech bubbles as a guide. This could be used as an on-going speaking assessment. They could add this to their tape of prepared speaking tasks.

Further practice of the language and vocabulary of this spread is provided as follows:

À l'oral, page 37: Prepared talk

Cahier d'exercices, pages 14–15

4 Les problèmes en famille

(Student's Book pages 34–35)

Main topics and objectives

● Talking about relationships

Key language

Je m'entends bien avec …
J'en ai marre de …
Ma mère m'énerve/me respecte/me critique.
On discute/se dispute/s'entend bien/mal.
Je peux sortir/me confier à (ma mère)/faire ce
  que je veux.
J'ai le droit de sortir/fumer.

Grammar

● Direct object pronouns: *le/la/les*

Skills/Strategies

● Working out unknown words
● Picking out details while listening

Resources

Cassette A side 2
À toi! A and B, pages 182–183
Cahier d'exercices, pages 16–18

It may be useful to allow students to approach this fairly lengthy reading text on their own so that they develop independent reading strategies. However, remind them that they should read first for gist, then identify key words which will help them answer the questions. Point out the tip box and remind students not to spend too long on any one text.

1a Find the meanings of the phrases in bold.

Reading. Students find out the meanings of the phrases in bold. This should help them understand more detail in each text.

Answers

> **Sabrina**
> *je m'entends bien avec* – I get on well with
> *C'est ma mère qui m'énerve. Elle me critique tout le temps.* – It's my mother who gets on my nerves. She criticises me all the time.
> **Éric**
> *Mes parents sont toujours fatigués et de mauvaise humeur. Ils ne comprennent pas moi, j'ai des choses à faire aussi.* – My parents are always tired and in a bad mood. They don't understand that I also have things to do.
> **Sébastien**
> *Il est très sévère et j'ai l'impression qu'il ne m'aime pas. Mes parents disent que c'est de ma faute et que je dois travailler plus dur mais je fais déjà tout ce que je peux.* – He is very strict and I have the impression that he doesn't like me. My parents say that it's my fault and that I must work harder, but I am already doing all that I can.
> **Juliette**
> *on s'entend bien! On discute ensemble* – we get on well. We talk about things together
> *On se dispute très rarement.* – We argue very rarely.
> *elle me respecte et je la respecte* – she respects me and I respect her

1b Read the letters and answer the questions.

Reading (1–4). Students read the letters again and answer the questions in English. Having done the pre-reading activities, they should find this task more accessible.

Answers

> **1a** She criticises her all the time, she won't allow her to go out with her friends during the week and she does not like her boyfriend. (3)
> **b** Leave home and go to live with her boyfriend. (2)
> **2a** He loves it; it's interesting and useful. (2)
> **b** He is very strict and he thinks that the teacher does not like him. (2)
> **c** That it's his fault and that he should work harder. (2)
> **d** Because he does not want him to speak to his maths teacher. (1)
> **3a** He has a lot of it. (1)
> **b** Shopping, set and clear the table and do the vacuuming. He has also to do his own washing. (any 2)
> **c** They are always tired and in a bad mood. They don't realise that he has things to do too. (2)
> **4a** She is not writing with a problem. She gets on well with her parents. (1)
> **b** He is understanding, has a sense of humour and helps her with her homework. (3)

Le détective

Direct object pronouns. Practise the construction with some other verbs, e.g. I see him, I like her.

1c Write a letter of your own to Tante Monique. You may have to invent a problem! Use the phrases in the key language box and the letters to help you.

Writing. Students write their own letter to Tante Monique. Encourage them to write as accurately as they can by allowing them to use the written texts as models. Writing for Standard Grade assessment and for Intermediate N.A.B.s must be produced under controlled conditions but students can base their initial drafts on texts they know to be correct and impressive.

Tip box

Listening skills. This reminds students not to panic if they don't understand everything and to think in advance of the sort of vocabulary they might hear.

2 Listen to these people. Are they happy or sad? Give one reason for each person.

Listening (1–5). Students say whether each person is happy or sad and give one reason for each.

Tapescript

1 Pour moi, ça va très bien à la maison, parce que mes parents sont très très sympa, et je peux leur parler de mes problèmes.

2 Je ne m'entends pas bien avec mon frère. Il me critique tout le temps: 'tu es trop grosse', 'tu manges trop de bonbons', 'tu es bête'… Il est vraiment casse-pieds.

3 Moi, j'aimerais bien avoir un petit chien, mais mes parents refusent de me donner la permission d'avoir un animal. Je suis vraiment triste à cause de ça.

4 À la maison, il n'y a pas de problèmes. Toute la famille a un bon sens de l'humour, et quand il y a des problèmes, on discute ensemble et on ne se dispute pas.

5 Je ne suis pas très content en ce moment, parce que mes parents sont en train de divorcer, et il y a beaucoup de disputes tous les jours entre eux.

Answers

1 happy – gets on well with parents
2 sad – brother is very annoying
3 sad – parents won't allow him to have a dog
4 happy – family all have sense of humour, talk together and don't argue
5 sad – parents getting divorced

3 Listen to these teenagers talking about their parents. Note one or two details for each person.

Listening (1–6). Students listen and note one or two details for each person.

Tapescript

1 J'ai de super bonnes relations avec mes parents. J'ai le droit de boire de l'alcool avec modération. Ils sont cools. Je peux me confier à mes parents. La seule chose qui m'embête, je n'ai pas le droit de rentrer après onze heures du soir. Ça m'énerve!

2 Mes parents ne sont pas difficiles. Je peux sortir quand je veux, j'ai le droit de partir en vacances avec des amis et ils me donnent beaucoup de liberté et de responsabilité. On se respecte – je pense que c'est important, ça.

3 Mes parents ne s'entendent pas bien et c'est moi qui souffre. Je ne peux rien faire. J'ai pas le droit de sortir en semaine et je dois faire mes devoirs avant de regarder la télé. J'en ai marre. Ils n'ont qu'à divorcer – ce serait mieux pour tout le monde.

4 C'est bien chez moi, je peux fumer dans ma chambre, je peux regarder la télé quand je veux. Je peux parler à mes parents comme à des amis. J'ai le droit de faire ce que je veux, quoi. J'ai beaucoup de chance, je le sais bien.

5 Je m'entends très bien avec ma mère, mais mon père ne respecte pas mes idées. Puisqu'il est adulte, il croit être supérieur. Je n'aime pas du tout son attitude, moi aussi j'ai le droit d'avoir des opinions. On se dispute tout le temps et ma mère n'aime pas ça du tout.

6 Mes parents sont assez jeunes, mais ils sont stricts dans un sens. Je n'ai pas le droit de sortir pendant la semaine par exemple. Mais le week-end, je peux rentrer après minuit. Ils savent que je fume, mais je n'ai pas le droit de fumer à la maison. C'est un peu contradictoire, mais voilà, c'est comme ça!

Answers

1 Gets on well with parents, can drink alcohol in moderation, can talk to them. However, can't come home after 11pm.
2 Can go out, go on holidays with friends, parents give her freedom and responsibility. They respect each other.
3 Parents don't get on, can't go out in the week, has to do homework before watching the TV. Thinks parents should divorce.
4 Can smoke in bedroom, watch the TV at any time. Can speak to parents like friends. Can do as he wants.
5 Gets on with mother, but dad does not respect her ideas. Doesn't like dad's attitude, thinks she has the right to have own opinions. Argues with dad all the time – mum not happy with that.
6 Can't go out in the week but can come back after midnight at the weekend. They know he smokes but not allowed to in the house.

4a In pairs. Discuss how you get on with people.

Speaking. Students discuss how they get on with people, using the example dialogue as support.

4b Prepare a short presentation on someone you get on well with and why. It could be a member of your family, a friend or a teacher. Try to use some phrases from the letters.

Speaking. This brings together much of the language from the module. It can be added to students' tape of prepared speaking tasks.

Further practice of the language and vocabulary of this spread is provided as follows:

À toi! A and B, pages 182–183

Cahier d'exercices, pages 16–18

All the key vocabulary and structures from this module are listed on the **Mots** pages 38–39. These can be used for revision by covering up either the English or the French. Students can check here to see how much they remember from the module and use them to prepare for the assessments.

Assessment materials for Modules 1 and 2 are available in the separate Assessment Pack.

Further speaking and grammar practice on the whole module is provided on **Cahier d'exercices** pages 17–18.

Entraînez-vous: À l'oral

MODULE 2 — CHEZ MOI

(Student's Book pages 36–37)

These spreads give regular practice in the three types of speaking activity required for the internally assessed speaking elements of the Standard Grade and Intermediate courses: conversations, transactions and prepared talks.

The activities on the speaking pages are designed to allow students to build up their speaking skills while working with a partner independently of teacher support. They also include handy hints on how students can improve their speaking grades.

Page 36 provides speaking activities for Module 1: conversations on the school day, school subjects and future plans and a prepared talk on future plans.

Page 37 provides speaking activities for Module 2: a conversation on helping at home, an interview for a job as an au pair and a prepared talk about a friend.

À toi! A & B

MODULE 2 — CHEZ MOI

(Student's Book pages 182–183)

These pages are designed to give students extra practice in reading and structured writing. There are two differentiated pages relating to each chapter: A and B. Page A is at an easier level and page B more challenging. You may wish students to work on the page most appropriate to their level or work through both pages. You may feel it is useful to work with students on the activities, but it should be possible for most students to work on them independently. The most appropriate time to use each page is indicated within the relevant teaching notes.

À Toi! A, page 182

This page is best used after pages 34–35 of the Student's Book.

1a Read the letters above and answer these questions in English.

Answers

> 1 Because she has a problem with her father. (1)
> 2 He criticises her all the time, won't allow her to go out with her friends, does not like her clothes or her friends and forbids her from seeing them. (3)
> 3 They get on well. (1)
> 4 She makes fun of him, criticising his clothes, his hobbies, the music he likes, even his way of talking. (4)

1b Find the French for the following.

Answers

> 1 il me faut des conseils
> 2 je m'entends bien avec ma mère
> 3 Il me critique tout le temps
> 4 veut m'interdire de les voir
> 5 j'en ai marre   6 Je suis très malheureuse
> 7 tout allait bien   8 quand nous sommes seuls
> 9 Elle est toujours très gentille.
> 10 c'est complètement différent
> 11 Elle se moque de moi
> 12 je ne peux pas continuer comme ça

1c Write a summary in English of one of the letters (about 50 words).

Answers

> Possible answers
> **Letter A**
> She has a problem with her dad. She gets on with her mum but her dad won't give her pocket money and she has to do all the housework. He criticises her, won't let her go out or see her friends. He doesn't like her clothes or her friends.
> **Letter B**
> He has a girlfriend who he has been seeing for 3 months. When they're alone all is well, but when they are with others she criticises him and makes fun of him.

2 Write a letter about a problem you would like to share with the readers (you could make one up).

À Toi! B, page 183

This page is best used after pages 34–35 of the Student's Book.

1a Read the text and answer the questions in English.

Answers

> 1 Because she gets jealous when her best friend speaks to other people. (1)
> 2 Jealousy is normal because everyone is a bit self-centred. (2)
> 3 It can develop someone's character (1)
> 4 They risk becoming isolated from their other friends and then their friendship will not last a long time (2)

1b Find the French for the following.

Answers

> 1 Tout le monde est un peu égoïste.
> 2 tout à fait normale
> 3 leur amitié ne durera pas longtemps
> 4 il est important d'avoir beaucoup d'amis
> 5 ta meilleure amie

2 You have seen this article in a magazine. What kind of friend are you? Write in French to the magazine.

Cahier d'exercices, page 11

4a (individual task)

4b (writing task)

5
Answers

> Michel Baudouin – Cognac – seize avril 1987 – Paris –
> trois – une – sympa, sociable et très patient –
> sens de l'humour – un peu paresseux et bruyant

1
Answers

> **a** Le cinq février deux mille.
> **b** Le quinze mars mille neuf cent quatre-vingt-quatre.
> **c** Le premier mai mille sept cent quatre-vingt-dix-neuf.
> **d** Le douze octobre mille neuf cent quarante et un.
> **e** Le vingt-sept juillet deux mille trois.

2
Answers

> **a** Loulou **b** none **c** 3
> **d** 17 (*until 30/6/02*) **e** Justin

3
Answers

> **a** son **b** ma **c** ton **d** sa **e** ses **f** sa
> **g** votre **h** son **i** ses **j** mon

Cahier d'exercices, page 12

Cahier d'exercices, page 13

6a (writing task)

6b (writing task)

Cahier d'exercices, page 14

7
Answers

a I hate vacuum cleaning.
b Clearing the table is OK.
c I hate taking the rubbish bin out.
d I love working in the garden.
e I never go (food) shopping.
f I often wash the car.

8 (writing task)

9
Answers

a Xavier's mother.
b She works in a small shop.
c She does the shopping, looks after the house, cooks, cleans the house.
d He does the vacuum cleaning.
e He looks after the garden and the car.
f He makes his bed, sets the table and does the washing-up.
g Because he forgets to take the rubbish bin out.

Cahier d'exercices, page 15

10
Answers

a Émilie lives in Bécherel, near Rennes.
b The eldest brother is called Bruno and is 18. The other is called Benjamin and will be 3 in December.
c She has a dog and a budgerigar.
d She says she is of average height, has brown eyes and brown hair, she is rather shy and hard-working.
e They annoy her when she must do her homework.
f Bruno listens to very loud music.
g Benjamin watches cartoons on TV.
h She does the cooking and the housework.

11 (writing task)

Cahier d'exercices, page 16

12
Answers

	Who do they have a problem with and why?	One detail about their appearance + one detail about their personality	What question do they ask?
Norbert	older brother – they do not get on	slim, handsome – kind, modest, generous	Why should they be friends just because they are brothers?
Yvonne	parents – they treat her like a baby	short (1m 50) – mature	How can I explain to my parents that I am almost an adult?
François	step-parents – he is fed up with them	curly blond hair – good sense of humour	How can I change their attitude?

Cahier d'exercices, page 17

2 Chez moi

Grammaire

1 Fill in the spaces using the correct form of the verb indicated.

a Élodie _____ casse-pieds. (*être*)
b Mes parents _____ trois enfants. (*avoir*)
c Nous _____ le ménage le week-end. (*faire*)
d Elles _____ la vaisselle dans la cuisine. (*faire*)
e Tu _____ un animal? (*avoir*)
f Vous _____ les yeux bleus. (*avoir*)
g Vous _____ jolie. (*être*)
h Je _____ petit. (*être*)

If you hesitated on some of these, copy the verb tables down (you will find them in the grammar section of the textbook) and LEARN THEM!!

2 Make these adjectives agree.

a Ma mère est _____ (*grand*)
b Ma tante est _____ (*petit*)
c Mon oncle est _____ (*mince*)
d Mes parents sont _____ (*aimable*)
e Mes nièces sont _____ (*équilibré*)
f Mes frères sont _____ (*bête*)
g Ma demi-sœur est _____ (*bavard*)
h Mes grands-parents sont _____ (*sévère*)
i Ma femme est _____ (*plein de vie*)
j Mes cousines sont _____ (*sage*)

Rappel
Mon père (*masc. sing.*) est amusant.
Ma mère (*fém. sing.*) est amusante.
Mes frères (*masc. pl.*) sont amusants.
Mes sœurs (*fém. pl.*) sont amusantes.

3 Choose the correct form of *devoir* to write out 6 correct sentences.

Mon frère	**dois**	ranger sa chambre.
Vous	**dois**	passer l'aspirateur.
Ma sœur et moi	**doit**	faire la vaisselle.
Tu	**devons**	faire ton lit?
Mes parents	**devez**	faire les courses tous les week-ends.
Je	**doivent**	beaucoup aider à la maison.

Métro pour l'Écosse © Heinemann Educational 2002

17

Cahier d'exercices, page 18

2 Chez moi

Bilan

1 Parle-moi de ta famille.

2 Tu t'entends bien avec tes parents?

3 Comment sont-ils?

4 Décris-toi physiquement.

5 Quelles sont tes qualités et tes défauts?

6 Décris un copain/une copine. Pourquoi est-ce un bon copain/une bonne copine?

7 Parle-moi d'une personne que tu admires.

8 Avec qui as-tu de bonnes relations? Pourquoi?

9 Décris quelqu'un que tu ne respectes pas et dis pourquoi.

10 Qu'est-ce que tu fais et ne fais pas pour aider à la maison? Pourquoi?

Métro pour l'Écosse © Heinemann Educational 2002

18

1
Answers

| **a** est | **b** ont | **c** faisons | **d** font | **e** as |
| **f** avez | **g** êtes | **h** suis | | |

2
Answers

a grande	**b** petite	**c** mince	**d** aimables
e équilibrées	**f** bêtes	**g** bavarde	**h** sévères
i grande	**j** sages		

3
Answers

Mon frère doit ranger sa chambre.
Vous devez passer l'aspirateur.
Ma sœur et moi devons faire la vaisselle.
Tu dois faire ton lit?
Mes parents doivent faire les courses tous les week-ends.
Je dois beaucoup aider à la maison.

MODULE 3 — TEMPS LIBRE

Temps libre

(Student's Book pages 40–57)

Topic area	Key language	Grammar	Skills/Strategies
Déjà vu (pp. 40–43) Talking about sports and leisure Talking about more leisure activities Inviting someone out	*Je lis. Je nage. Je joue avec l'ordinateur. Je vais à la pêche.* *Je fais du sport/du vélo/de la musculation/du ski nautique/du surf/du skate/du roller/du théâtre/de la gymnastique/de la danse/de la natation/ de l'équitation.* *Je regarde la télé. Je joue au tennis/volley. Je vais au cinéma.* *le lundi matin/après-midi/soir/le week-end* *C'est …/Je trouve ça … génial/super/passionnant/chouette/amusant/pas mal/barbant/affreux/pénible.* *faire de la musculation/du snowboard/du tir à l'arc/des arts martiaux/ une randonnée* *Tu veux aller au cinéma/au théâtre/au concert/à la piscine/en boîte?* *On se retrouve devant/derrière/dans la piscine/le cinéma/le stade.* *en face du théâtre/chez moi/toi/Benjamin* *aujourd'hui/ce soir/mercredi prochain/demain/après-demain/dans deux heures/à trois heures/vers dix heures*	*faire du/de la/de l'/des* *jouer au/à la/à là l'/aux* Comparatives and superlatives Ways of asking questions	Being careful of 'faux amis'
1 Les opinions (pp. 44–45) Saying what you like and don't like doing	*C'est affreux/agréable/barbant/choquant/chouette/cool/dangereux/ ennuyeux/extraordinaire/génial/impressionnant/intéressant/ magnifique/nul/pas mal/passionnant.* *faire du tir à l'arc/du snowboard/des arts martiaux/de la musculation/des randonnées/du rallye/du parapente/du patin sur glace/de l'athlétisme* *Ça me tient en forme. C'est bon pour la santé. Il y a le goût du risque.* *Ça ne coûte pas cher.*		How to agree and disagree Reading: not necessary to understand all the text
2 Les prix et les heures (pp. 46–47) Finding out about leisure facilities and buying tickets	*Vous ouvrez/fermez à quelle heure? C'est combien par personne?* *Il y a une réduction pour les étudiants? Je peux avoir des places au balcon/à l'orchestre?* *Le concert commence à quelle heure? Je voudrais un/deux ticket(s) d'entrée.* *Ça dure combien de temps?*		

TEMPS LIBRE ● MODULE MÉTRO 3

Topic area	Key language	Grammar	Skills/Strategies
3 On va au cinéma (pp. 48–49) Going to the pictures	*Tu veux aller au cinéma/au concert ce soir?* *Ça commence/finit à quelle heure?* *Un ticket d'entrée, c'est combien?* *On se voit où et à quelle heure?* *Séances à … film d'aventures/film romantique/comédie/drame psychologique/ film de science-fiction* *Les effets sont … superbes/passionnants/incroyables.* *Les acteurs sont … excellents/très naturels.*		Using IT for research
4 Invitations (pp. 50–51) Asking people out	*Tu veux aller à la boum/en boîte/au cirque/au concert?* *Tu voudrais voir le match de foot/un film?* *On pourrait faire un pique-nique/une excursion à vélo.* *D'accord. Je veux bien.* *Je suis désolé(e). Je regrette. Je m'excuse.* *Je suis contre (les cirques). J'aimerais mieux rester à la maison.* *Je dois faire mes devoirs. Ça ne me dit rien.*	Modal verbs	
5 Ça s'est bien passé? (pp. 52–53) Talking about the past	*Je suis allé(e) (à une boum/au club/à la piscine/en ville). Je suis resté(e) (à la maison).* *J'ai regardé (la télé). J'ai joué (aux cartes/jeux vidéo, du violon, au foot).* *J'ai mangé (un hamburger). J'ai écouté (des cassettes).* *J'ai passé (un week-end actif). J'ai surfé sur Internet. J'ai fait (une promenade, du VTT).* *J'ai lu (un livre). J'ai vu (un film). J'ai bu (un Coca). J'ai promené (mon chien).* *Je me suis reposé(e). Je me suis bien amusé(e).*	Perfect tense with *avoir* and *être*	Telling the difference between the perfect and present tenses Using useful phrases Using time expressions and opinions
Entraînez-vous: À l'écrit (pp. 54–55) Les copains et les loisirs	Language from Module 3		Extended writing Writing an e-mail Using different tenses and opinions Writing longer sentences
À toi! A and B (pp. 184–185)	Language from Module 3		Reading and writing skills

The vocabulary and structures taught in Module 3 are summarised on the **Mots** pages of the Student's Book, pages 56–57.
Further speaking practice on the language of the module is provided on **À l'oral**, page 72.
Assessment tasks for Modules 3 and 4 combined are provided in the separate Assessment Pack.

Main topics and objectives

- Talking about sport and leisure
- Talking about different leisure activities
- Inviting someone out

Key language

Je lis. Je nage.
Je joue avec l'ordinateur. Je vais à la pêche.
Je fais du sport/du vélo/de la musculation.
du ski nautique/du surf/du skate/du roller
du théâtre/de la gymnastique/de la danse
de la natation/de l'équitation
Je regarde la télé. Je vais au cinéma.
Je joue au tennis/volley.
le lundi matin/après-midi/soir/le week-end
C'est … /Je trouve ça …
   génial/super/passionnant/chouette/amusant/pas mal.
   barbant/affreux/pénible
faire de la musculation
faire du snowboard
faire du tir à l'arc
faire des arts martiaux
faire une randonnée

*Tu veux aller au cinéma/au théâtre/au concert/à la
   piscine/en boîte?*
*On se retrouve devant/derrière/dans la piscine/le
   cinéma/le stade.*
en face du théâtre/de la piscine
chez moi/toi/Benjamin
aujourd'hui/ce soir/mercredi prochain
demain/après-demain
dans deux heures/à trois heures/vers dix heures

Grammar

- *jouer à/faire de*
- Comparative and superlative
- Ways of asking questions

Skills/Strategies

- Being careful of *faux amis*

Resources

À l'oral, page 72: Conversation 1
Cassette B side 1
Cahier d'exercices, page 19

Introduce these spreads by brainstorming hobbies. Make separate lists of those which are *jouer à/faire de* and those which go with other verbs. Look at the *Rappel* box with students. Introduce any hobbies from the key language box which have not already been mentioned by the class.

1a Write a sentence for each picture.

Writing. Using the key language box for support, students write a sentence to describe each picture.

Answers

> **a** Je fais du roller.   **b** Je fais du ski nautique.
> **c** Je fais du sport.   **d** Je fais de la danse.
> **e** Je joue avec l'ordinateur.   **f** Je fais du vélo.
> **g** Je fais du théâtre.   **h** Je fais du surf.
> **i** Je fais du skate.   **j** Je fais de la gymnastique.
> **k** Je nage.   **l** Je fais de la musculation.
> **m** Je vais à la pêche.   **n** Je lis.

1b Replace the pictures with the right phrases.

Writing. Students complete the text replacing the pictures with the hobby phrases.

Answers

> Normalement le week-end, je <u>fais du sport</u>. Le samedi matin, je <u>vais à la pêche</u> et je <u>fais du skate</u>. Quelquefois, je <u>fais du vélo</u> avec mes copains ou je <u>fais de la musculation</u>. Le dimanche, je <u>nage</u> et je <u>lis</u> des magazines. Souvent je <u>joue avec l'ordinateur</u>.

Before moving on to 1c, revise/present the opinion phrases in the key language box. Make a comment on a particular hobby, e.g. *La natation, c'est chouette.* Students agree or disagree with you.

1c Listen. Note the activity and the opinion.

Listening (1–8). Students listen and note the activity and each person's opinion.

Tapescript

1 Le sport, je trouve ça affreux.
2 La pêche, c'est passionnant.
3 Je pense que la natation est vraiment géniale.
4 À mon avis, l'équitation n'est pas mal.
5 Je lis beaucoup. La lecture, c'est super.
6 Le volley est très amusant.
7 Je pense que le ski, c'est chouette. J'adore les sports
   d'hiver.
8 La télé, c'est barbant.

Answers

activity	🙂	😐	🙁
1 sport			✔
2 fishing	✔		
3 swimming	✔		
4 horse-riding		✔	
5 reading	✔		
6 volley-ball	✔		
7 skiing	✔		
8 TV			✔

Tip box

False friends. Remind students that not all words which look like English words mean the same thing. Brainstorm words which look alike but which have different meanings in French and English. See how long a list they can build up.

1d In pairs. Take turns to make sentences from the prompts.

Speaking. Using the key language box as support, students make up a sentence to describe the prompts given. Point out how to say <u>on</u> Monday morning, etc., reminding them that there is no equivalent for 'on' in French.

Le détective

Comparatives and superlatives. Practise the comparative by comparing the heights of people in the class. Then look at some superlatives: *Quelle est la montagne la plus haute du monde / la rivière la plus longue / le pays le plus peuplé / l'animal le plus rapide / la personne la plus riche?*, etc. This could be given as a research activity for homework.

2 Look at the survey results and say whether these sentences are true or false. Correct the false sentences.

Reading (1–5). Students study the grid and decide whether the sentences are true or false, then correct the false ones.

Answers

1 true **2** false **3** true **4** false **5** true	
2 Le hockey est moins populaire que le cyclisme./Le cyclisme est plus populaire que le hockey.	
4 Les activités les plus populaires sont la natation, le football et le tennis.	

3a In pairs. Practise this conversation, then change the underlined words to make a new conversation.

Speaking. Students practise the example conversation and then change the words underlined to make a new conversation.

Student's Book pages 42–43

3b Write about 50 words on your hobbies. You should include when you do them and what you think of them.

Writing. Students use the language already covered to write briefly about their hobbies. This could be used as practice for the writing exam.

Before moving on to activity **4**, revise times quickly with a large clock. Also, look at the different sporting

activities in the key language box and ask students to guess what they mean. You could ask them to match each with a picture in activity **4**.

4 Listen. Match the times to the pictures.

Listening. Students listen and match the pictures to the correct times.

Tapescript

Alors, à huit heures trente pour commencer la journée, on fait de la musculation.

À neuf heures, vous avez la possibilité de faire une randonnée qui dure trois heures.

À dix heures, on fait du snowboard. Je suis sûre que je vous verrai tous là-haut à un moment donné.

Continuons, à midi on a donc une heure de tir à l'arc avant de manger.

On repart à quatorze heures quand on fait de la moto ou bien des arts martiaux. Ça dure deux heures normalement. Après, c'est le goûter et ensuite vous avez du temps libre. Voilà.

Answers

1 e	**2** b	**3** c	**4** d	**5** a

5 Read the programme of activities and choose a suitable activity for each person.

Reading (1–5). Students read the programme, using a dictionary if required, and choose an activity for each person from the programme below.

Answers

1 b	**2** a	**3** d	**4** e	**5** c

6 Listen. Copy and complete the grid.

Listening. Students listen and complete the grid. This practises general vocabulary relating to dates and prices.

Tapescript

Alors ce soir sur NRF c'est le programme d'été pour les jeunes – tout ce qu'il y a pour vous amuser partout en Europe. Spectacles, événements, animations, vous n'avez qu'à vous déplacer. Alors, bougez, les enfants!

Par exemple, le 30 juin et le premier juillet, il y a un festival de rock. Le rock dans tous ses états à Évreux. Ça a l'air bien, il y aura Massilia et toute la bande. Billets entre €14,50 et €24,50. Pour avoir plus de renseignements, faites le 02 32 39 16 24.

Ensuite, entre le premier et le 9 juillet, si vous vous intéressez au cinoche, il y a le festival du cinéma 'Résistances' qui comprend une programmation pour vous les jeunes avec 12 films contre le racisme. Ça aura lieu à Tarascon-sur-Ariège. Le prix, €5 par séance.

Moi, je vais certainement au festival d'Avignon 'Théâtre enfants et tout public'. Ça m'intéresse. Ça commence donc le 10 juillet et continue jusqu'au 29. Prix d'entrée €3. Voici le numéro de téléphone si ça vous tente: 04 90 85 59 55.

Quoi encore? Eh bien, il y a un concert qui sera génial le 30 juillet, c'est de la musique classique, certes, mais ce concert va avoir lieu dans une grotte, oui, à Aven-Armand dans les Cévennes. Prix d'entrée, €6,50. L'ambiance sera cool – moi, j'y cours.

Answers

	date	prices	one other detail
Evreux rock festival	30.6–1.7	€14,50–€24,50	Tel 02 32 39 16 24
film festival	1.7–9.7	€5	12 films against racism
Avignon festival	10.7–29.7	€3	Tel 04 90 85 59 55
classical music concert	30.7	€6,50	Takes place in cave

Before moving on to **7a**, introduce simple ways of asking people out from the key language box on page 43. Ask students to make different combinations of the phases from the key language box. How many can they make in two minutes?

7a Copy and complete the grid in English.

Reading (1–6). Students read the notes and copy and complete the grid in English.

Answers

when?	where?
1 tomorrow morning	my house
2 12.00 next Thursday	at Anne-Claire's house
3 today, in 2 hours	at the swimming pool
4 8pm the day after tomorrow	in front of the cinema
5 tonight at about 7pm	at your house
6 7pm	opposite the station

Le détective

Asking questions. Remind students how important it is to be able to ask questions. You may wish to point out the difficulties in inverting the subject and verb and suggest it may be better to avoid it. Give students a question and ask them to form the same question in two different ways.

7b In pairs. Practise this conversation. Change the underlined words to make a new conversation, using the words in the key language box.

Speaking. Using the key language box for support, students practise the example conversation and then change the underlined words to make a new conversation.

7c Listen. Copy and complete the grid.

Listening (1–3). Students listen and complete the grid in English.

Tapescript

1 – *Allô, Françoise? Veux-tu aller en boîte ce soir?*
  – *Oui, je voudrais bien.*
  – *On se retrouve où?*
  – *Chez toi ?*
  – *OK. À quelle heure?*
  – *À neuf heures.*
2 – *Paul? Je vais à un concert ce soir. Tu veux venir avec moi?*
  – *Oui, pourquoi pas. On se retrouve où?*
  – *Devant le théâtre?*
  – *Et on se retrouve à quelle heure?*
  – *À six heures et demie.*
3 – *Tu voudrais aller à la piscine cet après-midi?*
  – *Oui, bonne idée. On se retrouve où?*
  – *Devant la piscine? À deux heures et quart?*
  – *D'accord. À bientôt !*

Answers

	activity	meeting place	time
1	go to club	at your house	9.00
2	concert	in front of theatre	6.30
3	swimming	in front of the pool	2.15

7d Write these invitations in French. Begin each with: …

Writing. Students write out the invitations in French following the prompts.

Answers

1 On se retrouve chez moi vers trois heures.
2 On se retrouve devant le stade, demain à deux heures et demie.
3 On se retrouve mercredi prochain, chez toi.
4 On se retrouve après-demain, chez Benjamin.
5 On se retrouve dans une heure au stade.
6 On se retrouve aujourd'hui vers midi.

Further practice of the language and vocabulary of this spread is provided as follows:

À l'oral, page 72: Conversation 1

Cahier d'exercices, page 19

MODULE 3 TEMPS LIBRE

1 Les opinions

(Student's Book pages 44–45)

Main topics and objectives

● Saying what you like and don't like doing

Key language

*C'est affreux/agréable/barbant/choquant/chouette/
cool/dangereux/ennuyeux/extraordinaire/génial/
impressionnant/intéressant/magnifique/nul/pas
mal/passionnant.
faire du tir à l'arc/du snowboard/des arts martiaux/
de la musculation/des randonnées/du rallye
faire du parapente/du patin sur glace/de l'athlétisme
Ça me tient en forme.*

*C'est bon pour la santé.
Il y a le goût du risque.
Ça ne coûte pas cher.*

Skills/Strategies

● How to agree and disagree
● Reading: not necessary to understand all the text

Resources

Cassette B side 1

Introduce the spread by revise hobbies with students, but this time asking them for an adjective to describe the activity. Encourage them to use adjectives they know first and then identify others which would be useful. Introduce any not mentioned from the key language box. Remind them that the adjective remains unchanged after *c'est*. Introduce/revise the six activities from the key language box and ask students for their opinions on them.

1a Divide the adjectives in the key language box into 2 groups – positive and negative.

Reading. Students divide the adjectives in the key language into two groups. They could include any other new adjectives they have found in the initial brainstorming.

Answers (open to interpretation)

Positive: agréable, chouette, cool, extraordinaire, génial, impressionnant, intéressant, magnifique, passionnant
Negative: affreux, barbant, choquant, dangereux, ennuyeux, nul, pas mal

1b Listen to these people. Do they like (✔) or dislike (✗) the activities?

Listening (1–6). Students listen and decide whether the speakers like or dislike the activities.

Tapescript

1 *Faire du tir à l'arc? J'ai horreur de ça. Je déteste regarder ça à la télé. C'est franchement nul, et qu'est-ce que c'est ennuyeux. Non merci!*
2 *Ce qui est bien c'est le snowboard, c'est un peu dangereux, mais c'est passionnant. J'aime bien faire ça. C'est génial.*
3 *Je fais des randonnées tous les étés. J'adore ça, j'aime bien être en plein air, c'est chouette.*
4 *Mes copains me prennent pour un fou puisque je fais du rallye toutes les semaines, mais moi, je trouve ça trop cool, c'est passionnant. J'adore la vitesse.*

5 *Je fais des arts martiaux, je suis très petite, mais je suis forte quand je me bats – c'est extraordinaire.*
6 *Ma mère insiste pour que j'aille au club de gym tous les vendredis soirs. Je fais de la musculation. C'est agréable de se détendre le vendredi soir après le collège.*

Answers

1 ✗	2 ✓	3 ✓	4 ✓	5 ✓	6 ✓

1c Listen again and note any adjectives mentioned.

Listening. Students listen again and note the adjectives mentioned from those in the key language box.

Answers

1 nul (rubbish), ennuyeux (boring)
2 dangereux (dangerous), passionnant (exciting), génial (great)
3 chouette (great)
4 cool (cool), passionnant (exciting)
5 extraordinaire (extraordinary)
6 agréable (pleasant)

Tip box

Agreeing and disagreeing. Remind students of how useful these expressions are. Practise them round the class by asking their opinion on various issues, e.g. *les hommes sont plus intelligents que les femmes (!), le mariage est démodé, le français est ennuyeux.*

1d In pairs. What do you think of the activities in the pictures?

Speaking. With a partner, students give their opinion of the activities in the pictures using the example as support.

Before moving on to 2a, introduce the language from the box at the bottom of the page. Read out the four reasons in turn and ask students to name any sports which fit each reason.

2a Listen and answer the questions in English.

Listening. Students listen and answer the questions in English. Remind them that the points after each question tell them how many pieces of information they are looking for.

Tapescript

– Voici Annick, Rahel et Charles qui vont nous parler de leur passe-temps. Alors, Annick, tu es fanatique des sports d'hiver, c'est ça?

– Oui, tout ce qui est ski, snowboard, patin sur glace, j'adore ça. C'est un peu cher pour aller dans les stations de ski, mais c'est bon pour la santé. Ça me tient en forme.

– Oui … Et toi, Rahel?

– Moi, je suis fou de parapente. C'est très cher, mais j'adore ça. Il y a aussi le goût du risque.

– Et finalement, Charles, qu'est-ce qui t'influence dans ton choix de passe-temps?

– Alors moi, je choisis des trucs qui ne coûtent pas cher. Je joue beaucoup au foot, ce qui est bon pour la santé, et je fais de l'athlétisme.

Answers

1a	skiing, snowboarding, ice-skating (3)
b	it's good for your health and it keeps her fit (any 1)
2a	there's the risk element (1)
b	it's very expensive (1)
3a	something which is not expensive (1)
b	football and athletics (2)

2b In pairs. Create sentences. (See p.112 for weather vocabulary.)

Speaking. With a partner, students build up sentences using the example and the key language box as support.

Answers

1 S'il fait beau, je fais du parapente. C'est fantastique.
2 S'il neige, je fais du snowboard. C'est super et il y a le goût du risque.
3 S'il pleut, je lis. C'est intéressant.
4 S'il fait froid, je fais du patin sur glace. C'est passionnant et ça me tient en forme.
5 S'il pleut, je fais de la musculation. C'est bon pour la santé.
6 S'il fait chaud, je fais du roller. Ça ne coûte pas cher.

➕ Ask students to make up some more examples of their own.

3a Look up the words in red in a dictionary and note their meaning. Match the sentences to the pictures.

Reading (1–5). Students look up the words in red, then match each sentence to the correct picture. To encourage dictionary skills – and add an element of fun – students could race each other at this activity.

Answers

1 b	**2** a	**3** d	**4** e	**5** c					

3b Choose 3 sentences from **3a** and translate them into English.

Reading. Students choose the three sentences they wish to translate.

Tip box

Reading strategies. Remind students that they do not need to understand all the text to answer the questions. They should always read a text first for gist, then look at the questions and read the text again in more detail. They should only look up a few necessary words.

4 Read the text and answer the questions in English.

Reading. Students read the text and answer the questions in English.

Answers

1	leisure in the 21st century (2)
2	for everyone (1)
3	to relax (1)
4	to forget work and to escape from everyday life (2)
5	to escape from their homework (1)
6	because of the risk element (1)

5a Write an article of 50 words about how you and one of your friends spend your free time. You should include: …

Writing. Students write about how they or a friend spend their free time, using language from this and previous spreads. This activity could be used as practice for the Writing exam.

5b CV Choose at least 5 statements about how you spend your leisure time and combine them in a paragraph under the title *Loisirs* on disc. Insert the data into your CV document.

Writing. Students write about their leisure activities to add to their CV from Modules 1 and 2.

2 Les prix et les heures

(Student's Book pages 46–47)

Main topics and objectives

● Finding out about leisure facilities and buying tickets

Key language

Vous ouvrez à quelle heure?
Vous fermez à quelle heure?
C'est combien par personne?
Il y a une réduction pour les étudiants?

Je peux avoir des places au balcon/à l'orchestre?
Le concert commence à quelle heure?
Je voudrais un/deux ticket(s) d'entrée.
Ça dure combien de temps?

Resources

Cassette B side 1

Before starting work on this spread, revise numbers, times and prices. Dictate them and ask students to write them down. Ask them to write down a variety of numbers, prices and times and dictate them to others in the class. Remind them that they must be able to cope with numbers out of sequence.

1a Listen. Copy and complete the grid.

Listening. Students listen and complete the grid with times and prices.

Tapescript

1 – Allô, ici la piscine municipale.
 – Bonjour, monsieur. Vous ouvrez à quelle heure aujourd'hui?
 – À sept heures et quart.
 – Et vous fermez à quelle heure?
 – À neuf heures et demie.
 – Merci. Et c'est combien par personne?
 – C'est €3 pour les adultes, et €2.30 pour les enfants.
 – Est-ce qu'il y a une réduction pour les étudiants?
 – Ah non.
 – Merci beaucoup. Au revoir, monsieur.
 – Au revoir.
2 – Allô, ici le théâtre Gallimard.
 – Bonjour, madame. Vous ouvrez à quelle heure aujourd'hui?
 – À six heures du soir.
 – Et vous fermez à quelle heure?
 – À minuit.
 – Merci. C'est combien par personne?
 – C'est €18.30 pour les adultes, et €15.20 pour les enfants.
 – Est-ce qu'il y a une réduction pour les étudiants?
 – Oui, les étudiants paient €15.20 la place.
 – Merci beaucoup. Au revoir, madame.
3 – Allô, ici la patinoire.
 – Bonjour, monsieur. Vous ouvrez à quelle heure, aujourd'hui?
 – À neuf heures et demie.
 – Et vous fermez à quelle heure?
 – À vingt-deux heures. C'est-à-dire, à dix heures du soir.
 – Merci. C'est combien par personne?
 – C'est €2.90 pour les adultes, et €1.70 pour les enfants.
 – Est-ce qu'il y a une réduction pour les étudiants?

 – Ah non, je suis désolé.
 – Merci beaucoup. Au revoir, monsieur.
 – Au revoir, mademoiselle.
4 – Allô, ici le stade municipal.
 – Bonjour, madame. Vous ouvrez à quelle heure aujourd'hui?
 – À deux heures, pour le match de rugby.
 – Et vous fermez à quelle heure?
 – À huit heures du soir.
 – Merci. C'est combien par personne?
 – C'est €5.80 pour les adultes, et €3 pour les enfants.
 – Est-ce qu'il y a une réduction pour les étudiants?
 – Ah non. Il n'y a pas de prix réduit pour les étudiants.
 – Merci beaucoup. Au revoir, madame.

Answers

	opening time	closing time	adult price	child price	student reduction (yes/no)
swimming pool	7.15	9.30	€3	€2.30	no
theatre	6pm	12.00	€18.30	€15.20	yes, €15.20
ice rink	9.30	22.00	€2.90	€1.70	no
stadium	2.00	8pm	€5.80	€3	no

1b In pairs. Practise the conversation. Change the underlined details to suit the other places shown on the right.

Speaking. With a partner, students practise the example conversation and then change the words underlined to suit the prompts.

2 In pairs. Practise the conversation. Change the underlined details to make a new conversation.

Speaking. With a partner, students practise the example conversation and then change the underlined words to make a new conversation using the key language box for support. Model some different conversations first with some student volunteers.

3a Read the sentences and note whether they apply to the pool, the sports centre, the cinema or the festival.

Reading (1–12). Students read the descriptions and decide which of the adverts they belong to. You can further exploit these texts in some whole class practice by asking questions in French or asking students to find the French for expressions you list in English.

Answers

1 sports centre	**2** cinema	**3** festival	**4** cinema
5 pool	**6** festival	**7** cinema	**8** pool	**9** festival
10 sports centre	**11** festival	**12** sports centre	

3b Write an advert for an event taking place in your school or college. Use expressions from the adverts above to help you. You should include: …

Writing. Students write an advert for an event taking place in their school or college, using the ones in **3a** as models. They may wish to produce this on computer.

3 On va au cinéma

(Student's Book pages 48–49)

Main topics and objectives

● Going to the cinema

Key language

Tu veux aller au cinéma/au concert ce soir?
Ça commence/finit à quelle heure?
Un ticket/billet d'entrée, c'est combien?
On se voit où et à quelle heure?
Séances à …
film d'aventures
film romantique
comédie
drame psychologique

film de science-fiction
Les effets sont superbes/passionnants/incroyables.
Les acteurs sont excellents/très naturels.

Skills/Strategies

● Using IT for research

Resources

À l'oral, page 72: Transaction 4
Cassette B side 1
Cahier d'exercices, page 20

Introduce the spread by brainstorming the topic of cinema with students. Ask them questions such as: *Quel était le dernier film que tu as vu?* and *Quelle sorte de film aimes-tu?* Introduce some types of film from the key language box on page 49.

1 Listen. Copy and complete the grid.

Listening. Students listen and complete the grid. This gives practice in the 24-hour clock.

Tapescript

Vous avez bien le répondeur de l'Odéon à Libourne. Vos billets sont à €8.50. Si vous voulez réserver une place, faites le 04 67 29 16 48.

Voici le programme pour cette semaine:

Salle 1: un film comique français, 'Les Insaisissables' avec Daniel Prévost. Séances à 14h, 16h30 et à 20h.

Salle 2: 'Seule contre tous' avec Julia Roberts. Séances à 14h10, 16h45 et 20h15.

Salle 3: 'Le dégoût', avec Jean Pierre Adelay. Ce film est interdit aux moins de dix-huit ans. Séances à 18h05, 20h55, et 22h10.

Answers

film	performance times
Les Insaisissables	14h, 16h30, 20h
Seule contre tous	14h10, 16h45, 20h15
Le dégoût	18h05, 20h55, 22h10

2a In pairs. Practise these conversations then make three new conversations using the notes below.

Speaking. With a partner, students practise the example conversations and then make up three new conversations to correspond with the information given. Read the conversations with the class first if necessary to make sure the meaning is clear.

2b Write out one of the conversations from exercise 2a.

Writing. Students write out one of the new conversations from 2a.

3 Read the e-mail and put the pictures in the correct order.

Reading. Students put the pictures into the correct order based on the e-mail.

Answers

e, f, a, c, b, d

4a Read the film advert and answer the questions in English.

Reading (1–9). Students read the advert and answer the questions in English. Remind them that they do not have to understand every word of the text.

Answers

1 2 hours 8 minutes (1)
2 to protect King (1)
3 an important man from industry (1)
4 he is assassinated (1)
5 King's daughter (1)
6 blame James Bond and avenge her father (2)
7 around the world (1)
8 the special effects are fantastic (1)
9 19 including this one (1)

Find out what films are popular in French-speaking countries at the moment. How do they compare with films here? Are there as many American films? Are there more comedies, thrillers, etc? Find one French film review and make up questions in English for your partner.

Students use the Internet to find out as much as they can on French films.

4b Design a poster for a film. Use the advert above as a model.

Writing. Students design their own poster for a film, perhaps on computer. To support students, give them a list of film titles in French. Do they know what they are in English? Examples include: *Trois hommes et un couffin, Le patient anglais, Les aventuriers de l'arche perdue, 101 dalmatiens, La belle et la bête, La belle au bois dormant, Le seigneur des anneaux, Les dents de la mer, Vendredi 13.*

Further practice of the language and vocabulary of this spread is provided as follows:

À l'oral, page 72: Transaction 4

Cahier d'exercices, page 20

4 Les invitations

(Student's Book pages 50–51)

Main topics and objectives

● Asking people out

Key language

Tu veux aller à la boum/en boîte/au cirque/au concert?
Tu voudrais voir le match de foot/un film?
On pourrait faire un pique-nique/une excursion à vélo.
D'accord. Je veux bien.
Je suis contre les cirques.
J'aimerais mieux rester à la maison.
Je dois faire mes devoirs.
Ça ne me dit rien.

Grammar

● Modal verbs

Resources

À toi! A, page 184
À l'oral, page 72: Conversation 3
Cassette B side 1
Cahier d'exercices, page 21

Introduce the spread by brainstorming/revising the language of asking someone out. Students have already met some on the **Déjà vu** spreads. Start with a template question – *Veux-tu aller au cinéma avec moi ce soir?* See how many more suggestions they can come up with.

1 Read and listen to the dialogue. Find the French for the sentences below.

Reading and listening (1–6). Students listen to the dialogue and read it at the same time. Tell them to pay particular attention to pronunciation. Students find the French for the phrases.

Tapescript

– *Tu es libre demain soir? Il y a un très bon concert à l'hôtel de ville.*
– *Non, je suis désolé, mais je n'aime pas les concerts.*
– *Alors, tu veux aller au cirque?*
– *Non, je regrette, mais je suis contre les cirques.*
– *Tu voudrais voir un film?*
– *Je m'excuse mais le cinéma, ça ne me dit rien.*
– *On pourrait voir le match de foot au stade.*
– *Je suis désolé mais j'aimerais mieux rester à la maison. Je dois faire mes devoirs.*

Answers

1 J'aimerais mieux rester à la maison.
2 Je suis contre les cirques.
3 Je dois faire mes devoirs.
4 Ça ne me dit rien.
5 Tu es libre demain soir?
6 Je n'aime pas les concerts.

Before moving on to activity **2a**, introduce some reasons for not going out from the key language box. Invite students to go somewhere. They must reply with a reason why they can't go.

2a Listen. For each conversation, note the activity and whether the person accepts(✓/✗).

Listening (1–8). Students listen to the conversation and note whether each person accepts or not.

Tapescript

1 – *Est-ce que tu voudrais m'accompagner à la boum, samedi soir?*
 – *C'est très gentil, mais malheureusement je ne suis pas libre.*
2 – *Si on allait voir le match de foot?*
 – *Avec plaisir. On se retrouve à quelle heure?*
3 – *Tu voudrais sortir avec moi ce soir? Je voudrais aller voir un film.*
 – *Je veux bien, c'est quel film?*
4 – *Est-ce que tu as envie d'aller au cirque samedi?*
 – *Ça ne me dit rien, je suis plutôt contre les cirques, tu sais.*
5 – *Es-tu libre demain soir? Il y a un très bon concert à l'hôtel de ville. C'est un groupe que j'aime beaucoup.*
 – *Bonne idée, j'ai vraiment envie de voir ce concert aussi, moi.*
6 – *Veux-tu aller en boîte avec moi ce week-end?*
 – *Je m'excuse, mais j'aimerais mieux rester à la maison.*
7 – *J'aimerais bien faire un pique-nique à la campagne aujourd'hui. Est-ce que tu peux venir?*
 – *Bien sûr, merci beaucoup. On va partir à quelle heure?*
8 – *Si tu es libre demain, on pourrait faire une excursion à vélo ensemble. Qu'est-ce que tu en penses?*
 – *Zut, j'aimerais bien t'accompagner, mais je dois faire mes devoirs demain.*

Answers

1 party ✗
2 football match ✓
3 cinema ✓
4 circus ✗
5 concert ✓
6 night club ✗
7 picnic (in the country) ✓
8 cycle ride ✗

2b Listen to the conversations again and note the reasons for those who don't accept.

Listening (1–8). Students listen again and note the reasons in English for those who do not accept.

Answers

1 not free
4 against circuses
6 prefer to stay at home
8 has to do homework

3 Translate these sentences into French. Use the key language box to help you.

Writing. Students translate the sentences into French. All the sentences use one of the modal verbs.

Answers

1 Tu veux faire un pique-nique?
2 Tu voudrais voir le match de foot?
3 On pourrait faire une promenade en vélo.
4 Tu voudrais aller en boîte?
5 On pourrait regarder un film.

➕ Ask students to form new sentences using the sentences from **3** as a template. You could also ask them to change the sentences to the *vous* part of the verb.

4 Read the article and answer the questions in English.

Reading (1–10). Students read the article and answer the questions in English. Remind students not to panic if they don't understand every word. They should read first for gist, look carefully at all the questions and then read for more detail.

Answers

1 Go to a concert, to the theatre or watch a film. (3)
2 You can't talk much. (1)
3 Party, salsa club or night club (3)
4 There is lots to see and do during the day and if all goes well you can continue into the evening. (2)
5 Friendship or love (2)
6 Don't be too sad. Ask why they can't. If the reason is a good one, try another date or time. (any 2)
7 I have to wash my hair. (1)
8 If you lose one, there are ten more to find. (1)
9 Time, date, place, and how you're going to get back home (4)
10 Good luck! (1)

5a In pairs. Practise this conversation. Change the underlined words to make new conversations. Try to be as imaginative as possible.

Speaking. With a partner, students practise the example conversation and then change the words underlined to make new conversations. Encourage them to be imaginative or funny. Brainstorm some excuses with the class first. Provide some verbs that they might need.

5b In groups. Make a list of the most interesting excuses you thought of in **5a**.

Writing. In groups, students make a list of the best knock backs!

Further practice of the language and vocabulary of this spread is provided as follows:

À toi! A, page 184

À l'oral, page 72: Conversation 3

Cahier d'exercices, page 21

5 Ça s'est bien passé?

(Student's Book pages 52–53)

Main topics and objectives

● Talking about the past

Key language

Je suis allé(e) (à une boum/au club/à la piscine, en ville).
Je suis resté(e) (à la maison).
J'ai regardé (la télé).
J'ai joué (aux cartes/jeux vidéo, du violon, au foot).
J'ai mangé (un hamburger).
J'ai écouté (des cassettes).
J'ai passé (un week-end actif).
J'ai surfé sur Internet.
J'ai fait (une promenade, du VTT).
J'ai lu (un livre).
J'au vu (un film).
J'ai bu (un Coca).
J'ai promené (mon chien).
Je me suis reposé(e).
Je me suis bien amusé(e).

Grammar

● The perfect tense with *avoir* and *être*

Skills/Strategies

● Telling the difference between the perfect and present tenses
● Using useful phrases
● Using time expressions and opinions

Resources

À toi! B, page 185
À l'oral, page 72: Conversation 2
Cassette B side 1
Cahier d'exercices, pages 22–23

Introduce the spread by talking about your weekend in the perfect tense. Write some key verbs on the OHT/board. Look at the *Le détective* box and remind students of the rules of the perfect tense. Which verbs will take *être*? Finally, brainstorm what students did last weekend.

1 Listen. What did Laurent do last weekend? Put the pictures in the right order.

Listening. Students listen to the boy describing his weekend and put the pictures in the correct order. As a follow-up, ask them to make a phrase for each picture using the key language box.

Tapescript

J'ai passé un week-end plutôt nul. Vendredi soir, je suis allé à une boum chez mon copain Fred. C'était très ennuyeux. Je n'aime pas danser. Pendant la boum, je suis monté dans la chambre de Fred et on a joué aux cartes avec d'autres copains. Bien sûr, j'ai perdu. On a aussi joué aux jeux vidéo, mais les jeux de Fred sont très démodés.

Samedi matin, ma mère m'a emmené en ville pour mon orchestre. J'ai joué du violon pendant deux heures. C'était pénible. Samedi soir, je suis resté à la maison et j'ai lu un livre. C'est passionnant, n'est-ce pas? Samedi soir, à la maison, en train de lire et écouter des CDs. Bof!

Dimanche, j'ai fait une promenade à la campagne avec mes parents. Oh, c'était ennuyeux. Après, j'ai dû jouer au foot avec mon petit frère dans le jardin. Il n'est pas Zidane, euh? Quelle perte de temps.

Dimanche soir, je suis allé à la piscine avec mes copains, et j'ai fait du VTT. Ça, c'était mieux mais je pensais déjà au collège le lendemain.

Answers

b, e, d, h, g, a, c, j, i, f

Tip box

Present and perfect tenses. This reminds students that the present tense has one main part to the verb and the perfect (past) tense has two parts (part of *avoir* or *être* + a past participle).

2a Last weekend was an odd one! Organise these sentences into 2 lists: normally, and last weekend.

Reading. Students organise the sentences into two lists, those in the present and those in the perfect tense.

Answers

Normally	Last weekend
Je vais au club de basket.	J'ai regardé un concours de ménage.
Je mange un hamburger.	
Je bois un Coca.	J'ai promené mon éléphant à la campagne.
Je regarde un match de foot au stade.	J'ai bu du jus de chaussettes.
Je fais mes devoirs de maths.	
Je promène mon chien à la campagne.	Je suis allé au club de saut à l'élastique.
Je lis des magazines d'ordinateur.	J'ai lu l'annuaire téléphonique.
	J'ai fait mes devoirs de jardinage.
	J'ai mangé un aspirateur.

2b Write at least six sentences like this: …

Writing. Students write at least six sentences using the present and perfect tenses, following the example. This contrast of tenses should help them see the relationship and differences between one and the other.

65

3a Read the texts and find a penfriend for each of these people.

Reading. This is reading for gist. Students read the text and find a suitable penfriend for each person.

Answers

| **1** Gilles | **2** Stéphanie | **3** Nourdine | **4** Fabienne |

3b Pick out all the different verbs in the text which are in the perfect tense and translate them.

Reading. Students now read the text in more detail to identify all the verbs which are in the perfect tense in French and English.

Answers

Stéphanie: *je suis allée* – I went, *je l'ai trouvé* – I found it, *j'ai passé* – I spent, *j'ai écouté* – I listened to, *j'ai surfé* – I surfed, *j'ai joué* – I played
Gilles: *j'ai passé* – I spent, *je suis parti* – I went away, *on a fait* – we did, *on a même pu* – we were able to, *on s'est très bien amusé* – we had a good time, *on a discuté* – we talked
Nourdine: *je me suis entraîné* – I trained, *on a fait de la musculation* – we did training
Fabienne: *j'ai fait un stage* – I did a course, *j'ai joué* – I played, *on a répété* – we rehearsed, *on a dansé* – we danced, *j'ai eu* – I had, *j'ai fait de la lecture* – I did some reading, *on s'est baladé* – we went for a walk, *je suis allée* – I went

3c In pairs. Describe one of these people. Your partner guesses who it is.

Speaking. Students describe one of the people from **3a** and their partner works out who it is. This gives practice in using the 3rd person singular of the perfect tense.

4a In pairs. Find out what your partner did last weekend. Note it down, beginning with *il* or *elle*.

Speaking. Students ask their partner what they did last weekend and then note it down using the 3rd person singular of the verb. It may be useful to practise a couple of examples on the board with the whole class first.

Tip boxes

Useful phrases. This lists some phrases in the perfect tense.

Time phrases and opinions. This encourages students to make what they say more interesting by adding time expressions and some opinions. Remind students of the importance of adding these extra details. It can improve their grade. Brainstorm any further time phrases or opinions.

4b Write approximately 150 words about what you did last weekend.

Writing. Students write about what they did last weekend. This could be used as practice for the writing exam.

Further practice of the language and vocabulary of this spread is provided as follows:

À toi! B, page 185

À l'oral, page 72: Conversation 2

Cahier d'exercices, pages 22–23

All the key vocabulary and structures from this module are listed on the **Mots** pages 56–57. These can be used for revision by covering up either the English or the French. Students can check here to see how much they remember from the module and use them to prepare for the assessments.

Assessment materials for Modules 3 and 4 are available in the separate Assessment Pack.

Further speaking and grammar practice on the whole module is provided on **Cahier d'exercices** pages 24–25.

Entraînez-vous: À l'écrit

(Student's Book pages 54–55)

Writing practice: Les copains et les loisirs

The **À l'écrit** spreads give regular, guided practice in preparing for the writing sections of Standard Grade and Intermediate examinations. Each double-page spread always starts with a model text which acts as a stimulus, giving students ideas about what they might want to include in their own writing. Students are encouraged to look at the detail of the text through the structured reading activities, and are guided gradually towards producing their own sentences in French, in preparation for the final task in which they are asked to produce an extended piece of writing. The **Au Secours!** column is a feature on all the **À l'écrit** spreads. It presents language and structures that students can include in their writing, and reminds them of general points that will help them to get a better grade.

To qualify for the writing components at Standard Grade or Intermediate writing N.A.B.s, final versions must be produced under controlled conditions. Students should be encouraged to use the language they understand and are familiar with so as to learn what they have written with a high degree of accuracy. They should be warned about the dangers of copying. At Standard Grade, students should be guided to write over 25 words at Foundation level, 50 words at General level and 100 words at Credit level.

Students should be encouraged to see that they can get Credit marks at Standard Grade and A grades at Intermediate 2 in Writing! Remind them of the following tips to help them get a better grade.

Handy tips for students

1 Structure your writing: a good beginning and ending, and 3 distinct paragraphs!
   Choose formats which structure themselves, e.g. a letter.
2 Focus your writing on one aspect of a module.
3 Choose aspects which give you opportunities to write about your opinions.
4 Choose aspects which allow you to use impressive vocabulary and phrases.
5 Make sure you include examples of different tenses in your writing.
6 It is very important to write accurate French! Make sure the language you choose for your writing is memorable for **you**. Only you can know how much new and impressive French you can learn to write out accurately in exam conditions!

This spread guides students towards producing an extended piece of writing on the topics of **friends** and **free time**. It takes them from understanding single items of vocabulary, through understanding phrases and comments in a variety of tenses, to structuring a letter to a French student. Students should be encouraged to write as accurately and as much as they can.

1a Find the French for the following in the text above.

Answers

> **1** vendredi dernier **2** c'était l'anniversaire de ma copine **3** il y avait plein de monde **4** un très beau garçon **5** elle était ravie **6** on discute du film **7** rigolos et pleins de vie **8** j'adore faire les courses **9** l'équipe scolaire **10** je voudrais sortir **11** aller en boîte **12** je vais devoir aider

1b Copy and use this grid to note the verb phrases highlighted in blue in the text and what they mean in English. (In paragraph 1 they are all past tense, in paragraph 2 they are all present tense and in paragraph 3 they either mean 'would' or 'going to'.)

Answers

past tense	English	present tense	English
je suis allée	I went	j'adore	I love
j'ai parlé	I spoke	je regarde	I watch
Vivienne a reçu	Vivienne received	on boit un Coca	we drink Coke
elle était ravie	she was enchanted	je joue au volley	I play volleyball
		je fais souvent de la natation	I often go swimming

would/going to	English
je voudrais sortir	I would like to go out
je voudrais aller manger	I would like to go to eat
je vais faire le ménage	I am going to do the housework

1c Say what the 6 comments (in red) mean.

Answers

> c'était génial – it was great
> c'était incroyable – it was unbelievable
> je trouve ça vraiment amusant – I find that very funny
> c'est fantastique – it's fantastic
> ce serait bien – it would be good
> ce serait fantastique – it would be fantastic

2 Write an e-mail to your pen-pal about your friends and what you do together. Use the *Au Secours!* panel to help.

Au secours!

This section reminds pupils of the following points:
- describing people
- using more than one tense
- sentence pattern: when, what, where, who with, comment
- giving reasons for opinions.

À toi! A & B

(Student's Book pages 184–185)

Self-access reading and writing at two levels

These pages are designed to give students extra practice in reading and structured writing. There are two differentiated pages relating to each chapter: A and B. Page A is at an easier level and page B more challenging. You may wish students to work on the page most appropriate to their level or work through both pages. You may feel it is useful to work with students on the activities, but it should be possible for most students to work on them independently. The most appropriate time to use each page is indicated within the relevant teaching notes.

A Toi! A, page 184

This page is best used after pages 50–51 of the Student's Book.

1a Read the speech bubbles and put the pictures in the correct order.

Answers

1 e	**2** f	**3** g	**4** h	**5** a	**6** b	**7** c	**8** d

1b Answer the questions in English.

Answers

1 She has always wanted to go out with him. (1)
2 Go to a Ziggy Marley concert. (1)
3 He does not really like music. (1)
4 Go to the theatre or cinema. (2)
5 Go to eat something. (1)
6 At the bus stop at 8pm. (2)
7 Because she is a bit fed up with Joël and she sees someone else who asks her to go to Cédric's house. (1)

2 Write your own cartoon story about a date.

A Toi! B, page 185

This page is best used after pages 52–53 of the Student's Book.

1 Read the text. Then copy and complete the English translation.

Answers

1 really   **2** went   **3** family   **4/5** Friday afternoon
6 at about   **7** evening   **8** stayed   **9** grandparents
10 suburbs   **11** town centre   **12** shopped
13 boring   **14** bought   **15** bad   **16** afternoon
17 interesting   **18** people   **19** Moroccan
20/21 too much   **22** visited   **23** adventure
24 evening   **25** soon

2 Imagine a fantastic weekend you spent somewhere wonderful with somebody famous. Write an account of it, in approximately 100 words.

Cahier d'exercices, page 19

1
Answers

| **1** d | **2** h | **3** f | **4** g | **5** c | **6** a | **7** e | **8** b |

2
Answers

| **a** plus | **b** moins | **c** plus | **d** moins |

3a
Answers

a Friday   **b** football, cycling, fishing, table tennis, sailing
c open to all   **d** under 18s

3b
Answers

a coup d'envoi   **b** tout compris
c course de vélo   **d** bibliothèque municipale

Cahier d'exercices, page 20

4
Answers

| **1** d | **2** e | **3** f | **4** a | **5** c | **6** b |

5
Answers

Produced by Luc Besson, a science fiction film set in the 23rd century. A taxi driver meets an extra-terrestrial woman (5th element). Unconventional and exciting.

6
Answers

a	23:14 = vingt-trois heures quatorze
b	19:35 = dix-neuf heures trente-cinq
c	15:45 = quinze heures quarante-cinq
d	22:40 = vingt-deux heures quarante
e	13:10 = treize heures dix
f	18:06 = dix-huit heures six
g	17:48 = dix-sept heures quarante-huit
h	14:55 = quatorze heures cinquante-cinq

Cahier d'exercices, page 21

7
Answers

| **1** = b + d | **2** = c + a | **3** = e + f |

8a
Answers

difficiles = pas faciles	tu aimes = ça t'intéresse
mignonne = jolie	les joueurs = l'équipe
aimerais-tu = on pourrait	super = génial
extrêmement triste = super déçu	le flirt = la drague

8b
Answers

Flirting is not easy! I sat next to a gorgeous girl at the football match. I told her I wanted Kilmarnock to win because they have French players and I asked her out for a drink but she shouted that if I was interested in football, I should stop talking! Not easy the Scottish girls! Kilmarnock lost too, what a disappointment!

Cahier d'exercices, page 22

9
Answers

a 4   **b** 2   **c** 7   **d** 6   **e** 1   **f** 5   **g** 8   **h** 3

10 (writing task)

Cahier d'exercices, page 23

11a
Answers

a handball, aerobics and gymnastics
b It is the best in the school.   **c** the aerobics class
d they are very strict and demanding
e because she arrived late   **f** chatting

11b
Answers

on s'y amuse bien: a
comme d'habitude: b
saut à l'élastique: c
J'ai hâte de te voir: d

12 (writing task)

Cahier d'exercices, page 24

1
Answers

a Il a pratiqué le football hier.
b Nous avons joué au basket lundi.
c Nous sommes allés au cinéma.
d Je suis resté(e) à la maison le week-end dernier.
e Sophie et Annie sont venues mardi.
f Tu as écouté de la musique.
g Il est allé en boîte.
h Ils/Elles ont regardé la télévision.

2
Answers

a Veux-tu aller au concert? Tu veux aller au concert?
b Tu aimes faire du snowboard? Est-ce que tu aimes faire du snowboard?
c Voudrais-tu aller à la boum? Est-ce que tu voudrais aller à la boum?
d Tu joues au foot? Est-ce que tu joues au foot?
e Vas-tu à la piscine? Tu vas à la piscine?

3
Answers

a 3	**b** 5	**c** 1	**d** 2	**e** 4

Cahier d'exercices, page 25

3 *Temps libre*

Bilan

1 Parle-moi de ton passe-temps préféré.

2 Qu'est-ce que tu aimes faire le week-end?

3 Qu'est-ce que tu fais normalement le soir?

4 Qu'est-ce qu'il y a pour les jeunes là où tu habites?

5 Qu'est-ce que tu fais comme sports? Décris où et quand tu les fais.

6 Qu'est-ce que tu n'aimes pas faire? Pourquoi?

7 Qu'est-ce que tu penses du foot? Pourquoi?

8 Quel nouveau passe-temps voudrais-tu commencer?

9 Qu'est-ce que tu as fait hier soir?

10 Qu'est-ce que tu as fait le week-end dernier?

25

MODULE 4 — AU BOULOT

Au boulot

(Student's Book pages 58–75)

Topic area	Key language	Grammar	Skills/Strategies
Déjà vu (pp. 58–59) Talking about different jobs	*Je suis … Il/Elle est … médecin, dentiste, secrétaire, professeur, coiffeur(-euse), chauffeur de camion, caissier(-ière), boulanger(-ère), agent de police, fermier(-ière), steward/hôtesse de l'air, vétérinaire, serveur(-euse), mécanicien(ne), infirmier(-ère), opérateur(-trice) d'ordinateur, vendeur(-euse), technicien(ne) de laboratoire, garçon/fille au pair, jardinier(-ière). Je voudrais travailler dans un magasin, en plein air, dans un bureau/une usine, dans le commerce/le secteur informatique/le secteur du tourisme. avec les gens/enfants/animaux/personnes âgées combien/combien de temps/combien d'argent combien d'heures/à quelle heure?*	No article in sentences with jobs Masculine and feminine forms of jobs	Asking and answering questions
1 Avez-vous un job? (pp. 60–61) Talking about part-time jobs and work experience	*Je travaille dans un (hypermarché/centre sportif). Je commence/finis à … Je vais au travail en (bus/vélo/voiture). Le trajet dure (15 minutes). Je gagne (€5) par heure/de l'heure. C'est bien/mal payé. C'est varié/intéressant/monotone/ennuyeux/facile/ difficile/dur/chouette. Je me suis levé(e) à …. J'y suis allé(e) à pied/en vélo/en autobus. J'ai fait …/appris …/répondu. J'ai classé…/gagné…/travaillé… J'ai dû + infinitive. Je me suis amusé(e). C'était + adjective(s)*	Perfect tense with reflexive verbs Interrogative verbs and adverbs (*comment, quand*)	Giving opinions Answering questions
2 Le monde du travail (pp. 62–63) Looking for a job in France	Language from previous spreads Language used in CV		Writing formal letters Using the Internet
3 Au téléphone (pp. 64–65) Using the phone	*Allô. C'est (Anne) à l'appareil. Je peux vous aider? Je voudrais parler à … C'est de la part de qui? Ne quittez pas. Je regrette, il/elle n'est pas là. Est-ce que je peux laisser un message? Votre nom, comment ça s'écrit? Quel est votre message? Quel est votre numéro de téléphone? À quelle heure est-ce que je peux rappeler? Je vous téléphone à propos de l'annonce. Je voudrais un poste comme (serveur).*	Talking about the past, present and future	Being polite Saying French phone numbers

Topic area	Key language	Grammar	Skills/Strategies
4 Qu'est-ce que vous voulez faire dans la vie? (pp. 66–67) Talking about your future career	*Je travaillerai/Je ne travaillerai pas comme serveur/gardien(ne)/chez McDo/dans le tourisme/dans un bureau/à l'étranger. Je trouverai (un travail). Je ferai (un diplôme). J'irai (à la fac/aux États-Unis). Je serai (joueur de foot). Je continuerai (mes études). Je voyagerai (autour du monde). Je gagnerai (un bon salaire). J'étudierai (l'anglais). Je rencontrerai l'homme de ma vie.*	The future tense Using the future with *quand* Other ways of expressing the future: *j'espère …/ je désire …*	
5 Les différents emplois (pp. 68–69) Talking about different kinds of work	*J'aimerais/Je voudrais … aider (les gens malades)/ travailler avec des enfants/des animaux/les personnes âgées en équipe/seul(e)/en plein air/dans un bureau dans le domaine de l'informatique/du marketing/de l'éducation dans le commerce/dans le tourisme Je préférerais … m'occuper (d'animaux/d'enfants)/être (infirmier/ère)/avoir (de longues vacances)/voyager/gagner beaucoup d'argent.*	Conditional tense	Reading authentic texts
6 Les études et le travail (pp. 70–71) Discussing work, studies and taking a year out	*Il faut trouver un équilibre travail-études. Mes examens sont plus importants que mon petit boulot. L'argent, c'est le plus important. Il devrait être possible de combiner un boulot et ses études. Gagner un peu d'argent te donne de l'indépendance. Le plus important, c'est de réussir dans ses examens. Étudier, c'est important – je ne veux pas être au chômage.*	Modal verbs in the conditional	Translating into natural English Using opinion phrases Planning an essay
Entraînez-vous: À l'oral (pp. 72–73)	Language from Modules 3 and 4		Practice for the speaking exam Using tenses and opinions Presentation skills
À toi! A and B (pp. 186–187)	Language from Module 4		Reading and writing skills

The vocabulary and structures taught in Module 4 are summarised on the **Mots** pages of the Student's Book, pages 74–75.
Further writing practice on the language of the module is provided on **À l'écrit**, pages 88–89.
Assessment tasks for Modules 3 and 4 combined are provided in the separate Assessment Pack.

Main topics and objectives

● Talking about different jobs

Key language

Je suis .., Il/Elle est …
médecin, dentiste, secrétaire, professeur, coiffeur
(-euse), chauffeur de camion, caissier(-ière),
boulanger(-ère), agent de police, fermier(-ière),
steward/hôtesse de l'air, vétérinaire, serveur(-euse),
mécanicien, infirmier(-ière), opérateur(-trice)
d'ordinateur, vendeur(-euse), technicien(ne) de
laboratoire, garçon/fille au pair, jardinier(-ière)
Je voudrais travailler …
dans un magasin, en plein air, dans un bureau/une
usine, dans le commerce/le secteur informatique/
le secteur du tourisme

avec les gens/enfants/animaux/personnes âgées
comment/combien de temps/combien d'argent
combien d'heures/à quelle heure?

Grammar

● No article in sentences with jobs
● Masculine and feminine forms of jobs

Skills/Strategies

● Asking and answering questions

Resources

Cassette B side 2
Cahier d'exercices, pages 26–27 (exs 1–3)

Introduce the spread by brainstorming any jobs the
class already know in French, then put the students
into groups, give each group an OHT and a pen and
allow them five minutes to find at least a further 10
jobs using dictionaries. When collating the different
jobs the students have found, write them in both
masculine and feminine forms, pointing out the
invariable words for jobs, e.g. *boulanger(-ère)*,
chauffeur(-).

1a Listen. Note the jobs you hear, in English. If
you understand any other details, note them too.

Listening (1–10). Students apply knowledge from
previous units (likes and dislikes, *depuis*, etc.) to
newly acquired/revised work-based vocabulary. They
may wish to listen once for the jobs and a second
time for any extra details.

Tapescript

1 Ma sœur est coiffeuse. Elle aime bien ça. Elle discute tout
le temps avec les clients.
2 Mon père est boulanger. Ça fait dix ans qu'il travaille dans
la même boulangerie. Il doit se lever très tôt le matin.
3 Mon grand-père était fermier. J'aime bien lui rendre visite,
je l'aide à s'occuper de tous les animaux, mais c'est dur
comme travail.
4 Ma mère est professeur. Elle travaille dans un collège
près de chez nous.
5 Ma grand-mère était serveuse. Maintenant, elle a pris sa
retraite, mais elle dit que le travail lui manque.
6 Je voudrais être infirmier. J'aimerais bien aider les gens
malades.
7 Mon frère voudrait être steward. Il veut voyager. Il
n'arrête pas de nous raconter son désir de voyager
autour du monde.
8 Ma tante est agent de police. C'est dangereux des fois, si
on se fait agresser.
9 Mon oncle est médecin. Il travaille dans un très grand
hôpital où il y a souvent des cas difficiles.

10 Je ne voudrais pas être secrétaire. Ça ne me dirait pas de
passer toutes mes heures devant un ordinateur à faire le
travail de quelqu'un d'autre.

Answers

1 hairdresser, likes job, talks to clients
2 baker, 10 years in same bakery, gets up very early
3 farmer, likes visiting to help with the animals, hard work
4 teacher, works in school nearby
5 waitress, now retired but misses work
6 nurse, would like to help ill people
7 steward, wants to travel around the world
8 policewoman, can be dangerous
9 doctor, works in very big hospital where there are often
   difficult cases
10 secretary, would not like to do it because does not
   want to spend hours in front of a computer doing
   someone else's work

1b Write sentences in French.

Writing (1–8). Students apply the structure in the
example and in the key language box to form correct
sentences about other people's jobs. Draw their
attention to the fact that *un/une* are not used with
jobs in French (see the tip box next to **1a**).

Answers

1 Ma sœur est secrétaire.
2 Mon père est vétérinaire.
3 Ma belle-mère est caissière.
4 Mon grand-père est chauffeur de camion.
5 Mon copain est coiffeur.
6 Mon oncle est médecin.
7 Ma mère est opératrice d'ordinateur.
8 Mon frère est infirmier.

1c Listen. Make notes for each person, then choose a job for them from the box on the right.

Listening. (1–8). Students listen to the people's preferences and then choose the most appropriate job for them from the list. This gives practice in both recognition of job preferences and choosing the correct gender of job to match the person's voice heard.

Tapescript

1 Je voudrais travailler dans un magasin, avec des gens, parce que j'aime le contact avec d'autres personnes.

2 J'aimerais travailler avec les enfants. Ça me plairait de faire le ménage et un peu de cuisine aussi.

3 Je voudrais travailler dans le secteur du tourisme, peut-être dans le restaurant d'un de nos grands hôtels.

4 Mon rêve, c'est de travailler en plein air. Je n'ai pas envie de passer mon temps derrière un ordinateur. J'aime être dehors.

5 Moi, je veux travailler avec les animaux. Je trouve que les animaux sont plus gentils que les gens!

6 Soigner les malades, c'est ce que je veux faire dans la vie. Ça me permettra de travailler avec les enfants et les personnes âgées aussi.

7 Je voudrais travailler dans un bureau, ou dans le commerce, mais surtout dans le secteur informatique.

8 Je voudrais travailler dans une usine, ou peut-être dans un collège, mais je dois absolument faire un métier scientifique, parce que j'adore les sciences.

Answers

> **1** wants to work in a shop/with people: *vendeur*
> **2** wants to work with children, would like to do the housework and a bit of cooking: *fille au pair*
> **3** wants to work in tourism, in a restaurant or hotel: *serveur*
> **4** wants to work outside, does not want to be at a computer: *jardinier*
> **5** wants to work with animals, thinks animals are nicer than people: *vétérinaire*
> **6** wants to care for ill people, with children and old people: *infirmier*
> **7** wants to work in an office or in commerce in the area of computers: *opérateur d'ordinateur*
> **8** wants to work in a factory or a school, wants a scientific job: *technicienne de laboratoire*

➕ Ask students where/with whom they would like to work, to exploit the key language further. Introduce the structure *je voudrais être technicien(ne)*.

2a Match the questions to the correct answers. Then write what each pair means.

Reading (1–9). Students revise question forms and are introduced to work-related questions and statements.

Answers

> **1 e** What time do you start? I start at 9 o'clock.
> **2 a** What time do you finish? Normally, I finish at 3 o'clock.
> **3 d** How long do you have for lunch? I have one hour for lunch.
> **4 f** Do you work every day? No, normally I work at the weekend.
> **5 c** How many hours do you work per week? I work 5 hours a week.
> **6 i** How much do you earn? I earn £5.50 an hour.
> **7 b** Do you think it's well paid? Yes, quite well.
> **8 g** Do you like your work? Yes, but sometimes I get bored.
> **9 h** How do you get to work? I get there on foot.

Key language box

Question words. Students met these words first in Module 1. Revise them thoroughly. Questions are often difficult for students to learn because they recognise them easily and do not make the effort to learn them so that they can use them flexibly themselves.

2b In pairs. Take turns to ask and answer the questions in **2a**. Adapt the answers slightly to give different details.

Speaking. Students use the same questions to give structured practice of question/answer about jobs. You could brainstorm different possible answers with the class first.

2c Copy this text and fill in the blanks with the words in the box.

Reading. Students fill in the gaps in this account of a part time job.

Answers

> **1** chez   **2** à   **3** caisse   **4** tôt   **5** finis
> **6** gagne   **7** gentil

➕ Students should be encouraged to copy-type the text. They can then use the text as a basis for writing about their own part-time jobs (real or imaginary!).

> Further practice of the language and vocabulary of this spread is provided as follows:
>
> Cahier d'exercices, pages 26–27 (exs 1–3)

1 *Avez-vous un job?*

(Student's Book pages 60–61)

Main topics and objectives

- Talking about part-time jobs and work experience

Key language

Je travaille dans un (hypermarché/centre sportif).
Je commence/finis à …
Je vais au travail en (bus/vélo/voiture).
Le trajet dure (15 minutes).
Je gagne (€5) par heure/de l'heure.
C'est bien/mal payé.
C'est varié/intéressant/monotone/ennuyeux/facile/
   difficile/dur/chouette.
Je me suis levé(e) à …
J'y suis allé(e) à pied/à vélo/en autobus.
J'ai fait …/appris …/répondu …
J'ai classé …/gagné …/travaillé …

J'ai dû + infinitive
Je me suis amusé(e).
C'était + adjective

Grammar

- Perfect tense with reflexive verbs

Skills/Strategies

- Giving opinions
- Answering questions

Resources

À l'oral, page 73: Prepared talk
Cassette B side 2
Cahier d'exercices, page 27 (ex. 4), pages 28–29

Introduce the spread by asking your students the questions on the clipboard. They could answer about their own jobs, about jobs shown them on an OHT or flashcards, or the class could play 'What's My Line' and guess the job based on the answers given.

1a Listen. Copy and complete the grid. Note: Valérie works 2 different shifts and Fanch has 2 jobs.

Listening. Students listen to three people being asked the questions revised at the beginning of the spread. Ensure your students leave enough space for two answers in the table and for several answers at the bottom of the table.

Tapescript

– *Est-ce que c'est une bonne idée d'avoir un petit job le soir, le week-end ou pendant les vacances? Valérie, 15 ans, Fanch, 16 ans, et Coralie, 15 ans, répondent à nos questions:*
– *Bonjour, Valérie. Tu travailles où?*
– *Je travaille dans un grand hypermarché.*
– *Tu commences à quelle heure?*
– *Je commence à 8h30 ou à 11h.*
– *Tu finis à quelle heure?*
– *Si je commence à 8h30, je finis à 17h00, mais si je commence à 11h, je termine plus tard, à 20h.*
– *Comment vas-tu au travail?*
– *Je vais au supermarché en bus.*
– *Et le trajet dure combien de temps?*
– *Le trajet dure 20 minutes.*
– *Combien est-ce que tu gagnes?*
– *Je gagne €5.90 par heure.*
– *Tu aimes ton job? Et pourquoi?*
– *Oui, j'aime mon job parce que c'est bien payé et assez varié.*

– *Et toi, Fanch?*
– *Moi, je distribue des journaux tous les matins, et parfois, je fais du baby-sitting le samedi soir.*

– *Tu commences à quelle heure?*
– *Je commence à 5h30 … oui! C'est fatigant! Pour le baby-sitting, ça dépend. D'habitude, c'est entre 19h et 21h.*
– *Tu finis à quelle heure?*
– *Pour distribuer les journaux, il me faut environ une heure. Quand je garde les enfants, je finis quand les parents rentrent à la maison.*
– *Comment vas-tu au travail?*
– *J'y vais à pied ou parfois à vélo.*
– *Et le trajet dure combien de temps?*
– *Oh, cinq minutes maximum: c'est tout près de chez moi.*
– *Combien est-ce que tu gagnes?*
– *Je gagne €12 par semaine pour les journaux. Pour le baby-sitting, je gagne €3 de l'heure.*
– *Tu aimes ton job? Et pourquoi?*
– *C'est ennuyeux de livrer les journaux, et c'est assez mal payé. Mais le baby-sitting, c'est facile, si les enfants sont sages…*

– *Bonjour, Coralie. Tu travailles où?*
– *Je travaille dans le centre sportif dans mon village. Je travaille tous les samedis.*
– *Tu commences à quelle heure?*
– *Je commence à 9h15.*
– *Tu finis à quelle heure?*
– *D'habitude, je finis vers 1h15 – je ne fais que 4 heures par jour.*
– *Comment vas-tu au travail?*
– *J'y vais à vélo, parce que c'est tout près de chez moi.*
– *Et le trajet dure combien de temps?*
– *Le trajet dure 5 minutes.*
– *Combien est-ce que tu gagnes?*
– *Je gagne €6.10 de l'heure.*
– *Tu aimes ton job? Et pourquoi?*
– *Oui, c'est chouette, parce que j'adore le sport, et j'ai l'occasion d'en faire pendant la journée. En plus, j'ai le droit d'avoir une réduction de prix pour les activités sportives, pendant le reste de la semaine.*

Answers

	Valérie	Fanch	Coralie
Job	hypermarket	delivers papers and babysitting	sports centre
Start	8.30 or 11h	5h30 or between 19h and 21h	9h15
Finish	17h or 20h	1 hour or when parents return	1h15
Transport	bus	walk or bike	bike
Journey time	20 mins	5 mins	5 mins
Pay	€5.90	€12 for papers, €3 an hour for babysitting	€6.10 an hour
Opinion(s)	likes it: well paid and varied	papers: boring and badly paid, babysitting: easy if children are good	good, she likes sport, gets reductions

1b In pairs. Ask each other the questions on the clipboard. Use the details below and the key language to answer.

Speaking. Students are directed to give specific answers to the same questions as in **1a**.

1c Use your answers to **1b** to write about 100 words about your job. Invent one if you haven't got one!

Writing. Students write about their own part-time jobs. They could expand the follow-up exercise to **2c** on page 59 if this has been word-processed.

Tip box

Students are reminded to give opinions. Remind them that *c'est* + adjective does not require agreement, whereas *mon patron/ma patronne* does!

2a Read and listen to this text. Find the French for the phrases below.

Reading (1–14). Students now concentrate on the details of work-based routine. The phrases will be useful to them in writing and speaking about work experience, so make sure they note both the French and English.

Tapescript

J'ai fait un stage dans une entreprise. J'ai dû organiser beaucoup de choses. En fait, j'ai appris beaucoup de choses. Je me suis levée tous les jours à six heures du matin. C'était affreux. J'y suis allée en autobus et j'ai commencé le travail à sept heures et demie. C'était très tôt. Vers dix heures, j'ai préparé le café. Pendant les quinze jours j'ai utilisé le fax, et la machine de traitement de texte. À part ça, j'ai répondu au téléphone et j'ai classé les documents. Le travail était un peu monotone, mais je me suis bien amusée. C'était mieux que l'école, quoi!

Answers

1 *j'ai fait un stage* – I did work experience
2 *j'ai dû organiser* – I had to organise
3 *j'ai appris beaucoup de choses* – I learned lots of things
4 *je me suis levée* – I got up
5 *tous les jours* – every day
6 *c'était affreux* – it was awful
7 *j'y suis allée* – I went there
8 *vers dix heures* – at about 10 o'clock
9 *pendant les quinze jours* – for two weeks (15 days)
10 *la machine de traitement de texte* – word processor
11 *j'ai répondu au téléphone* – I answered the telephone
12 *le travail était un peu monotone* – the work was a bit dull
13 *je me suis bien amusée* – I had a good time
14 *c'était mieux que l'école, quoi* – it was better than school

Le détective

The perfect tense with reflexive verbs. A good way of teaching this structure, and vocabulary for daily routine, is through a song (tune: 'The Flower of Scotland'):
Pour aller au collège
Je me suis levé(e)
Et puis j'ai bu un bon café
Je me suis lavé(e)
Et je me suis habillé(e)
Je me suis dépêché(e)
Pour prendre le bus, mais
Je me suis rendu(e) compte, que
C'était dimanche!

2b Use the underlined parts of the text above and the key language to help you talk about the 2 jobs shown in the pictures below.

Speaking. Students use the language from the text in **2a** to help them to practise speaking about past work experience.

3a Write about 75 words about your own work experience. Use the text in **2a** to help you.

Writing. Students write about work experience in the past.

✚ Students could use their writing as preparation for speaking. They can benefit greatly from learning paragraphs of text they themselves have created.

3b CV Choose at least 5 statements about your work experience and combine them in a paragraph under the title *Expérience* on disc. Insert the data into your CV document.

Further practice of the language and vocabulary of this spread is provided as follows:

À l'oral, page 73: Prepared talk

Cahier d'exercices, page 27 (ex. 4), pages 28–29

2 Le monde du travail

(Student's Book pages 62–63)

Main topics and objectives

- Looking for a job in France

Key language

Language from previous spreads
Language used in CV

Skills/Strategies

- Writing formal letters
- Using the Internet

Resources

Cassette B side 2
Cahier d'exercices, page 30

Introduce the spread with a discussion of the importance of languages in the world of work, and the likelihood of many of your students working abroad. Students may well have started work on their personal statements in their PSE classes. Brainstorm how many personal characteristics students can remember in French, and add to their word lists any they will need to express their own characteristics.

1a Find the words and phrases below in Alice's job application letter.

Reading (1–10). Students find phrases which will be of relevance to them when they write similar letters of application for jobs in France. They should write down the English and French phrases for easy reference later on.

Answers

```
 1  j'ai vu votre annonce
 2  je vous écris …
 3  pour poser ma candidature au poste
 4  j'ai déjà travaillé dans un restaurant
 5  pendant mon stage
 6  j'ai un petit boulot
 7  le week-end
 8  je suis travailleuse
 9  je m'entends bien avec mon patron
10  veuillez trouver ci-joint
```

Tip box

French business letters are very formal! Draw students' attention to phrases such as *Je vous écris pour poser ma candidature au poste de …*, *Veuillez trouver* and the possibility of including phrases like *je vous remercie infiniement*.

1b Write a letter of application for one of the jobs in this hotel. Use Alice's letter as a model and change the words printed in red.

Writing. Students write their own letter of application for one of these jobs. Tell them about the importance of making work experience relevant to the job advertised (this is particularly important for Intermediate 2 candidates).

This letter and the CV in **2a**, **2b** and **2c** could be copy-typed and made available to all students via the school/college intranet.

2a Copy the CV. Put the details below in the right places.

Reading. Students demonstrate understanding by putting the details for the CV under the right headings.

Answers

Nom: Provost
Prénom: Franc
Adresse: 6 rue des Lilas, Angoulême
Date de naissance: 3/07/1983
Lieu de naissance: Paris
Nationalité: française
Famille: J'ai une sœur. Elle s'appelle Natalie. Elle a 13 ans.
Domicile: J'habite à Angoulême. C'est une grande ville. J'aime habiter ici.
École: Mon école s'appelle le Lycée de l'Image. Je fais français, histoire, géo, maths, anglais, sciences et théâtre. Ma matière préférée est l'histoire.
Expérience: J'ai fait un stage dans une école primaire. Je travaille dans un supermarché.
Loisirs: J'aime le théâtre. Je vais au cinéma. Je joue au foot.

2b Listen to the interview with Alice. Copy the CV and fill in her details in French.

Listening. Students fill in a CV with the details they have heard. Encourage them to answer in full sentences where the original CV has them.

Tapescript

– *Merci d'avoir téléphoné, mademoiselle, je vais vous poser quelques questions, d'accord? Vous êtes donc Mademoiselle Reid, Alice Reid?*
– *Oui, madame.*
– *Et vous habitez au numéro 24, Tay View, Dundee. Quelle est votre date de naissance, s'il vous plaît?*
– *Je suis née le 21 juin, 1988, à Dundee, en Écosse.*
– *Vous êtes écossaise, alors.*
– *Oui, bien sûr.*

MÉTRO **4**

– *Vous avez des sœurs ou des frères?*
– *Oui, j'ai deux frères. Ils s'appellent Paul et Richard. J'habite avec mon père.*
– *Et vous habitez à Dundee?*
– *Oui, j'habite à Dundee. C'est une grande ville dans l'est de l'Écosse. Il y a beaucoup de choses à faire à Dundee.*
– *Mais vous parlez très bien français, Alice.*
– *Oui, j'apprends le français à mon collège, Harris Academy.*
– *Alors, vous étudiez le français, quelles autres matières faites-vous ?*
– *Je fais anglais, mathématiques, français, … sciences, allemand, histoire, musique et informatique. Ma matière préférée, c'est la musique.*
– *Avez-vous de l'expérience qui pourrait vous servir?*
– *Oui, j'ai fait un stage en industrie dans un restaurant pendant une semaine. J'ai servi les clients et j'ai pris des réservations au téléphone. Pendant le week-end, je travaille dans un café où je sers les clients et je prépare les sandwichs.*
– *Merci. Et qu'est-ce que vous faites pendant votre temps libre?*
– *J'aime beaucoup regarder le sport, surtout le football. J'aime aussi la lecture et le dessin.*
– *Eh bien, merci beaucoup mademoiselle. Je dois encore voir d'autres personnes, mais je vous téléphonerai dès que possible pour vous dire si on vous prend, d'accord?*
– *Merci beaucoup, madame. Au revoir.*

Answers

Nom: Reid
Prénom: Alice
Adresse: 24 Tay View, Dundee
Date de naissance: 21 juin 1988
Lieu de naissance: Dundee
Nationalité: écossaise
Famille: J'ai deux frères. Ils s'appellent Paul et Richard. J'habite avec mon père.
Domicile: Dundee. C'est une grande ville dans l'est de l'Écosse.
École: Harris Academy. Je fais anglais, mathématiques, français, sciences, allemand, histoire, musique et informatique. Ma matière préférée est la musique.
Expérience: J'ai fait un stage dans un restaurant. Le week-end, je travaille dans un café.
Loisirs: J'aime regarder le sport. J'aime aussi la lecture et le dessin.

2c
CV Now write your own CV in French. Use the models above to help you.

Writing. Students should update their CV (CV.doc) using the extra details from Alice's CV.

Internet project. Surf the Internet to find an advert for a job you could do in your summer holidays. Focus your search as much as you can.

If possible, search the Internet in advance of your students in order to direct their search more accurately.

Further practice of the language and vocabulary of this spread is provided as follows:

Cahier d'exercices, page 30

3 Au téléphone

(Student's Book pages 64–65)

Main topics and objectives

● Using the phone

Key language

Allô.
C'est (Anne) à l'appareil.
Je peux vous aider?
Je voudrais parler à …
C'est de la part de qui?
Ne quittez pas.
Je regrette, il/elle n'est pas là.
Est-ce que je peux laisser un message?
Votre nom, comment ça s'écrit?
Quel est votre message?
Quel est votre numéro de téléphone?

À quelle heure est-ce que je peux rappeler?
Je vous téléphone à propos de l'annonce.
Je voudrais un poste comme (serveur).

Grammar

● Talking about the past, present and future

Skills/Strategies

● Being polite
● Saying French phone numbers

Resources

À l'oral, page 73: Transaction 2
Cassette B side 2
Cahier d'exercices, page 31 (exs 8–9)

Introduce the spread by practising phone numbers (and thereby numbers up to 100) with your students. Get them used to understanding and giving phone numbers at speed. Look at the first tip box with students.

1a Are the printed telephone numbers correct? Listen and correct any mistakes.

Listening (1–8). Students start to develop their speed in recognition and recording of phone numbers by listening to phone numbers which are correct, by and large. They have only to spot which element is incorrect.

Tapescript

1 *L'Office du tourisme est fermé jusqu'à 2 heures, appelez le 04 89 27 29 49.*
2 *Ici la maison Cachin, 04 68 73 15 13.*
3 *Vous êtes bien au coin du feu – 05 62 66 71 56. Veuillez laisser un message.*
4 *Hôtel Yaka, Biarritz – 05 78 04 33 52.*
5 *Atelier Gill, 02 89 71 94 14. Merci de votre appel, veuillez patienter.*
6 *L'Association Clément est fermée en raison des vacances. Contactez-les au 01 45 67 67 42. Nous vous remercions de votre appel.*
7 *La nef vous prie de rappeler ce numéro – 02 97 71 85 87.*
8 *01 99 76 64 96 – Gérard Darel à votre service.*

Answers

```
1 ✓
2 04 68 73 15 13
3 ✓
4 05 78 04 33 52
5 02 89 71 94 14
6 ✓
7 02 97 71 85 87
8 01 99 76 64 96
```

1b In pairs. Take turns to give the telephone numbers from **1a**, and to say who is calling.

Speaking. Students develop their skills further by giving the numbers they have seen and heard in **1a**.

Tip box

Being polite. Remind students that they have already come across the use of *madame* in the letter on page 62.

2a In pairs, listen to this conversation, then practise it with a partner, changing the underlined details each time.

Speaking. Students practise a model phone conversation, then change details where they can.

Tapescript

– *Good morning, Eau Naturelle, can I help you?*
– *Bonjour, monsieur, parlez-vous français?*
– *Ah oui, bonjour madame. C'est Matthew à l'appareil. Je peux vous aider?*
– *Je voudrais parler à Monsieur Foley, s'il vous plaît.*
– *C'est de la part de qui?*
– *Je suis Fabienne Alalain.*
– *Merci. Ne quittez pas … Ah, je regrette, mais il n'est pas là.*
– *Est-ce que je peux vous laisser un message?*
– *Bien sûr. Votre nom, comment ça s'écrit?*
– *Ça s'écrit A… L… A… L… A… I… N.*
– *Et quel est votre message?*
– *Dites-lui que je ne peux pas venir à la réunion demain.*
– *Merci beaucoup, c'est noté. Quel est votre numéro de téléphone, s'il vous plaît?*
– *C'est le 02 45 75 89 23.*
– *Et Monsieur Foley peut vous rappeler à quelle heure?*
– *À partir de dix heures et demie.*
– *Merci … Merci, madame. Au revoir!*

2b Find the French in the conversation for the following.

Reading (1–10). Students find phrases in the printed conversation in **2a**, which are particularly useful for telephone conversations.

Answers

> 1 C'est Matthew à l'appareil.
> 2 Je voudrais parler à …
> 3 C'est de la part de qui?
> 4 Ne quittez pas …
> 5 Il n'est pas là.
> 6 Est-ce que je peux vous laisser un message?
> 7 Votre nom, comment ça s'écrit?
> 8 Quel est votre numéro de téléphone?
> 9 Monsieur Foley peut vous rappeler à quelle heure?
> 10 À partir de dix heures et demie.

3a Can you work out what these questions mean?

Reading (1–5). Students use their revision of question words to help them translate five questions which will be particularly useful to them when phoning about a job or in a job interview.

Answers

> 1 What time does work begin?
> 2 What is the salary?
> 3 What exactly is the work?
> 4 Can I speak to Madame Nabotin?
> 5 Can I leave a message?

Le détective

Talking about the past, present and future. Students now need to be able to use past, present and future tenses in the same conversation. Draw their attention to the practice of mirroring a question in its answer: *tu as/avez-vous → j'ai; tu peux/pouvez-vous → je peux*, etc. Make sure students have a clear idea that *j'ai* + past participle are markers for the past tense and that *je* alone is not!

3b You would like to apply for one of these jobs. Prepare answers to these questions in French. You can make up details if you like.

Writing. Students complete the sentences. This activity will help them conduct the telephone interview in activity **4**.

4 In pairs. Use the telephone conversation in **2a** and the answers you have prepared for **3b** to help you.

Speaking. Students use all of the language they have gathered so far to help them answer questions in a telephone enquiry/job interview. Model it with student volunteers first if you wish.

> Further practice of the language and vocabulary of this spread is provided as follows:
>
> À l'oral, page 73: Transaction 2
>
> Cahier d'exercices, page 31

4 Qu'est-ce que vous voulez faire dans la vie?

MODULE 4 AU BOULOT

(Student's Book pages 66–67)

Main topics and objectives

- Talking about your future career

Key language

*Je travaillerai/Je ne travaillerai pas
comme serveur/guardien(ne)/chez McDo
dans le tourisme/dans un bureau/à l'étranger
Je trouverai (un travail).
Je ferai (un diplôme).
J'irai (à la fac/aux États-Unis).
Je serai (joueur de foot).
Je continuerai (mes etudes).
Je voyagerai (autour du monde).
Je gagnerai (un bon salaire).
J'étudierai (l'anglais).
Je rencontrerai l'homme de ma vie.*

Grammar

- The future tense
- Using the future with *quand*
- Other ways of expressing the future

Resources

À l'oral, page 73: Conversation 1
À toi! A, page 186
Cassette B side 2
Cahier d'exercices, page 31 (ex. 10)

Introduce the spread by asking, in English, how many students already have career intentions. Discuss how to express these in French. Students should look up unusual jobs for themselves in the dictionary.

1a Read the future plans of these young people and answer the questions.

Reading (1–8). A reading activity which expands students' vocabulary by giving them some alternative expressions to those used in the text.

Answers

1 Luc	2 Anne	3 Feyrouze	4 Romain
5 Yoann	6 Anne	7 Feyrouze	8 Romain

Le détective

The future tense. One way of presenting the future (and conditional) to your students is by means of a song! This is sung to the tune of 'With a Little Help from my Friends' (Lennon/McCartney).

What do you do to say 'will' or say 'would'?
In French there is no separate word.
You take the infinitive and add an ending
(*avoir* for the future I've heard).
Oh, so you leave the little 'r' before the end.
Mmm, always leave the little 'r' before the end.
Je finirai, tu finiras, il/elle/on finira, nous finirons, vous finirez, ils and *elles finiront.*
Oh, so you leave the little 'r' before the end, etc.

1b Note all the verbs in the future tense in **1a** (*Projets d'avenir*). Then say what they mean in English.

Writing. Students practise recognition of the future

tense (point out the characteristic 'r' before the end and the use of *avoir* for endings), and also formal recognition of meanings.

Answers

Romain: *je ferai (faire)* – I will do, *je chercherai* – I will look for, *permettra* – will allow
Yoann: *je ferai* – I will do, *je chercherai* – I will look for
Anne: *j'irai* – I will go
Feyrouze: *je travaillerai* – I will work
Luc: *je serai* – I will be, *je continuerai* – I will continue

2 Work out what the sentences mean, then listen to the tape. Who says what?

Listening (1–4). Students prepare for this listening activity by reading and accessing the meanings of key phrases. They then hear the future tense in a format they will instantly recognise and understand.

Tapescript

1 Je me présente, je m'appelle Valérie Fossey et je vais vous parler de mes ambitions. J'irai donc au mois de septembre aux États-Unis où je vais travailler à la rédaction d'un magazine français. Je gagnerai environ $40,000 – je suis ravie!! Quand je serai à New York, je visiterai aussi d'autres villes: Boston, Washington … et je poursuivrai mes études le soir. Ce sera dur, mais je suis impatiente.
2 Bonjour tout le monde, Marie-Annick Buffon. Je vous parle en direct de la Martinique. Alors moi, je viendrai en France à Paris et j'étudierai les langues étrangères à la Sorbonne. Pour gagner de l'argent afin de financer mes études, je travaillerai dans un café, c'est déjà prévu. Je rencontrerai bien sûr l'homme de ma vie, je me marierai avec lui et on aura 2,4 enfants et deux voitures!
3 Bonjour, je m'appelle Laurent Châtelain et je vais vous parler de mes projets … enfin, ce que j'espère faire dans

l'avenir. Je continuerai mes études à la fac de Nancy. Je vais étudier la gestion avec une langue étrangère afin de voyager ultérieurement. Question d'argent, oui, c'est important pour moi. En tant que vendeur, je gagnerai un bon salaire et mon niveau de vie pourra largement payer le loyer et les frais d'une petite famille.

4 *L'avenir ... je voyagerai autour du monde, je rencontrerai des gens intéressants, je trouverai un travail fantastique à Hollywood. Je gagnerai des milliers de francs. Mes enfants seront très beaux, voilà, c'est tout.*

Answers

1 a, d	2 b, i, c, j	3 f, h	4 e, g, k

Le détective

Using *quand* and the future tense. Show your students some examples of this before they listen to **3a**, e.g. *Quand j'irai à Glasgow, j'achèterai... Quand Paul viendra, il trouvera...*

3a Listen. Join up the beginnings and ends of the sentences.

Listening (1–6). Students hear examples of *quand* being used with the future tense, and write out the completed sentences.

Tapescript

Quand j'aurai dix-huit ans, je travaillerai comme au pair. Je vivrai en Italie, et je serai heureuse.
Quand j'aurai dix-neuf ans, j'irai à la fac.
Quand j'aurai vingt-trois ans, je travaillerai chez Dior ... et je toucherai un gros salaire.

Answers

1 d	2 b	3 a	4 c	5 f	6 e

3b What will you be doing in two years' time? Write 2 things in answer to each question in the speech bubble, then tape what you have written!

Writing. Students write what they think they will be doing in the future. Encourage them to write imaginative answers.

Rappel

Other ways of expressing the future. Draw students' attention to the need to vary what they say and write.

3c In pairs. Take turns to ask and answer the questions: Qu'est-ce que tu feras quand tu auras 18 ans/20 ans/30 ans/40 ans?

Speaking. In pairs, students practise the structure *quand* + future.

Further practice of the language and vocabulary of this spread is provided as follows:

À l'oral, page 73: Conversation 1

À toi! A, page 186

Cahier d'exercices, page 31 (ex. 10)

5 Les différents emplois

(Student's Book pages 68–69)

Main topics and objectives

● Talking about different kinds of work

Key language

J'aimerais/Je voudrais …
 aider (les gens malades)
 travailler avec des enfants/des animaux/les personnes âgées
 en équipe/seul(e)/en plein air/dans un bureau
 dans le domaine de l'informatique/du marketing/de l'éducation
 dans le commerce/dans le tourisme
Je préférerais …
 m'occuper (d'animaux/d'enfants)

être (infirmier/ère)
avoir (de longues vacances)
voyager/gagner beaucoup d'argent

Grammar

● The conditional tense

Skills/Strategies

● Reading authentic texts

Resources

Cassette B side 2
Cahier d'exercices, page 32 (ex. 11)

Introduce this spread by revising preferences for work environment and personal characteristics. This can be done in the form of a quiz or as 'What's My Line?'. Draw students' attention to the key language box on page 68 and introduce any new expressions from it.

1a Find the ideal job for each person (there may be more than one).

Reading (1–10). Students read people's preferences for work environment and select the most appropriate job for each person from the pictures.

Answers (any sensible answers accepted)

1 a or f	**2** e or g	**3** i	**4** h	**5** e	**6** b	**7** a or f
8 d	**9** a, b, f or i	**10** c or d			

1b Conduct a survey in your class about people's ideal jobs. Make your results into a graph.

Speaking. Students practise asking the same question several times and recording the answers in graph form. Ensure that they can all ask and remember this question before allowing them to conduct the survey.

Le détective

The conditional tense. Remind students of the song used to teach the future tense endings. Point out that the same stem is used for the conditional tense, but with different endings. Teach the endings by spelling them out to the tune of 'This old man':
-ais, -ais, -ait; -ions, with an *-iez* and an *-aient*, that's what the conditional endings should be!

2a Read the bubbles and make notes about where these people want to work.

Reading (a–e). Students expand their vocabulary by reading more preferences for working environment.

Answers

a in marketing
b in computers
c in the private sector – commerce
d in education
e in tourism

2b Now listen and match your notes from **2a** with what the speakers say.

Listening (1–5). Students listen and match the speakers to their notes from **2a**. They have prepared for this by reading and accessing the meanings of key phrases.

Tapescript

1 *Je suis très branché sur les ordinateurs et la technologie. Il est donc très important pour moi qu'il y ait un élément technologique dans mon boulot.*
2 *Je m'intéresse énormément aux autres pays et aux autres cultures. Je fais des économies pour pouvoir voyager. J'ai choisi ce métier afin de m'adonner à ma passion pour les langues étrangères.*
3 *Je veux gagner beaucoup d'argent pour moi et prendre ma retraite à un très jeune âge. J'ai choisi ce secteur, parce que je pense que ce sera plus facile d'arriver à mon but que si je faisais autre chose. C'est très simple.*
4 *J'aime bien avoir le contact avec des gens et je peux convaincre les gens de ce qu'ils veulent. Mon père me dit que j'arriverais à vendre mon grand-père si je m'y mettais.*
5 *L'enseignement, c'est important pour l'avenir de tous et pour le bien-être de tous. C'est d'une importance capitale. C'est pour ça que j'ai choisi de faire le métier que je fais, être instituteur.*

Answers

1 b	**2** e	**3** c	**4** a	**5** d

3 Read this article and answer the questions in English.

Reading (1–7). Students answer comprehension questions on a passage containing a certain amount of unfamiliar vocabulary. They should be exposed to an increasing amount of vocabulary they have either to work out from its context or look up in a dictionary.

Answers

1 Perfect a foreign language, learn about another culture, gain experience of another country and it's good for your CV. (4)
2 It's a beautiful country. He likes the Italians. They are open, friendly and dynamic. (2)
3 He would go out, eat and speak like an Italian. (3)
4 Managing director. (1)
5 Wants to work with people and money is important. More interesting to work in marketing. (2)
6 Does not want to work with them – would be boring. (2)
7 To perfect his languages. (1)

4 Use the following questions to help you write a paragraph about your ambitions.

Writing. Students use the questions to give them vocabulary and to structure a piece of writing about their career intentions.

Further practice of the language and vocabulary of this spread is provided as follows:

Cahier d'exercices, page 32 (ex. 11)

6 Les études et le travail

(Student's Book pages 70–71)

Main topics and objectives

● Discussing work, studies and taking a year out

Key language

Il faut trouver un équilibre travail-études.
Mes examens sont plus importants que mon petit boulot.
L'argent, c'est le plus important.
Il devrait être possible de combiner un boulot et ses études.
Gagner un peu d'argent te donne de l'indépendance.
Le plus important, c'est de réussir dans ses examens.
Étudier, c'est important – je ne veux pas être au chômage.

Grammar

● Modal verbs in the conditional

Skills/Strategies

● Translating into natural English
● Using opinion phrases
● Planning an essay

Resources

À toi! B, page 187
Cassette B side 2
Cahier d'exercices, page 32 (ex 12)

Introduce the spread by eliciting positive and negative opinions on taking a year out, first in English, then in French, from your students.

1a What are these French students saying about having to work as well as study? Put the opinions into 3 groups.

Reading. Students show understanding by organising statements into columns. This activity also gives them help with identifying positive and negative opinions later on.

Answers

a 3, 5	**b** 2, 6, 7	**c** 1, 4

1b Translate the opinions into English.

Reading (1–7). Students practise translation techniques: using the dictionary to get a raw, word-for-word translation and then making sense out of all the information they have gathered.

Answers

1 You have to find a balance between working and studying.
2 My exams are more important than my job.
3 Money is the most important.
4 It should be possible to combine a job and studying.
5 Earning a little money gives you independence.
6 The most important is to succeed in your exams.
7 Studying is important – I don't want to be unemployed.

Le détective

Modal verbs. Point out to students the conditional meaning of these verbs and brainstorm some sentences where they could be used.

1c In groups of 4–5. Take turns to give your opinion about working and studying. The rest of the group have to agree or disagree.

Speaking. This gives further practice in the use of *je suis d'accord* and *je ne suis pas d'accord*.

Tip box

Opinion phrases. Encourage students to use a variety of opinion phrases every time they speak or write opinions.

1d Write about 100 words, giving your own opinion about working and studying.

Writing. Students use the opinions given, either as they stand or changed slightly, to represent their own opinions.

2a Are these opinions for or against the idea of a gap year? Translate the ones you agree with.

Reading. Students prepare for exercises **2b** and **4**, firstly by identifying positive and negative statements, and then by translating the phrases they may well use in their own writing.

Answers

For: 1, 2, 3, 5, 7
Against: 4, 6, 8
1 It's good to have the experience of another country.
2 You make friends when you travel. It's a privilege.
3 I think that a gap year widens your horizons.
4 It would be hard to go away for a whole year.
5 You learn lots of things during a gap year, without mentioning the experience.
6 I would miss my friends.
7 I would like to get to know another culture.
8 The language could pose some problems.

2b Listen. Answer the questions in English.

Listening (1–2). Students apply the language they have read in **2a** to understanding spoken French. Point out to them that the (3) after the question should indicate to them that they must find three reasons. A useful technique is to concentrate on a different reason each time they listen.

Tapescript

– *C'est bien de voyager à mon avis. C'est bien de faire une petite pause avant de se lancer dans les études. Une année sabbatique vous donne l'occasion de vous reposer, de réfléchir un petit peu – et c'est important, ça. En plus on peut gagner un peu d'argent avant d'aller à la fac. C'est ce que je vais faire, moi.*

– *Je ne suis pas d'accord. Si on fait une pause, on risque de tout oublier et c'est pas un risque à courir. En plus, si on continue, c'est nettement moins cher. Moi, j'irai directement à l'université.*

Answers

1 It's good to have a break before studying. It's gives you the chance to rest and to reflect. Also, you can earn some money. (3)
2 You risk forgetting everything. It's less expensive if you go straight to university. (2)

3 Which headline says each of these things?

Reading (1–6). Students use matching techniques to work out the meaning of opinions expressed as headlines. This is also language which can be used in their personal writing in activity **4**.

Answers

| **1** b | **2** c | **3** e | **4** f | **5** a | **6** d |

Tip box

Planning an essay. This reminds students that it is very important to structure pieces of writing. Marking criteria for Credit at Standard Grade and for A/G at Intermediate 2 stress the need for clear structure.

4 Write an article of about 100 words in French about work. Use the opinions in **2a** and these questions to help you.

Writing. Students now pull together all the language they have learned to write at length on a specific subject. Encourage more able students to write well over 100 words.

Further practice of the language and vocabulary of this spread is provided as follows:

À toi! B, page 187

Cahier d'exercices, page 32 (ex. 12)

All the key vocabulary and structures from this module are listed on the **Mots** pages 74–75. These can be used for revision by covering up either the English or the French. Students can check here to see how much they remember from the module and use them to prepare for the assessments.

Assessment materials for Modules 3 and 4 are available in the separate Assessment Pack.

Further speaking and grammar practice on the whole module is provided on **Cahier d'exercices** pages 33–34.

Entraînez-vous: À l'oral

(Student's Book pages 72–73)

Speaking practice: Modules 3 & 4

These spreads give regular practice in the three types of speaking activity required for the internally assessed speaking elements of the Standard Grade and Intermediate courses: conversations, transactions and prepared talks.

The activities on the speaking pages are designed to allow students to build up their speaking skills while working with a partner independently of teacher support. They also include handy hints on how

students can improve their speaking grades.

Page 72 provides speaking activities for Module 3: conversations on hobbies, past activities and inviting someone out and a transaction on finding information at the cinema.

Page 73 provides speaking activities for Module 4: a conversation on future plans, a transaction on the telephone and a prepared talk on work experience.

À toi A & B

(Student's Book pages 186–187)

Self-access reading and writing at two levels

These pages are designed to give students extra practice in reading and structured writing. There are two differentiated pages relating to each chapter: A and B. Page A is at an easier level and page B more challenging. You may wish students to work on the page most appropriate to their level or to work through both pages. You may feel it is useful to work with students on the activities, but it should be possible for most students to work on them independently. The most appropriate time to use each page is indicated within the relevant teaching notes.

À toi! A, page 186

This page is best used after pages 66–67 of the Student's Book.

1 Read the magazine article and answer the questions in English.

Answers

1 go to university to study languages (2)
2 English and Spanish (2)
3 German (1)
4 freer than life at school (2)
5 what he wants to do in life (1)
6 when he is 18 (1)
7 aid work (1)
8 It will be a fantastic experience and it will broaden his horizons. (2)
9 leave school and start work in an office or a bank (3)
10 She will learn more at work than at school. Staying at school is not worth it! (2)
11 electronic communications (1)
12 studying whilst doing a job (he will do work placements in industry) (2)

2 What do you intend to do after you have left school? Write about 75 words. Use expressions from the texts above.

Tip box

Different ways of talking about the future. This reminds pupils that they can use *aller* + infinitive, the proper future, *j'ai l'intention* … and *j'espère* … to talk about their plan for the future.

À toi! B, page 187

This page is best used after pages 70–71 of the Student's Book.

1a Does the article claim that the following ideas are myths or reality?

Answers

1 myth	**2** reality	**3** myth	**4** reality	**5** myth

1b Answer these questions in English. Remember to look for the number of points asked for.

Answers

1 Stay at home whilst staying in contact with colleagues, communicate, choose, buy, sell, thanks to e-mail and websites. (4)
2 It remains quite popular but mostly with women. (2)
3 Traditional industry is disappearing but machines will never replace people in hospitals, schools and other service industries. (3)

2 Write at least 100 words about working conditions in the future. Try to answer these questions.

AU BOULOT

MODULE **4**

Cahier d'exercices, page 26

1
Answers

a agent de police – *cap* – au commmissariat
b boulanger – *baguette* – dans une boulangerie
c hôtesse de l'air – *aeroplane* – dans le monde entier
d professeur – *blackboard* – au collège
e facteur – *envelope* – à la poste
f infirmier – *syringe* – dans un hôpital
g mécanicien – *car* – dans un garage
h secrétaire – *computer* – dans un bureau
i fermier – *farm animals* – dans une ferme
j caissier – *cash till* – au supermarché

2
Answers

a serveur **b** infirmière **c** vétérinaire **d** boulanger
e coiffeuse **f** dentiste **g** médecin **h** maçon
i hôtesse de l'air **j** camionneur/chauffeur de camion

Cahier d'exercices, page 27

3
Answers

a quel **b** combien **c** comment **d** quelles **e** que

4
Answers

a She works in a bank.
b She starts at 9 and finishes at 5.
c Saturdays and Sundays
d answer the telephone, work at the counter, check the figures
e her boss – she is rather unfriendly
f underground or tram
g She doesn't want to be unemployed.

Cahier d'exercices, page 28

5a
Answers

	Éric	Amélie	Arthur	Gérard
Job	waiter	hairdresser's assistant	bank employee	works in an old people's hospice
Tasks (x2)	wash the glasses, serve customers	wash hair, sweep the floor	work on the computer, sort the mail	chat to old people, make teas and coffees
Start (time)	07:00	12:00	09:00	10:00
Finish (time)	23:00	18:00	17:00	16:00
Advantage	the customers and the boss are nice	it is easy	it is well paid	she learns a lot from talking to the old people
Drawback	it is very tiring and poorly paid	her feet hurt sometimes	it is far to cycle	it is a little boring sometimes

5b
Answers

a je ne travaille que **b** mal payé **c** les clients sont gentils **d** je ne commence qu'à **e** quelquefois
f chaque été **g** les horaires ne sont pas mal
h la journée passe vite

5c (writing task)

Cahier d'exercices, page 29

6a
Answers

a presque toutes les grandes vacances
b j'ai travaillé comme serveur
c c'était un travail assez intéressant
d j'ai rencontré beaucoup de gens
e j'étais bien payé
f le travail était aussi assez dur
g À la fin du service, j'ai balayé.
h C'était un travail fatigant, mais varié.
i mon patron était très gentil
j j'ai servi les boissons

6b (writing task)

Cahier d'exercices, page 30

7 (writing task)

Cahier d'exercices, page 31

8
Answers

a 3	**b** 9	**c** 10	**d** 5	**e** 8	**f** 1	**g** 6
h 2	**i** 7	**j** 4				

9
Answers

a 02 38 12 05 63	**b** 03 44 15 23 80
c 06 88 52 14 78	**d** 04 00 99 11 30
e 01 36 19 42 72	

10 (writing task)

Cahier d'exercices, page 32

11
Answers

a 3	**b** 7	**c** 7	**d** 7	**e** 3	**f** 7	**g** 7

12
Answers

a You must succeed in your exams.
b It is good to live in a foreign country.
c The most important thing is to find a balance between work and study.
d You learn a lot of things when you do work experience.
e I think there are a lot of people who do not want to work.

Cahier d'exercices, page 33

Cahier d'exercices, page 34

1
Answers

a professeur   b infirmière
c coiffeuse   d hôtesse de l'air
e boulangère   f caissière
g secrétaire   h opératrice

2
Answers

a present   b future   c perfect
d present   e future

3
Answers

a 4   b 7   c 2   d 9   e 3

4
Answers

Je passerai mes examens en juin et je réviserai beaucoup. J'étudierai le dessin à l'université et mes parents m'aideront financièrement. Ma petite amie et moi irons en vacances cet été.

MODULE 5
MA VILLE

Ma ville

(Student's Book pages 76–91)

Topic area	Key language	Grammar	Skills/Strategies
Déjà vu (pp. 76–79) Talking about where you live Talking about what you can do Describing special occasions	C'est un/une grand(e)/petit(e)/joli(e)/beau(belle)/vieux(vieille) ville/village important(e)/ancien(ne)/historique/animé(e)/magnifique, industriel(le)/typique/moderne/calme/pittoresque/moyen(ne). Ma ville/Mon village est situé(e)/se trouve … à la montagne/au bord de la mer/à la campagne/dans les Alpes/au bord d'un lac. Il y a /Il n'y a pas de … une piscine/gare/église/école/cathédrale/ un hôpital/château/stade/musée/parc/syndicat d'initiative/hôtel de ville des magasins. On peut visiter le théâtre/cinéma/café/pont/centre commercial/marché/ centre de recyclage/jardin des plantes/casino/l'aquarium l'office de tourisme/la patinoire/mairie/zone piétonne/place/plage/citadelle/ les monuments/remparts/caves. Nous, on fête …, le …. Le matin/L'après-midi/Le soir, il y avait … un défilé/un marché/bal/ concours/concert/des feux d'artifice/un match de foot/un spectacle. On a dansé/chanté/mangé/bu/joué (à) … On est allé à … On s'est amusé. On s'est déguisé en …	Il n'y a pas de … Position of adjectives Using on Perfect tense	Listening strategy: predictions
1 Qu'est-ce qu'il y a à faire ici? (pp. 80–81) Saying what there is and is not in a town	Dans mon village/ma ville/mon quartier/ma région, il y a beaucoup/plein/pas mal de … Il n'y a pas de … maisons individuelles/jumelées/mitoyennes/HLM. C'est isolé. Il n'y a pas de (bus/cinéma/centre sportif/maison des jeunes). Il n'y a rien à faire. Il n'y a rien ici pour les jeunes. Il y a trop de bruit/voitures/pollution de l'air. On ne peut pas sortir seul(e)/ aller en boîte/se déplacer facilement. Je ne me sens jamais en sécurité.	Negatives	Using useful words/ expressions in writing
2 La ville et la campagne (pp. 82–83) Comparing the town and country	Il y a beaucoup de distractions. Il y a plein/peu de choses à faire. C'est (très) animé/(plus) calme/(moins) sale/(moins) pollué/(trop) bruyant/(extrêmement) ennuyeux/(plus) sain/propre. On peut sortir/se détendre. On est plus près de la nature. Tout le monde est pressé. Il y a trop de pollution/de voitures. Il y a plus de voitures/plus de gens/moins de monde/moins de bruit.	Le mieux/Le pire, c'est de … The conditional tense	Expressing pros and cons

92

Topic area	Key language	Grammar	Skills/Strategies
3 L'environnement (pp. 84–85) Discussing environmental issues	*Pour moi, la pollution/l'emballage/le gaspillage d'énergie/le matérialisme/ le bruit/les papiers par terre … est/sont plus important(s) que …* *Il faut/On devrait … acheter des produits verts/utiliser les transports en commun/conserver l'énergie et l'eau/trier les déchets/utiliser les produits recyclés/éteindre la lumière.* *Il ne faut pas/On ne devrait pas … gaspiller l'eau/jeter les papiers par terre.*	Comparisons *Il faut* + infinitive The passive voice	Extended reading: Working out meaning from context/cognates Using 'marker' words in an essay
4 Les pays francophones (pp. 86–87) Discussing the French-speaking world	Language from the whole module		Using the Internet for research
Entraînez-vous: À l'écrit (pp. 88–89) Ma ville	Language from Module 5		Writing a brochure Accuracy Using exclamations
À toi! A and B (pp.188–189)	Language from Module 5		Reading and writing skills

The vocabulary and structures taught in Module 5 are summarised on the **Mots** pages of the Student's Book, pages 90–91.
Further speaking practice on the language of the module is provided on **À l'oral**, page 106.
Assessment tasks for Modules 5 and 6 combined are provided in the separate Assessment Pack.

Déjà vu

(Student's Book pages 76–79)

Main topics and objectives

- Talking about where you live
- Talking about what you can do
- Describing special occasions

Key language

*C'est un/une grand(e)/petit(e)/joli(e)/beau(belle)/
  vieux(vieille) ville/village.
important(e), ancien(ne), historique,
  animé(e), magnifique, industriel(le),
  typique, moderne, calme, pittoresque, moyen(ne)
Ma ville/Mon village est situé(e)/se trouve …
  à la montagne/au bord de la mer/à la
  campagne/dans les Alpes/au bord d'un lac
Il y a/Il n'y a pas de …
  une piscine/gare/église/école/cathédrale
  un hôpital/château/stade/musée/parc/syndicat
  d'initiative/hôtel de ville
  des magasins
On peut visiter …
  le théâtre/cinéma/café/pont/centre commercial/
  marché/centre de recyclage/jardin des plantes/casino
  l'aquarium/l'office de tourisme*

*la patinoire/mairie/place/plage/citadelle/zone piétonne
les monuments/remparts/caves
Nous, on fête … le ….
Le matin/L'après-midi/Le soir, il y avait …
  un défilé/marché/bal/concours/concert
  des feux d'artifice/un match de foot/un spectacle
On a dansé, chanté, mangé, bu, joué (à)
On est allé à … On s'est amusé.
On s'est déguisé en …*

Grammar

- *Il n'y a pas de….*
- Position of adjectives
- Using *on*

Skills/Strategies

- Listening: predicting content

Resources

Cassette B side 2
Cahier d'exercices, pages 35–37

Introduce this module by revising vocabulary to describe the region/town your students live in (e.g. *c'est un village/une ville, c'est à la campagne, c'est près de …, c'est à … km de …*, etc.). Introduce adjectives used to describe towns (see key language box on page 76). Look at the *Rappel* box which points out normal and exceptional word order for adjectives.

1a Read the texts above. Copy this table and fill in the gaps.

Reading. Students read the three texts and use dictionaries to help them to fill in the required details in the table.

Answers

	type of place	where
Alicia	city	south-west France, 730 km from Paris
Pierre	small village	north of Martinique, in the Caribbean
Sébastien	medium-sized town	countryside, south-east of Belgium.

1b Find the following in the bold text above: 3 locations, 5 types of place and 9 descriptions. Write or type them in English and in French.

Reading. Students categorise the words they have found. This activity will help them with text substitution techniques.

Answers

locations	types of place	descriptions
dans la banlieue – on the outskirts of town	*la capitale* – the capital	*calme* – quiet
à la campagne – in the country	*une grande ville* – a big town	*moderne* – modern
dans un quartier – in an area	*un petit village* – a small village	*industrielle* – industrial
	une île – an island	*agréable* – pleasant
	une ville moyenne – an average-sized town	*historique* – historic
		joli – pretty
		touristique — touristic
		rurale – rural
		animée – lively

1c Categorise these words and phrases under the headings from **1b**.

Reading. Students add further words and phrases to their existing lists from **1b**.

Answers

locations	types of place	descriptions
à la montagne	une station balnéaire	important
au bord de la mer		vieux
		beau
		ancien
		typique

Rappel

Point out the *Rappel* box on page 77 which reminds students about the position of adjectives.

Before moving on to activity **2**, revise *à la montagne*, etc. from the key language box on page 77.

2 Listen. Match the pictures to the descriptions.

Listening (1–5). Students listen and match the descriptions with the photographs.

Tapescript

1 *J'habite à la Baule. C'est une station balnéaire, c'est-à-dire que c'est une ville touristique située au bord de la mer. J'aime bien y habiter, il y a plein de choses à faire.*
2 *J'habite à Vandré, c'est un petit village très pittoresque qui se trouve à la campagne.*
3 *J'aime bien habiter à Genève. Genève se trouve près des Alpes, et c'est pas loin des stations de ski. J'adore faire du ski, c'est génial.*
4 *J'habite à Montréal au Canada. Montréal est une grande ville industrielle mais aussi une très belle ville historique.*
5 *J'habite à Annecy. C'est une très jolie ville située au bord d'un lac, tout près des Alpes.*

Answers

1 a	**2** b	**3** e	**4** c	**5** d

Tip box

il n'y a pas de … Point out the structure quantity + *de* to students, including the negative quantity *pas de*. Remind them also of *trop de, beaucoup de, peu de*.

3a Make a list of what there is and isn't in these villages/towns.

Reading (1–5). Students revise the names for places in town by identifying them in these descriptions.

Answers

1 swimming pool, shops, hospital, station, churches, no castle
2 no school, one shop
3 big hospital, football stadium, museum, cathedral
4 no pool, large park, 9 or 10 shops, church and school
5 town hall, tourist office, large castle, lots of shops

3b Write two paragraphs.

Writing. Students now write about their home town/village, saying what is and isn't there. Point out that long lists are not impressive in writing or in speaking. If lists are called for, it is best to limit them to three items and then to impress with a different structure (e.g. inserting *aussi*).

Student's Book pages 78–79

Introduce this spread by inviting your students to finish off the sentence *Ici dans la région/ville, on peut …* in as many different ways as they can (thereby reinforcing the structure *on peut* + infinitive). Introduce any language from the key language box on page 79 that has not already been mentioned.

4a Listen. What is there in these towns?

Listening (1–6). Students write in English the places they hear.

Tapescript

1 *Il y plein de distractions dans ma ville, y compris un théâtre, une patinoire et un cinéma.*
2 *Il n'y a pas de centre sportif dans mon village, il y a seulement la mairie et un café.*
3 *Dans ma ville, il faut visiter le pont sur la Seine. C'est la seule chose qui vaut une visite.*
4 *Il n'y a pas de grand centre commercial dans ma ville, mais il y a beaucoup de magasins, et un marché le mardi.*
5 *Ce qui est bien dans mon village, c'est le centre de recyclage, où on peut tout recycler.*
6 *Dans ma ville, il faut visiter les monuments historiques et la grande place.*

Answers

1 theatre, ice rink, cinema
2 no sports centre, only town hall and café
3 bridge over the Seine
4 no shopping centre but lots of shops and a market
5 recycling centre
6 historic monuments and the main square

Tip box

Remind students that they can prepare for listening by working out the words that they expect to hear *before* they listen. They can put this into practice for activity **4b** below.

4b Look at these pictures. Write the numbers under each place name. Then listen and tick the places off as you hear them. Which places are not mentioned?

Listening (1–4). Students have to listen to the whole of each passage to work out which place is not mentioned.

Tapescript

1 *Donc, à Avallon, on peut visiter l'église Saint Lazare qui date du onzième siècle, c'est magnifique, vraiment magnifique. Ensuite, il y a un marché où on trouve de tout mais il ne faut pas rater les fromages de la région. On y trouve des époisses délicieux! Ensuite, vous avez beaucoup de magasins et de cafés. Notre syndicat*

d'initiative vous fournira des renseignements sur toute la Bourgogne. Vous pouvez faire un joli tour sur les remparts pour visiter la ville, et n'oubliez pas que la piscine est tout près, de l'autre côté de la vallée.

2 Qu'est-ce qu'on peut visiter à Arcachon? Eh bien, il y a le parc et la piscine, qui sont tout près l'un de l'autre. Vous avez un aquarium superbe, d'une certaine renommée, ça vaut la peine, surtout si vous avez des enfants. L'après-midi, vous pourriez visiter le musée et le soir, il y a le casino bien sûr.

3 À Montpellier, technopole surdouée, vous devez visiter le jardin des plantes. C'est très agréable d'y passer des heures à flâner. Il y a le polygone, le centre commercial où vous trouverez tous les magasins qu'il vous faudra. Vous avez la cathédrale et le musée Fabre. C'est une ville qui est très agréable. On l'appelle parfois la capitale de l'Europe du sud.

4 À Reims – capitale de la région de la Champagne charmante – vous pouvez visiter la cathédrale. Dans la zone piétonne, il y a l'office du tourisme, et des caves où vous pourrez faire une petite dégustation de champagne, ça fait un joli circuit. Si vous recherchez un peu d'animation, ou bien si vous avez des enfants, il y a la piscine.

Answers

Avallon: 5 (plage) **Arcachon:** 2 (marché) **Montpellier:** 3 (piscine) **Reims:** 5 (parc)

4c In pairs. Look at the pictures above. Choose a town and describe it. Your partner has to name the town.

Speaking. Students describe one of towns in **4b** for their partner to guess.

4d Prepare a description of your town/village and another one nearby, to present to the class.

Speaking. Students can use the text given, changing the details in bold as necessary to describe these places.

Before moving on to **5a**, make sure students know about the festivities on the 14th July and at Carnival, and that they are aware that Christmas celebrations differ from country to country. Introduce some key language by describing an event (imaginary if necessary) you have been to in France. Write some of the key phrases on the OHT/board. This is another good opportunity to revisit the perfect tense.

Tip box

Using *on*. Revise the use of *on*, particularly in expressions like *on peut*.

5a Which festival is it: 14th July, Christmas or the carnival?

Reading (1–8). Students identify the correct festival from reading the texts and the descriptions in past tenses.

Answers

14th July: 4, 7 **Christmas:** 1, 3, 6, 8 **carnival:** 2, 5

5b What do you do to celebrate? Describe a festival, celebration or street party you have been part of in Scotland.

Writing. Students now use the texts to help them write at length using past tenses about a festival they have been to. Model one on the OHT/board first if necessary, going over some useful verbs in the perfect tense.

Further practice of the language and vocabulary of these spreads is provided as follows:

Cahier d'exercices, pages 35–37

1 Qu'est-ce qu'il y a à faire ici?

MODULE 5 — MA VILLE

(Student's Book pages 80–81)

Main topics and objectives

- Saying what there is and is not in a town

Key language

Dans mon village/ma ville/mon quartier/ma région
  il y a beaucoup/plein/pas mal de …
  il n'y a pas de/d' …
  maisons individuelles/jumelées/mitoyennes/HLM.
C'est isolé.
Il n'y a pas de (bus/cinéma/centre sportif/maison des jeunes).
Il n'y a rien à faire.
Il n'y a rien ici pour les jeunes.
Il y a trop de bruit/voitures/pollution de l'air.
On ne peut pas sortir seul(e)/aller en boîte.

Je ne me sens jamais en sécurité.
On ne peut pas se déplacer facilement.

Grammar

- Negatives
- *ne … pas de/d'*

Skills/Strategies

- Using useful words/expressions in writing

Resources

À l'oral, page 106: Transaction 3
Cassette B side 2
Cahier d'exercices, page 38 (ex. 8)

Introduce this spread by getting your students to answer, in as many different ways as possible, the question *Qu'est-ce qu'il y a à faire ici?*.

1a Read the text on the right and try to fill the gaps with the words in the box. Listen and check your answers.

Reading. Students fill in the gaps in the text first, using reading strategies, then listen to check their answers.

Tapescript

J'habite à la campagne et j'adore ça! Mon père est fermier, nous habitons donc une ferme où il y a beaucoup d'animaux, des champs, et des bois. On a des chevaux. Je sais que j'ai beaucoup de chance d'avoir un cheval; il s'appelle Cacahuète.
J'adore la nature. Pour moi c'est la perfection, les fleurs et les arbres. Nous avons aussi un grand lac sur notre propriété où l'on peut pêcher à la ligne. Les gens aiment faire ça. Je vois mes vaches et mes moutons tous les jours, moi. Je n'y changerais rien!

Answers

1 campagne	2 fermier	3 champs	4 bois
5 chevaux	6 cheval	7 nature	8 fleurs	9 arbres
10 lac	11 vaches	12 moutons

1b Make up 5 questions in English for your partner to answer on this text. Think: Who? What? Where? When? Why?

Reading. Students have first to understand the text before they can make up questions on it.

Before moving on to **2a**, introduce the different types of housing as listed in the key language box. Ask about housing in the local area.

2a Match the housing described with a picture on the right.

Reading (1–5). Students match the pictures to the descriptions of housing.

Answers

1 c	2 d	3 b	4 e	5 a

2b CV Write at least 5 sentences about the housing in your town/village and combine them in a paragraph under the title *Ma ville* on disc. Insert the data into your CV document. Your CV is now complete – remember to update it!

Students finish the document they started in Module 1.

3a Who says the following? Write out the French sentence.

Reading (a–j). Students identify who said each sentence and also precisely what each sentence is in French.

Answers

a Frank: Il n'y a rien ici pour les jeunes.
b Alain: On ne peut pas se déplacer facilement.
c Danielle: Il y a trop de bruit.
d Frank: Il n'y a pas de maison des jeunes.
e Danielle: On ne peut jamais sortir toute seule.
f Alain: Il n'y a rien à faire.
g Danielle: Il y a trop de voitures.
h Danielle: Je ne me sens jamais en sécurité.
i Frank: Il n'y a pas de centre sportif.
j Frank: On ne peut pas aller au cinéma ou en boîte.

➕ Students choose one person and translate what they say.

3b Listen to these young people making the same complaints about where they live. Note the points each mentions from **3a**.

Listening (1–5). Students now identify the same phrases in a spoken context.

Tapescript

1 *Moi, j'habite à la campagne. Nous avons une grande maison, mais c'est assez ennuyeux. Il n'y a rien à faire et on ne peut pas se déplacer facilement.*
2 *En ville il y a beaucoup de distractions, mais moi, je ne me sens jamais tout à fait en sécurité. On ne peut jamais sortir toute seule, j'ai peur.*
3 *Mon village, c'est nul. Il n'y a rien ici pour les jeunes, pas de centre sportif, pas de cinéma. Rien.*
4 *J'habite une grande ville où il y a beaucoup de problèmes de circulation. Il y a simplement trop de voitures qui font trop de bruit et de pollution.*
5 *Moi, j'habite à la montagne. Ici il n'y a pas de maison des jeunes, et on ne peut pas sortir en boîte ou au cinéma, mais il y a plein d'autres choses à faire!*

Answers

1 f, b	**2** h, e	**3** a, i	**4** g, c	**5** d, j

Tip box

Using useful expressions. Students should add these to their own lists of 'useful expressions' for opinion writing.

Le détective

Negatives. This summaries the negatives met so far. Present the negatives to students in pictorial form, with the *ne* in a top slice of bread (or half baguette), the verb in the middle and the *pas/rien/jamais* in the bottom slice/half. Ask students to pick out all the negatives in the texts in **3a**. Make sure students are aware of all the different ways of translating negatives into English.

3c What can't you do where you live? What is missing from your town/village? Where would you prefer to live? Write 100 words. Be inventive!

Writing. Students are encouraged to include lots of negatives in their descriptions of where they live. If used accurately, a range of negatives can greatly increase the impressiveness of a piece of writing. Brainstorm some phrases first if necessary.

Further practice of the language and vocabulary of this spread is provided as follows:

À l'oral, page 106: Transaction 3

Cahier d'exercices, page 38 (ex. 8)

MODULE 5 MA VILLE

2 La ville et la campagne

(Student's Book pages 82–83)

Main topics and objectives

● Comparing the town and country

Key language

Il y a beaucoup de distractions.
Il y a plein/peu de choses à faire.
C'est très/trop/extrêmement/plus/moins animé/calme/
sale/pollué/bruyant/ennuyeux/sain/propre.
On peut sortir/se détendre.
On est plus près de la nature.
Tout le monde est pressé.
Il y a trop de pollution/de voitures.
Il y a plus de voitures/plus de gens/
moins de monde/moins de bruit.

Grammar

● *Le mieux/Le pire, c'est de …*
● Conditional tense

Skills/strategies

● Expressing pros and cons

Resources

À l'oral, page 106: Conversation 1 and Prepared talk
Cassette B side 2
Cahier d'exercices, pages 38–40 (exs 9–11)

Introduce this spread by brainstorming in French the advantages and disadvantages of living either in the town or in the countryside. Structure this by putting headings on the board/OHT and ensuring students know the meanings and the grammatical name for the word which follows each phrase:

il y a beaucoup de … (plein de …)   *il y a peu de …*
il y a trop de …   *il n'y a pas de …*
il y a plus de …   *il y a moins de …*
c'est plus …   *c'est moins …*
on peut … plus facilement   *on ne peut pas …*

1a Do you think these opinions are about the town or the countryside?

Reading (a–u). Students categorise phrases which will help them to express their own feelings about life in the town and in the countryside

Answers (open to interpretation)

Town: a, b, d, e, k, l, m, p, q, r
Countryside: c, f, g, h, i, j, n, o, s, t, u

1b Listen to these opinions. Copy and complete the grid.

Listening. Students hear similar opinions expressed in a spoken context, and complete the grid.

Tapescript

1 *Moi, j'habite la ville, et je m'y plais bien. Il y a beaucoup de distractions, c'est toujours très animé et il y a plein de choses à faire. Je n'aime pas la campagne, il y a peu de choses à faire et c'est trop calme.*
2 *Moi, je voudrais habiter en ville. Il y a plus de gens et il y a beaucoup de distractions. C'est plus intéressant, quoi! À présent, j'habite la campagne et j'ai horreur de ça. C'est extrêmement ennuyeux et c'est trop calme. L'année prochaine, j'irai à la fac et tout ira mieux!*
3 *Moi, j'aimerais mieux vivre à la campagne. C'est plus sain et plus calme et on est plus près de la nature. Je n'aime*

pas vivre en ville. C'est trop pollué et c'est trop bruyant. Quand j'aurai dix huit ans, je vais me barrer.

Answers

	likes/ would like to live in	reason(s)	dislikes	reason(s)
Hakim	town	lots to do, lively	country	too quiet, little to do
Rosalie	town	more people, lots to do, more interesting	country	boring, too quiet
Loïc	country	healthier, quieter, nearer nature	town	too polluted, too noisy

2a Are these opinions for (✓) or against (✗) life in the country?

Reading (a–j). Students now read more complex opinions and identify them as positive or negative.

Answers

a ✓   b ✗   c ✓   d ✗   e ✓   f ✓   g ✗   h ✗   i ✓   j ✗

Le détective

Comparisons. Go over these phrases with the students. Point out that they can use them as a set phrase where they would say 'the best thing is' or 'the worst thing is' in English.

2b Write 2 paragraphs: one in favour of living in a town, the other in favour of living in the country. Use these phrases.

Writing. Students now select from all the opinion phrases they have met so far in this spread to write two contrasting paragraphs. If necessary, prepare a model with the class first on the OHT.

99

2c In pairs. Take turns to ask and answer the questions in this magazine article.

Speaking. Students use the same opinion phrases to answer questions.

Point out the advantages of using parts of questions in their answers:
Quels sont les avantages d'habiter en ville?
Les avantages d'habiter en ville sont que …
Où voudrais-tu habiter plus tard dans la vie?
Plus tard dans la vie je voudrais habiter …

Le détective

The conditional. Revise the meaning and the conjugation of the conditional.

3a Listen to Fadéla. Match up the beginnings and ends of the sentences below.

Listening. Students listen to sentences in the conditional and provide the correct endings for each.

Tapescript

Ma ville idéale serait calme, mais pas trop calme. Il y aurait beaucoup de choses à faire, beaucoup de distractions, mais il n'y aurait pas beaucoup de bruit. J'aimerais habiter une station balnéaire. Je serais donc au bord de la mer. Ma ville idéale serait assez grande, mais tout près de la campagne aussi. Comme ça, je pourrais prendre le large si je voulais. Et toi, comment serait ta ville idéale?

Answers

1 d	2 a	3 b	4 c

3b Write a paragraph about your ideal town.

Writing. Students use a range of vocabulary and tenses to write at length about their ideal town. Remind them to look back at previous spreads and to use as much language as possible.

Further practice of the language and vocabulary of this spread is provided as follows:

À l'oral, page 106: Conversation 1 and Prepared talk

Cahier d'exercices, pages 38–40 (exs 9–11)

3 L'environnement

(Student's Book pages 84–85)

Main topics and objectives

● Discussing environmental issues

Key language

*Pour moi, la pollution/l'emballage/le gaspillage
d'énergie/le matérialisme/le bruit/les papiers
par terre …
est/sont plus important(s) que …
Il faut/On pourrait/Ou devrait …
acheter des produits verts
utiliser les transports en commun
conserver l'énergie/l'eau
trier les déchets
utiliser les produits recyclés
éteindre la lumière
Il ne faut pas/On ne devrait pas …
gaspiller l'eau
jeter les papiers par terre*

Grammar

● Comparisons
● *il faut* + infinitive
● The passive voice

Skills/Strategies

● Working out words without the dictionary
● Recording vocabulary
● Using 'marker' words in an essay

Resources

À l'oral, page 106: Conversation 2
À toi! A and B, pages 188–189
Cassette B side 2
Cahier d'exercices, pages 40–41 (exs 12–13)

Introduce the spread by brainstorming in English the problems which threaten the environment, and explaining that this spread will help your students express these in French.

1a Listen. Which of these environmental problems are the people talking about? Note any other details if you can.

Listening (1–6). Students have the French words for 6 environmental problems in front of them and have to identify which one is being talked about.

Tapescript

1 *Pour moi, le problème principal, c'est la pollution. Ça me dégoûte. Il y a trop de voitures, on ne fait pas attention à l'environnement, nous sommes en train de le détruire avec toutes ces voitures.*
2 *Ce qui m'énerve, c'est les emballages. Quand on achète des choses au supermarché, il y a tellement de plastique, de papier, c'est dingue.*
3 *Moi, j'ai horreur de trouver des papiers par terre. C'est un problème d'éducation. Les parents devraient apprendre à leurs enfants à ne pas jeter des papiers par terre. Ça nuit à l'environnement.*
4 *De nos jours, il y a trop de matérialisme. Nike, Diesel, Yves Saint Laurent, Moschino – ça n'a pas d'importance réelle.*
5 *Le bruit constitue le problème principal actuellement. Si on n'a pas de calme, pas de paix, on devient fou.*
6 *Pour moi, le problème principal, c'est le gaspillage d'énergie. C'est un gaspillage des ressources de la terre. On n'éteint pas la lumière parce qu'on n'y pense pas. Il faut changer la mentalité des gens.*

Answers

> 1 *La pollution* (pollution): too many cars
> 2 *L'emballage* (packaging): so much plastic and paper when you buy things from the supermarket
> 3 *Les papiers par terre* (litter): parent should tell their children not to drop litter
> 4 *Le matérialisme* (materialism): has no real importance
> 5 *Le bruit* (noise): you go mad if you don't have peace and quiet
> 6 *Le gaspillage d'énergie* (wasting energy): people don't switch lights off

Rappel

Comparatives. Students have met *plus/moins de …* and *c'est plus/moins …* on the previous spread. Ensure they know the meaning of these structures and how to use them.

1b In pairs. Put these problems in order of their importance to you.

Speaking. Students discuss the relative importance of environmental issues to them. They can use the expressions of agreement/disagreement to respond to each other.

Rappel

il faut. Students first met this construction in Module 1 (page 14). Revise *il faut* firstly in the context in which it was met (school uniform and rules), then transfer the structure to the environment.

2 What should we do to protect the environment? Match the pictures to the speech bubbles.

Reading (1–10). Students write out the phrases and allocate each to a picture. To help your students identify these phrases for use in later activities, establish labels in English for the pictures, so your students will write, e.g. 1 *Il faut acheter des produits verts* = h (environmentally-friendly products)

Answers

1 h	2 e	3 b	4 f	5 a	6 d	7 j	8 i	9 c	10 g

Tip box

Working out the meaning of words. The first two sentences of the text illustrate this point very well. Students ought to understand all of the first sentence apart from the phrase *de nos jours*, and all of the second sentence apart from *conscient* and *utiliser*. Write both sentences on an OHT, and write firstly a word-for-word translation of the words your students understand, then a more fluent translation, leaving gaps for the missing words. Students should be able to suggest words to fill in the gaps without recourse to a dictionary.

3a Read the text and list in English 6 ways people harm the environment, according to the article.

Reading. Students scan the whole text looking for the answers.

Answers

too many cars, not taking public transport, not switching off lights, not conserving water, water is polluted by chemical waste, throwing litter

3b Find the French for the following in the text above.

Reading (1–10). Students find phrases in the text which will help them express their own opinions on the environment.

Answers

1 on est conscient de la nécessité
2 des produits verts
3 trop de voitures particulières
4 les transports en commun
5 éteindre la lumière
6 l'énergie est gaspillée
7 de même pour la conservation de l'eau
8 les déchets chimiques
9 les papiers sont jetés partout
10 voilà la solution

Le détective

The passive. This grammar point is easy for students to grasp, provided that they know the past participles.

3c Conduct a survey in your class. Now write up your results like this.

Speaking. Students ask the same question of all the other students in their group and then record their findings.

Tip box

Using 'marker' words. Before drawing students' attention to the tip box, first try to brainstorm as many of these expressions as possible. The list will not seem as daunting if students see that they know most of these expressions already.

4 Write 50 words to answer these questions.

Writing. Establish with your students that all these phrases apart from *Le problème qui m'intéresse, c'est* … are followed by an infinitive. Prepare with the class first, asking the questions to elicit some different answers.

Further practice of the language and vocabulary of this spread is provided as follows:

À l'oral, page 106: Conversation 2

À toi! A and B, pages 188–189

Cahier d'exercices, pages 40–41 (exs 12–13)

4 Les pays francophones

(Student's Book pages 86–87)

Main topics and objectives

● Discussing the French-speaking world

Key language

Language from the module

Skills/Strategies

● Using the Internet to research

Resources

Cassette B side 2
Cahier d'exercices, page 41 (ex. 14)

Introduce the spread by discussing in English other French-speaking countries. Students are often surprised to discover how many different countries have French as (one of) their official language(s). Name the countries in French, too.

1a Answer the questions in English.

Reading (1–8). Students start their comprehension of this authentic text by means of questions in English.

This is the official web-page of the Guadeloupe Tourist Board. Naturally it contains a number of words and expressions which students will not know. To make the text more accessible, there are a number of strategies which you can use:
– Before allowing your students to answer the questions, first get them to locate the answers (e.g. question 1 is in paragraph 1, question 2 in the first sentence of paragraph 2, etc.).
– Get your students to identify in the questions words which may appear in French in the text (e.g. 'rich' question 3, 'industries' question 4, 'people/population' question 5).
– The language needed to answer the last question ranges from the very simple (identification *of tourisme* in Grande-Terre, not Basse-Terre) to the very complex (*faiblement vallonnée* and *aux massifs montagneux*). Encourage students to read for gist and to be satisfied when they have found two contrasting points.

Answers

1 7000 km from mainland France, 2700 km from New York, 16° latitude north and 60° longitude west, in the Antilles (West Indies) (any 3)
2 8 islands (1)
3 its population of 1000 faces, its history, environment, food, culture (5)
4 production of sugar cane, bananas and tourism (3)
5 varied, happy, welcoming and warm (4)
6 with coconut palms and a crystal blue sea (2)
7 Emerald Island (1)
8 Basse-Terre – more mountainous, has more rain, has a volcano, has fewer/no beaches, has less tourism (any 2)

1b Read the web page. Are these statements true or false?

Reading (1–6). Students' comprehension is then developed with a true/false activity.

Answers

1 ✓	2 x	3 ✓	4 x	5 ✓	6 x

2a Read this text and fill in the blanks. Then listen to check your answers.

Reading. Students work out the most appropriate words to fill in the blanks, then listen to check if they were right. They should write the whole text out to enable them to do the following activity.

Tapescript

La France est un pays immense. Les grandes villes telles que Paris, Marseille, Lyon, Bordeaux sont importantes bien sûr, mais l'agriculture compte et lorsqu'on visite la France on se rend compte que c'est un pays rural avec un paysage très, très varié. Dans le nord, vous avez les plaines et les villes industrielles. Dans l'est vous avez les montagnes, les Vosges et les Alpes. Au milieu, vous avez le Massif Central, et en bas, c'est un pays qui est bordé par les Pyrénées. Ensuite, il y a la mer Méditerranée et l'Atlantique, et puis les îles: l'île d'Oléron, l'île de Ré, et n'oublions pas la Corse. Les grands fleuves comme la Seine, la Loire et le Rhône forment les axes de l'industrie. Vous avez un climat du sud chaud, ensoleillé, et un climat du nord pluvieux, froid. Certains prétendent que c'est la même chose pour les gens, mais je n'en suis pas certaine …

Answers

1 immense	2 villes	3 l'agriculture	4 rural
5 paysage	6 industrielles	7 montagnes	
8 Pyrénées	9 mer	10 fleuves	11 climat
12 climat			

2b Find the French for the following in your completed text.

Reading (1–8). Students use their texts to find the French translations for the phrases.

Answers

> 1 La France est un pays immense
> 2 l'agriculture compte
> 3 on se rend compte que
> 4 un paysage très, très varié
> 5 n'oublions pas
> 6 un climat du sud chaud, ensoleillé
> 7 un climat du nord pluvieux, froid
> 8 mais je n'en suis pas certaine

3 Using the underlined words in the article above, write a description of your own country. Work with a partner or a group to brainstorm your ideas. Then structure your article for the school magazine or website if you have one.

Writing. Students use the given text to write a structured, accurate description of Scotland. Their own texts can stick very closely to the original, or can be more inventive, but encourage accuracy by offering the text in **2a** as a model.

4a Choose a French-speaking country to research. Make notes in French under these headings.

Writing. Students choose the country they want to research and the information they want to find out about the country. This can be a very motivating activity, even more so if students can down-load photographs from the web and print them in colour or use them on Powerpoint for their project.

🖰 There are lots of French-speaking countries: *La Réunion, le Québec, le Sénégal* … Try using www.yahoo.fr as a search engine, or limiting a web search by entering the headings as well as your chosen country.

Make sure your students know how to limit a web search. Most search engines require entries like: +"La Réunion" + habitants +"villes principales", etc.

4b Make a presentation on your chosen country. Use your notes and the phrases below to help you.

Students' presentations can be enlivened by photographs or by a Powerpoint presentation with photographs or other supporting web material.

Further practice of the language and vocabulary of this spread is provided as follows:

Cahier d'exercices page 41 (ex. 14)

All the key vocabulary and structures from this module are listed on the **Mots** pages 90–91. These can be used for revision by covering up either the English or the French. Students can check here to see how much they remember from the module and use them to prepare for the assessments.

Assessment materials for Modules 5 and 6 are available in the separate Assessment Pack.

Further speaking and grammar practice on the whole module is provided on **Cahier d'exercices** pages 42–43.

Entraînez-vous: À l'écrit

(Student's Book pages 88–89)

Writing practice: Ma ville

The **À l'écrit** spreads give regular, guided practice in preparing for the writing sections of Standard Grade and Intermediate examinations. Each double-page spread always starts with a model text which acts as a stimulus to give students ideas about what they might include in their ownwriting. Students are encouraged to look at the detail of the text through the structured reading activities, and are guided gradually towards producing their own sentences in French, in preparation for the final task in which they are asked to produce an extended piece of writing. The **Au Secours!** panel is a feature on all of the **À l'écrit** spreads. It presents language and structures that students can include in their writing, and reminds them of general points which will enable them to get a better grade.

To qualify for the writing components at Standard Grade or Intermediate writing N.A.B.s, final versions must be produced under controlled conditions. Students should be encouraged to use the language they understand and are familiar with so as to learn what they have written with a high degree of accuracy. They should be warned about the dangers of copying. At Standard Grade, students should be guided to write over 25 words at Foundation level, 50 words at General level and 100 words at Credit level.

Students should be encouraged to see that they can get Credit marks at Standard Grade and A grades at Intermediate 2 in Writing! Remind them of the following tips to help them get a better grade.

Handy tips for students

1 Structure your writing: a good beginning and ending, and 3 distinct paragraphs!

   Choose formats which structure themselves, e.g. a letter.

2 Focus your writing on one aspect of a module.

3 Choose aspects which give you opportunities to write about your opinions.

4 Choose aspects which allow you to use impressive vocabulary and phrases.

5 Make sure you include examples of different tenses in your writing.

6 It is very important to write accurate French! Make sure the language you choose for your writing is memorable for **you**. Only you can know how much new and impressive French you can learn to write out accurately in exam conditions!

This spread guides students towards producing an extended piece of writing on the topics of **work** and **town**. It takes them from understanding single items of vocabulary, through sentence completion, to producing their own brochure for their town or region in French. Students should be encouraged to write as accurately and as much as they can.

1 Complete these sentences about Villeneuve to provide the basic, essential information about the town.

Answers

1 Villeneuve se trouve dans le centre de la France, tout près de Clermont-Ferrand.
2 C'est une petite ville en pleine campagne.
3 Il y a une vieille église, un cinéma et un parc. Il y a aussi un vieux château, le musée de la poste et un centre commercial. Il y a des restaurants et cafés et une boîte de nuit.
4 On peut voir des spectacles théâtraux dans les jardins du château en été.
5 Il y a des magasins de mode dans le centre commercial.
6 Il y a une discothèque fabuleuse avec trois pistes différentes, un restaurant et une piscine.
7 Au lac on peut faire du ski nautique et de la voile.
8 Pour les jeunes il y a une maison des jeunes et beaucoup de choses à faire.

2 Choose **a**, **b** or **c** to complete these sentences with the right adjective endings.

Answers

1 a	2 a	3 b	4 a	5 b	6 b

3 Write a brochure to persuade young French people to visit your own town, area or region. Use the questions below and the *Au Secours!* panel to help you.

Au secours!

This section give advice on the following points:
● using the brochure for Villeneuve as a model
● writing accurate French
● including exclamations and speech bubbles
● using pictures to make work look more professional
● writing a page for the school/college website

MODULE 5 — MR VILLE

À toi! A & B

(Student's Book pages 188–189)

Self-access reading and writing at two levels

These pages are designed to give students extra practice in reading and structured writing. There are two differentiated pages relating to each chapter: A and B. Page A is at an easier level and page B more challenging. You may wish students to work on the page most appropriate to their level or work through both pages. You may feel it is useful to work with students on the activities, but it should be possible for most students to work on them independently. The most appropriate time to use each page is indicated within the relevant teaching notes.

À toi! A, page 188

This page is best used after pages 84–85 of the Student's Book.

1a Read the article and answer these questions in English.

Answers

> 1 recycling and the importance of public transport (2)
> 2 overpopulation (1)
> 3 causes global warming (1)
> 4 acid rain (1)
> 5 for money (1)

1b Find the French in the text for the following.

Answers

> 1 les baleines
> 2 le réchauffement de la planète
> 3 la pluie acide
> 4 l'extinction des espèces rares
> 5 surpopulation
> 6 la destruction des forêts tropicales

2 Choose from **1b** the 3 most important environmental problems for you and complete these sentences in French.

À toi! B, page 189

This page is best used after pages 84–85 of the Student's Book.

1a Read the text and answer these questions in English.

Answers

> 1 emptied into the sea (1)
> 2 burnt, buried or recycled (20%) (3)
> 3 reduce our production of rubbish by consuming less, recycle waste, think up/use all possible methods for protecting nature/reducing pollution (3)

1b Find the French for the following.

Answers

> 1 l'industrie et les ménages produisent des montagnes de déchets
> 2 les déchets dangereux
> 3 la majorité des déchets liquides industriels
> 4 un grave problème européen
> 5 50 tonnes de déchets par an
> 6 la grande majorité est brûlée ou enterrée
> 7 la disparition des espèces rares
> 8 diminution de la pollution

2 Write an article of 100 words or more on the main environmental problems we face. You can use the framework below to help you.

MA VILLE

Cahier d'exercices, page 35

1
Answers

a capitale, touristique
b nord, port
c jolie, historique
d petits, pittoresques
e Pays de Galles, Angleterre

2
Answers

1 c **2** f **3** g **4** i **5** b **6** d **7** a **8** j **9** h **10** e

3
Answers

a town   **b** bookshop   **c** square   **d** town hall
e shop   **f** pretty   **g** squeezed/in a hurry
h clean/own

Cahier d'exercices, page 36

4
Answers

a 24th December, in the evening
b No, it is a family celebration.
c oysters, turkey, vegetables, chocolate log; a lot of champagne
d people go to midnight mass
e Christmas tree, nativity scene
f marzipan or apple
g You are King or Queen and you choose your husband or wife.

5
Answers

fête – villes – concert – bal – feux d'artifice – chante – boit – matin
In Scotland, we really celebrate New Year's Eve. There are concerts, balls, fireworks in the towns. People dance, eat and drink till late the next day.

Cahier d'exercices, page 37

6
Answers

25th November – girls – 25 – cards and presents – their friends – hat – embarrassed – like – marry – grandmother – roses – old-fashioned

7 (writing task)

Cahier d'exercices, page 38

8
Answers

| 1 e | 2 b | 3 c | 4 h | 5 a | 6 g | 7 d | 8 f |

Cahier d'exercices, page 39

9
Answers

invitation – train – dear – town – north – geography – Belgium – north – river – historic – town – countryside – pedestrian streets – shops – celebrating – 6th December – Monday – September – enjoyed – three – nights

10
Answers

Mohamed

a À la campagne, c'est trop calme.

d Il n'y a pas grand-chose à faire.

e Il y a beaucoup de distractions.

i Il y a plus de transports en commun.

Lucie

b Les villes sont souvent polluées.

c Il y a beaucoup d'embouteillages, de circulation et de bruit.

f Les animaux, c'est chouette.

g Les rues sont sales.

h Les oiseaux chantent plus à la campagne.

j Tout le monde est pressé.

Cahier d'exercices, page 40

11 (writing task)

12
Answers

sauver notre monde – mère – seul – bêtes – protégez – pollution – conservation – gaspillage – recyclage
Go on everybody!
Come and save the world
Our planet earth is our mother
Our sole universe!
Don't be so stupid
Protect the planet!
Goodbye pollution
Hello conservation
Goodbye waste
Hello recycling!

MA VILLE • MODULE **5**

Cahier d'exercices, page 41

13

Answers

a ✗	b ✓	c ✗	d ✗	e ✓	f ✓	g ✗	h ✓

14

Answers

a ✓	b ✗	c ✓	d ✗	e 3	f ✗	g ✗	h ✗

Cahier d'exercices, page 42

1

Answers

> **a** grande – jolie – française
> *I live in a large and beautiful French town.*
> **b** petit – vieille – pittoresques – jolies
> *We live in a small flat in the old town. The picturesque houses have pretty facades.*
> **c** longue – beaux – très calmes
> *The long river flows around beautiful and very peaceful parks.*

2

Answers

> **a** J'habiterais en France.
> **b** Tu aimerais écouter de la musique.
> **c** Elle déménagerait.
> **d** Nous préférerions aller à la piscine.
> **e** Ils/Elles mangeraient tout.
> **f** Vous joueriez bien.

3

Answers

1 a/d/e	**2** a/d/e	**3** b	**4** c/f	**5** c/f	**6** a/d/e

Cahier d'exercices, page 43

MODULE 6

Aux magasins

(Student's Book pages 92–109)

Topic area	Key language	Grammar	Skills/Strategies
Déjà vu (pp. 92–95) Understanding types of shop Talking about opening hours Buying clothes Buying quantities of food Shopping in a department store	la charcuterie/la boulangerie/la confiserie/l'épicerie/la parfumerie/la pâtisserie/la pharmacie/la poste/le supermarché/le tabac Vous ouvrez/fermez à quelle heure? Votre magasin est ouvert à partir de quelle heure? Votre magasin ferme à quelle heure? une boîte de soupe/carottes, une bouteille/un litre de lait/jus d'orange/ Coca/vin/eau minérale une douzaine d'œufs, un pot de yaourt, un paquet de chips/biscuits un kilo/500 grammes de bananes/tomates/carottes/raisin/fromage un sac de pommes de terre Je porte … Il/Elle porte … une casquette/des chaussures/des chaussettes/des baskets/une chemise/un sweat/un survêtement/une jupe/une robe/un pantalon/un pull(over)/un bikini/une veste. blanc/bleu/gris/jaune/marron/noir/orange/rose/rouge/vert clair/foncé Je voudrais … Avez-vous …? Je cherche … Il n'y a plus de … C'est … au sous-sol/rez-de-chaussée/(premier/deuxième/troisième) étage.	de after quantities	Working out meaning from cognates
1 On fait des achats (pp. 96–97) Talking about a recent shopping trip Discussing shopping preferences	Je suis allé(e)/Nous sommes allé(e)s (à Glasgow). J'ai fait du lèche-vitrines. Nous avons trouvé … J'ai acheté … Nous avons mangé (à Pizzaland). Il y avait … C'était fantastique/cher/extra/grand. J'ai beaucoup aimé …	Perfect tense (revision)	
2 Les fringues (pp. 98–99) Shopping for clothes	Je cherche … Quelle taille/pointure? Taille … Est-ce que je peux l'essayer? Avez-vous quelque chose de plus (petit)? Je le/la/les prends. Je paye en espèces/par carte bleue. en soie/laine/coton/acrylique/plastique/jean délavé/cuir/à pois/à rayures C'est trop grand/petit/court/long. Où est la cabine d'essayage? Je fais du 34. Je ne le/la/les prends pas. Je ne les aime/l'aime pas. Il/Elle est troué(e)/déchiré(e). Il/Elle est trop cher/chère. Il manque un bouton. La fermeture éclair ne marche pas. Il y a une tâche. Il/Elle a rétréci. Je peux l'échanger? Pouvez-vous me rembourser? Avez-vous le reçu? Je pourrais vous donner un crédit?	Demonstratives Direct object pronouns	Useful phrases for complaining Checking shoe size

Topic area	Key language	Grammar	Skills/Strategies
3 L'argent de poche (pp. 100–101) Talking about your pocket money	*Je reçois … par semaine/mois de mes parents/mon père/ma mère.* *Mes parents me paient/m'achètent mes vêtements/chaussures pour l'école.* *Je fais des économies pour … une mobylette, un appareil-photo.* *J'achète … des jeux électroniques/billets de cinéma/cadeaux/ CD/affaires pour le collège/magazines/du chewing-gum/de la bijouterie/un portable/du maquillage.* *Je trouve que j'ai assez d'argent de poche. J'aimerais avoir un peu plus d'argent de poche. Je trouve que ce n'est pas juste.*	Indirect object pronouns	Recycling language from other topics
4 À la poste et à la banque (pp. 102–103) Sending letters and parcels Exchanging money	*Est-ce qu'il y a une boîte aux lettres/une poste/une cabine téléphonique près d'ici?* *Je voudrais envoyer une carte postale/lettre/un paquet (en Écosse).* *C'est combien pour envoyer (une carte postale) en Écosse?* *Je voudrais (quatre) timbres à (€0,40). Je voudrais une télécarte.* *Je voudrais changer des chèques de voyage/50 livres sterling. Voici mon passeport. J'ai oublié mon passeport. Donnez-moi des billets de (€50). Le taux est à combien en ce moment? Est-ce que je peux avoir quelques pièces de dix cents?*		
5 Je suis perdue! (pp. 104–105) Reporting a loss	*J'ai perdu mon appareil-photo/sac/porte-monnaie/parapluie/ma montre.* *Je l'ai laissé(e) … J'étais (dans le métro). (Le sac) était … Il y avait … dedans.*	Perfect/imperfect tenses	Using different tenses
Entraînez-vous: À l'oral (pp. 106–107)	Language from Modules 5 and 6		Practice for the speaking exam Learning useful phrases Presentation skills
À toi! A and B (pp. 190–191)	Language from Module 6		Reading and writing skills

The vocabulary and structures taught in Module 6 are summarised on the **Mots** pages of the Student's Book, pages 108–109.
Further writing practice on the language of the module is provided on **À l'écrit**, pages 124–125.
Assessment tasks for Modules 5 and 6 combined are provided in the separate Assessment Pack.
There is also an end-of-year assessment to be used after Module 6.

Déjà vu
(Student's Book pages 92–95)

MODULE 6 AUX MAGASINS

Main topics and objectives

- Understanding types of shops
- Talking about opening hours
- Buying quantities of food
- Buying clothes
- Shopping in a department store

Key language

*la charcuterie/la boulangerie/la confiserie/l'épicerie/
  la parfumerie/la pâtisserie/la pharmacie/la poste/
  le supermarché/le tabac
Vous ouvrez/fermez à quelle heure?
Votre magasin est ouvert à partir de quelle heure?
Votre magasin ferme à quelle heure?
une boîte de soupe/carottes
une bouteille/un litre de lait/jus d'orange/Coca/vin/
  eau minérale
une douzaine d'œufs, un pot de yaourt
un paquet de chips/biscuits
un sac de pommes de terre
un kilo/500 grammes de
  bananes/tomates/carottes/raisin/fromage*

*Je porte/Il porte/Elle porte…
  une casquette/une chemise/une jupe/une robe/une
  veste des chaussures/des chaussettes/des baskets
  un sweat/un survêtement/un pantalon/
  un pull(over)/un bikini
blanc/bleu/gris/jaune/marron/noir/orange/rose/
  rouge/vert/clair/foncé
Je voudrais … Avez-vous …
Je cherche … Il n'y a plus de …
C'est … au sous-sol/au rez-de-chaussée/
  au (premier/deuxième/troisième) étage*

Grammar

- Quantities: using *de*

Skills / Strategies

- Guessing words (cognates)

Resources

Cassette C side 1
Cahier d'exercices, pages 44–45

Introduce the spread by revising numbers. Point out to students that it is essential they can use numbers accurately **out of sequence**. Do warm-up exercises:
– show cards with random numbers (including times and prices) and ask students to say what they are
– ask students to give you their telephone number in French
– read out numbers, times and prices in French and ask students to write them down.
Then present names of shops. How many do they know? How many can they guess? How quickly can they look up those they do not know? Check comprehension by asking them to name a shop type in French and give you a British example, e.g. *une pharmacie – Boots* ; *une confiserie – Thorntons.*

1 What are they looking for? Listen and note the name of each shop in French and in English. Listen again and try to note where it is.

Listening (1–10). Students listen and note the names of the shops in French. They should then listen again and note where each shop is. You may wish to let students listen three times for each part of the activity.

Tapescript

1 – *Pardon, où est la pâtisserie, s'il vous plaît?*
   – *Continuez tout droit, c'est en face de la banque.*
2 – *Est-ce qu'il y a une pharmacie près d'ici?*
   – *Oui, à 22 mètres sur votre gauche.*
3 – *Pour aller à la poste, s'il vous plaît?*
   – *Elle se trouve dans le centre commercial, juste en face de la gare.*

4 – *Où est l'épicerie, s'il vous plaît?*
   – *Ah, il n'y a pas de magasins dans ce petit village, madame, il faut aller à Labastide.*
5 – *Excusez-moi, je cherche une boulangerie. Est-ce qu'il y en a une près d'ici?*
   – *Oui, il y en a même deux. Dans la rue de l'Horloge toutes les deux.*
6 – *Où est le tabac le plus proche, s'il vous plaît?*
   – *Dans le café des Sports là-bas.*
7 – *Où est le supermarché, s'il vous plaît?*
   – *Il se trouve à l'entrée de la ville, monsieur.*
8 – *Est-ce qu'il y a une parfumerie dans cette ville?*
   – *Voyons, non, il me semble qu'il faut aller dans les environs de Nice pour en trouver une.*
9 – *Excusez-moi. Où est la charcuterie?*
   – *À côté du Prisunic, mademoiselle.*
10 – *Je voudrais aller à la confiserie. C'est où exactement?*
   – *Sur la place des Fêtes, à dix minutes à pied.*

Answers

1 *la pâtisserie*/cake shop – opposite the bank
2 *la pharmacie*/chemist – 22m on the left
3 *la poste*/post office – in the shopping centre opposite the station
4 *l'épicerie*/grocer's – in Labastide
5 *la boulangerie*/baker's – 2 of them in the rue de l'Horloge
6 *le tabac*/tobacconist – in the café over there
7 *le supermarché*/supermarket – at the entry to the town
8 *la parfumerie*/perfume shop – in the Nice area
9 *la charcuterie*/delicatessen – next to Prisunic
10 *la confiserie*/sweet shop – on the *place des Fêtes*, 10 minutes walk away

Before moving on to **2a** and **2b**, practise the language needed to ask when places open and close. Remind students that they are required to use the *vous* form of the verb here. Do they know why? Practise the example conversation with other places, e.g. *Votre café est ouvert à partir de quelle heure?*

2a Listen and note the correct sign.

Listening (1–5). Students listen and note which sign matches which recorded item.

Tapescript

1 – *Vous ouvrez à quelle heure, s'il vous plaît?*
 – *À huit heures, mademoiselle.*
 – *Et vous fermez à quelle heure?*
 – *À midi trente. L'après-midi, nous sommes ouverts à partir de quatorze heures jusqu'à dix-neuf heures.*
2 – *Nous sommes fermés le lundi.*
3 – *Bienvenus à l'atelier Duprès. Nous sommes actuellement en vacances. Veuillez laisser un message après le signal sonore avec vos coordonnées, et nous vous contacterons dès notre retour.*
4 – *Oui, donc, nous sommes fermés du 23 décembre au 18 janvier. Mais autrement, nous sommes ouverts toute l'année. Notre restaurant ferme le jeudi à midi et toute la journée pour le mercredi entre octobre et avril.*
5 – *Pouvez-vous me renseigner? Votre magasin ouvre et ferme à quelle heure?*
 – *Oh, c'est compliqué. Il vaut mieux téléphoner au 04 08 87 00 53 pour prendre rendez-vous.*

Answers

1 c	2 e	3 a	4 d	5 b

2b In pairs. Practise these conversations. Change the underlined words to make new conversations.

Speaking. Students practise the example conversations before going on to make new ones. Remind them that their times must be realistic – not just any number that they can remember!

Rappel

Using *de* after quantities. Use the *Rappel* box to revise/present quantities. Ask students to make a list of 10 other examples. Together with quantities, brainstorm how many food items they remember.

3a Make appropriate phrases to describe these quantities. Use the key language.

Writing. Students use the key language given to describe the items in the pictures.

Answers

1 une douzaine d'œufs	**2** un kilo de bananes	
3 un pot de yaourt	**4** une boîte de jus d'orange	
5 un paquet de chips	**6** 500 grammes de fromage	
7 une bouteille de vin	**8** une boîte de soupe	
9 un paquet de biscuits		

3b Listen. Copy and complete the grid.

Listening (1–4). Students listen to the transactions and complete the grid.

Tapescript

1 – *Bonjour, monsieur. Vous désirez?*
 – *Avez-vous des bananes?*
 – *Oui, combien en voulez-vous?*
 – *Donnez-moi deux kilos, s'il vous plaît.*
 – *Voilà. Et avec ça?*
 – *Je voudrais une bouteille de vin rouge, s'il vous plaît.*
 – *Une bouteille de vin rouge, voilà. Voulez-vous autre chose?*
 – *Non, c'est tout. Ça fait combien?*
 – *Ça fait €4.90.*
2 – *Bonjour, madame. Vous désirez?*
 – *Avez-vous des tomates?*
 – *Oui, combien en voulez-vous?*
 – *Donnez-moi 500 grammes, s'il vous plaît.*
 – *Voilà. Et avec ça?*
 – *Je voudrais un paquet de biscuits au chocolat, s'il vous plaît.*
 – *Un paquet de biscuits au chocolat, voilà. Voulez-vous autre chose?*
 – *Non, c'est tout. Ça fait combien?*
 – *Ça fait €2.55.*
3 – *Bonjour, monsieur. Vous désirez?*
 – *Avez-vous des œufs?*
 – *Oui, combien en voulez-vous?*
 – *Donnez-moi une demi-douzaine, s'il vous plaît.*
 – *Voilà. Et avec ça?*
 – *Je voudrais deux litres de lait, s'il vous plaît.*
 – *Deux litres de lait, voilà. Voulez-vous autre chose?*
 – *Non, c'est tout. Ça fait combien?*
 – *Ça fait €2.75.*
4 – *Bonjour, madame. Vous désirez?*
 – *Avez-vous des carottes?*
 – *Oui, combien en voulez-vous?*
 – *Donnez-moi trois kilos, s'il vous plaît.*
 – *Voilà. Et avec ça?*
 – *Euh … Je voudrais un pot de yaourt, s'il vous plaît.*
 – *Un pot de yaourt, voilà. Voulez-vous autre chose?*
 – *Non, c'est tout. Ça fait combien?*
 – *Ça fait €1.95.*

Answers

	wants	amount	also	cost
1	bananas	2 kilos	bottle of red wine	€4.90
2	tomatoes	500 grammes	packet of biscuits	€2.55
3	eggs	$^1/_2$ dozen	2 litres milk	€2.75
4	carrots	3 kilos	pot of yoghurt	€1.95

3c In pairs. Practise this conversation. Change the underlined details to make 3 new conversations. Use the pictures on the right.

Speaking. Students practise the example conversation and then use the pictures to change the details underlined to make 3 new conversations.

4 You are preparing a buffet for your year-group disco. Write the shopping list.

Writing. Students could undertake this exercise in pairs or in small groups and then compare. Alternatively it could be done as a homework task.

Student's Book pages 94–95

Revise clothes vocabulary before moving on to **5a**, e.g. *Qu'est-ce que tu portes aujourd'hui? Qu'est-ce que tu portes le week-end? Qu'est-ce que tu portes pour aller à la disco?* Remind students that colours, like all other adjectives, must agree with the item they are describing. Point out the exceptions to this, including the fact that qualified colours (*foncé, clair,* etc.) do not agree.

Revise *je voudrais,* etc. from the key language box. Ask students to complete the phrases with various examples, e.g. *je voudrais un pull noir.*

5a Listen. What clothes do they want to buy? Note the item, the colour and whether the shop has it.

Listening (1–6). Students listen to the transactions and note what each person wants, the colour and whether the shop has it.

Tapescript

1 – *Bonjour, je voudrais une jupe.*
 – *Quelle couleur?*
 – *Bleu.*
 – *Voilà une jolie jupe bleue.*
2 – *Salut, je cherche un pantalon.*
 – *Quelle couleur voulez-vous?*
 – *Noir.*
 – *Voici un pantalon noir.*
3 – *Bonjour, avez-vous des vestes?*
 – *De quelle couleur?*
 – *Vert.*
 – *Ah, je regrette, il n'y en a plus.*
4 – *Bonjour, je voudrais des chaussures.*
 – *Quelle couleur cherchez-vous?*
 – *Rouge.*
 – *Excusez-moi, mais il n'y a pas de chaussures rouges.*
5 – *Salut, avez-vous une paire de chaussettes ?*
 – *Quelle couleur?*
 – *Jaune.*
 – *Oui, voilà.*
6 – *Bonjour, je cherche une robe.*

– *De quelle couleur?*
– *Blanc.*
– *Mmm … il n'y a plus de robes blanches dans ce magasin.*

Answers

> **1** skirt, blue, ✓
> **2** trousers, black, ✓
> **3** jacket, green, ✗
> **4** shoes, red, ✗
> **5** socks, yellow, ✓
> **6** dress, white, ✗

Tip box

Guessing words from English. Remind students they should **think** before rushing to look up a word. However, it may be worth reminding them here of false friends!

5b Read this advert and answer the questions in English.

Reading (1–8). Students read the advert and answer the questions in English. Remind students that questions in English mean answers in English!

Answers

> **1** light green, light blue and dark blue (3)
> **2** leather (1)
> **3** €18, 30 (1)
> **4** 1 size more than usual size (1)
> **5** wool (1)
> **6** white, beige, grey or black (4)
> **7** top has 2 zipped pockets, bottom has 2 side pockets, 100% polyester (4)
> **8** yes – *sur tous terrains* (2)

➕ As a supplementary homework task, you could ask students to make up their own advert – perhaps on computer.

5c Say these sentences in French.

Speaking. Students use the pictures to practise asking for items in French.

Answers

> **1** Je voudrais un pantalon vert.
> **2** Avez-vous une veste rouge?
> **3** Je cherche un pull noir.
> **4** Avez-vous des chaussures brunes?
> **5** Je voudrais une chemise rose.
> **6** Je cherche une casquette bleue, blanche et rouge.

Before moving on to activity **6**, introduce the language from the key language box. Can students guess what the phrases mean? How would they say '5th floor', '12th floor', '20th floor'? Can they guess what

the abbreviations SS and RC would mean in a lift?
Point out that *sous-sol* literally means underground
and that *rez-de-chaussée* literally means 'at the level
of the street'. Explain that *chaussée* is an old word –
can they think of any words that come from it ?
(*chaussure, chaussette*)

6 Look at the department store information.
Which floor should these customers go to?

Reading (1–8). Students read each statement and use
the Galeries Lafayette store guide to identify where
each person should go.

Answers

1 C'est au premier étage.
2 C'est au troisième étage.
3 C'est au rez-de-chaussée.
4 C'est au rez-de-chaussée.
5 C'est au troisième étage.
6 C'est au troisième étage.
7 C'est au sous-sol.
8 C'est au troisième étage.

Students could visit the Galeries Lafayette website.
How much more information can they find out?

Further practice of the language and vocabulary of
these spreads is provided as follows:

Cahier d'exercices, pages 44–45.

1 On fait des achats

(Student's Book pages 96–97)

Main topics and objectives

- Talking about a recent shopping trip
- Discussing shopping preferences

Key language

Je suis allé(e)/Nous sommes allé(e)s (à Glasgow).
J'ai fait du lèche-vitrines.
Nous avons trouvé …
J'ai acheté …
Nous avons mangé (à Pizzaland).
Il y avait …
C'était fantastique/cher/extra/grand.
J'ai beaucoup aimé ….

Grammar

- Perfect tense (revision)

Resources

Cassette C side 1
À l'oral, page 107: Prepared talk
À toi! B, page 191
Cahier d'exercices, page 46

Present the topic of the spread by describing a recent shopping trip that you have made, using the expressions from the key language box on page 97. Put the phrases on the board/OHT and point to them as you are describing your trip.

1a Listen and read. Then answer the questions in English.

Reading (1–5). Students read and listen to the text before answering the questions which follow in English. Remind students that the points after each question tell them how many pieces of information are required. You may wish to play one or two of the texts first before they read, and see how many facts they can pick out.

Tapescript

1 *Quand je suis allée à New York, c'était extra. C'est la capitale du shopping et c'est pas cher. Je suis allée dans tous les grands magasins – Macy's, Sak's, Bloomingdale's. Barney's New York était mon magasin préféré, mais j'ai beaucoup aimé les petites boutiques dans le quartier de Soho également – far out!*

2 *J'habite un tout petit village, alors quand je suis allée à Paris pour la première fois, ça m'a fait un effet. Je suis allée aux Halles avec ma mère et nous avons fait du lèche-vitrines. Nous sommes entrées dans la Fnac – une librairie immense, un magasin de chaînes hi-fi aussi, et des disques, et tout ce qui est photo. C'était impressionnant. Après, nous avons trouvé une parfumerie immense et nous avons essayé tous les parfums possibles.*

3 *Quand j'ai fait un échange scolaire, je suis allé à Berlin. J'ai beaucoup aimé comme ville et nous sommes allés au magasin KaDeWe. C'était très grand et très cher avec des produits de luxe. Quand il y avait le mur, les autorités de l'Ouest voulaient impressionner les habitants de l'Est – d'où KaDeWe. Ça vaut la peine.*

4 *J'ai passé les vacances de Noël à Londres et j'ai fait du shopping avec ma maman, mais c'était cher. C'était surtout les vêtements qui m'intéressaient. Nous sommes allés à Carnaby Street et au grand marché, à Camden.*

Nous avons fait les grands magasins aussi, Harrods et Selfridges et bien sûr, nous avons pris le thé à Fortnum and Mason.

5 *Quand je suis allée au Maroc, j'ai fait les souks à Marrakech. C'était génial! Toutes ces couleurs, c'était fantastique. Il y avait de tout, des tapis, des tissus, des chaussures, des jupes, des pantoufles, des épices, des miroirs. Il fallait marchander. Sinon, on ne vous respectait pas. Moi, j'avais du mal, mais mon frère a beaucoup aimé!*

Answers

1a the capital of shopping and not expensive (2)
b her favourite shop (1)
2a she lives in a small village (1)
b a huge book shop, also a hi-fi shop, has records and everything to do with photos (4)
c tried every possible perfume (1)
3a on a school exchange (1)
b very big, very expensive selling luxury goods (3)
4a during the Christmas holidays (1)
b the clothes (1)
5a carpets, fabrics, spices, mirrors, shoes, skirts, slippers (any 4)
b barter (1)

1b Find the French for the following.

Reading. Students find the French in the text for the English statements given.

Answers

1a Je suis allée dans tous les grands magasins.
b J'ai beaucoup aimé les petites boutiques.
2a Nous avons fait du lèche-vitrines.
b C'était impressionnant.
c Nous avons trouvé une parfumerie immense.
3a J'ai fait un échange scolaire.
b C'était très grand et très cher.
4a J'ai fait du shopping avec ma maman.
b Nous avons pris le thé.
5a C'était génial!
b Il y avait de tout.

Rappel

The perfect tense. The amount of time you have to spend on this will depend on how accurately students have previously grasped the perfect tense. It would certainly be useful for most students to do some oral and/or written revision exercises on the perfect tense, e.g. changing phrases in the present tense to the perfect or translating from English into French. Do some whole-class oral work to get students to use the phrases in the key language box. Ask questions such as *Où es-tu allé(e)? Qu'est-ce que tu as acheté?*, etc.

1c Write approximately 100 words about a recent shopping trip. Include where you went, what you did there and what you thought of it. Remember your opinions are important!

Writing. This piece of written work could be included as an exam piece or used as exam practice.

1d Use your writing from **1c** to prepare a presentation to your group/class.

Speaking. Students give a presentation on a recent shopping trip. This could be used as an on-going speaking assessment or as practice for one. It can be recorded onto their prepared speaking cassette.

2a Listen. What do these people think of hypermarkets? Say whether they are for (✓), against (✗) or undecided (?).

Listening (1–4). Students note what each person thinks of hypermarkets..

Tapescript

1 *Je ne sais pas, moi. Parfois je vais dans une grande surface, parfois je vais au marché. Ça dépend des jours.*
2 *Moi, j'aime bien les grandes surfaces – les marchés, c'est pour les mémés. Dans une grande surface, il y a plus de choix. En plus, c'est pratique. C'est rapide et on peut se garer facilement.*
3 *Je préfère les petits magasins ou les marchés, c'est plus intime. J'aime bien discuter avec les gens quand je fais mes courses.*
4 *Moi, j'adore aller au marché, j'y vais toutes les semaines. Il y a toujours beaucoup de monde. J'ai horreur de faire la queue au supermarché. Je n'y vais jamais.*

Answers

1 ?	2 ✓	3 ✗	4 ✗

2b Read the sentences. What do they mean? Listen again and pick out two statements for each person.

Listening (1–4). Before students listen, ask them to read the statements and work out what they mean. They then listen to the recording for **2a** again and pick out two statements for each speaker. As follow-up, ask students the question *Et toi, tu es pour ou contre les hypermarchés? Pourquoi?* They can use the expressions in the notepad at the bottom of the page to answer.

Answers

1 b, e	2 h, f	3 d, a	4 g, c

2c Which do you prefer, small shops or big department stores? Use some of the phrases on the right to give your opinion.

Writing. Students write about the kind of shops they prefer, using the phrases given for support. Point out the importance of justifying an opinion. Go over the phrases given first with students, and practise with some whole-class oral work.

2d In groups. Compare your opinions.

Speaking. Students use their notes from **2c** to discuss with others the kind of shops they like and why.

Further practice of the language and vocabulary of this spread is provided as follows:

À l'oral, page 107: Prepared talk

À toi! B, page 191

Cahier d'exercices, page 46

2 Les fringues

(Student's Book pages 98–99)

Main topics and objectives

● Shopping for clothes

Key language

Je cherche …
Quelle taille/pointure? Taille …
Est-ce que je peux l'essayer?
Avez-vous quelque chose de plus (petit)?
Je le/la/les prends.
Je ne l'aime/les aime pas.
Je ne le/la/les prends pas.
Je paye en espèces/par carte bleue.
en soie/laine/coton/acrilique/plastique/jean
  délavé/cuir
à pois/rayures
C'est trop grand/petit/court/long.
Où est la cabine d'essayage?
Je fais du 34.
Il/Elle est troué(e)/déchiré(e).
Il/Elle est trop cher/chère.
Il manque un bouton.
La fermeture éclair ne marche pas.

Il y a une tâche.
Il/Elle a rétréci.
Je peux l'échanger?
Pouvez-vous me rembourser?
Avez-vous le reçu?
Je pourrais vous donner un crédit?

Grammar

● Direct object pronouns: *le/la/l'/les*
● *celui-ci/là*, etc.

Skills/Strategies

● Useful phrases for complaining
● Checking shoe size

Resources

Cassette C side 1
À l'oral, page 107: Transaction 2
À toi! A, page 190
Cahier d'exercice, pages 47–48 (exs 7–10)

Draw students' attention to the title of this unit. This may be a good opportunity to introduce some other slang expressions (such as *les godasses, le boulot, une bagnole, une clope, la bouffe*, etc,) and talk about the importance of argot in French, which now includes *le verslen* (*un féca, une meuf*)and *le rap*.

Before embarking on **1a**, brainstorm with students the kind of language you would need to buy clothes. Can they find it here ?

1a Write out these speech bubbles in the right order to give a conversation in a clothes shop.

Reading. Students put the speech bubbles in the correct order to form a conversation.

Answers

d, i, e, c, h, g, f, a, b, m, k, j, l, o, n

1b Listen and check your answer to **1a**.

Listening. Students listen to the conversation and correct their version.

Tapescript

– *Bonjour, mademoiselle. Vous désirez?*
– *Je cherche un jean.*
– *Quelle taille?*
– *Taille 42.*
– *Et quelle couleur?*
– *Vert foncé, s'il vous plaît.*
– *D'accord, un moment … voilà.*
– *Est-ce que je peux l'essayer?*

– *Bien sûr.*
– *Malheureusement celui-ci est trop grand. Avez-vous quelque chose de plus petit?*
– *De plus petit? … Oui, j'ai celui-là en taille 40.*
– *Merci, je le prends.*
– *Très bien, vous payez à la caisse.*
– *Vous payez en espèces?*
– *Non, carte bleue.*

Rappel

Direct object pronouns. Revise these by putting phrases on the board or OHP and asking students to replace the words underlined with a pronoun, e.g. *j'aime la jupe rouge*.

1c In pairs. Make 3 conversations using the model you wrote out in **1a**. You are buying 3 of these items.

Speaking. Students use the pictures to create three new transactions in a clothes shop, following the model given.

Le détective

celui-ci/là, etc. Demonstrate this grammatical point using objects in the classroom, e.g. *j'ai deux crayons, celui-ci est rouge et celui-là est bleu*.

Before moving on to **2**, introduce the language in the key language box at the top of page 99. Can students describe in detail the clothes they are wearing? Or show students photos of clothes from catalogues/magazines – can they describe them in detail?

Encourage them to note their Marks and Spencer labels which are given in English and French! Remind students of the importance of knowing their size in French.

2 In threes. You are shopping with a friend. Practise this conversation. Change the underlined words to make 2 new conversations, using the key language.

Speaking. Students practise the example transaction before going on to create two new ones. They could act out their conversations to the class.

Now introduce the expressions for complaining from the other key language box. Point out how challenging but also how satisfying it can be to complain in French! You may have your own example you can share with them!

3 Listen. Match the conversations to the pictures.

Listening (1–6). Students listen and match the transactions they hear to the pictures.

Tapescript

1 – Bonjour, madame. J'ai acheté ce sac hier, mais quand je suis rentré à la maison, j'ai remarqué qu'il était troué. Pouvez-vous me rembourser?
– Vous avez le reçu?
– Oui, le voilà.
– Bon, vous devez aller à la section service après-vente, ils vous rembourseront.

2 – Bonjour monsieur, je peux vous aider?
– Oui, j'ai acheté ce pantalon il y a trois jours, mais il est déchiré et la fermeture éclair ne marche pas. Je peux l'échanger?
– Vous avez le reçu?
– Oui, voilà.
– Bon, d'accord. Prenez un autre pantalon et passez à la caisse.

3 – Je peux vous aider, mademoiselle?
– Oui, je suis désolée, mais j'ai acheté ce porte-monnaie la semaine dernière, et ma mère m'a dit que c'était beaucoup trop cher et elle a insisté pour que je le change.
– Oh là, là. Je sais pas, moi. Vous avez le reçu?
– Oui. Le voilà. Celui-ci à €20 me plaît. Est-ce que vous pourriez me rembourser la différence?
– Ah non, c'est pas possible ça, mais je pourrais vous donner un crédit.
– Bon, d'accord. Faisons comme ça.

4 – J'ai acheté ce T-shirt hier, mais il y a une tâche derrière. Est-ce que je peux l'échanger?
– Ah oui, je vois. Je suis désolée, mademoiselle. C'est quelle taille? Je vais vous en chercher un.

5 – Mon père m'a acheté cette veste avant-hier, mais il y manque un bouton. Est-ce que je peux l'échanger?
– Je regrette, monsieur, mais nous n'avons plus ce modèle. Je pourrais commander un bouton pour vous si vous voulez.

6 – J'ai acheté cette robe la semaine dernière, mais quand je l'ai lavée elle a rétréci et elle est beaucoup trop petite. Elle était chère en plus! Je voudrais me faire rembourser. C'est pas normal, ça!

Answers

1 e	2 a	3 f	4 c	5 b	6 d

Tip box

Useful phrases. This reminds students of phrases which they can use for activity **4**.

4 With a partner or group. Write a scene entitled *Le magasin d'enfer* – the shop from hell. The sales assistant is rude, the clothes are awful …Then act it out.

Writing. Students write their own sketch and then act it out, using as much of the new language as they can.

Further practice of the language and vocabulary of this spread is provided as follows:

À l'oral, page 107: Transaction 2

À toi! A, page 190

Cahier d'exercices, pages 47–48 (exs 7–10)

3 L'argent de poche

(Student's Book pages 100–101)

Main topics and objectives

● Talking about your pocket money

Key language

Je reçois … par semaine/mois de mes parents/mon père/ma mère.
Mes parents me paient/m'achètent mes vêtements/chaussures pour l'école.
Je fais des économies pour … une mobylette/ un appareil-photo.
J'achète …
 des jeux électroniques/billets de cinéma/cadeaux/ CD/affaires pour le collège/ magazines.
 du chewing-gum/de la bijouterie/un portable/ du maquillage.

Je trouve que j'ai assez d'argent de poche.
J'aimerais avoir un peu plus d'argent de poche.
Je trouve que ce n'est pas juste.

Grammar

● Indirect object pronouns

Skills/Strategies

● Recycling language from other topics

Resources

Cassette C side 1
À l'oral, page 107: Conversation 1

Using the key language box for support, brainstorm with students how much pocket money they receive and how they spend it.

1a Read the texts above. Who …? (Some questions have more than one answer!)

Reading (1–8). Students read the texts and say who the statements refer to.

Answers

1 Angélique	**2** Audrey
3 Yann and Audrey	**4** Angélique
5 Audrey and Angélique	**6** Yann
7 Angélique	**8** Yann and Angélique

1b Find the French for the following.

Reading (1–6). Students find the French in the texts for the English phrases.

Answers

1 Je fais des économies pour un portable.
2 J'achète aussi des bijoux.
3 Il me reste assez d'argent pour faire des économies.
4 Ce que j'aime acheter le plus, ce sont les vêtements.
5 Je n'ai pas assez d'argent.
6 J'aimerais avoir un peu plus d'argent par mois.

1c Choose one person and summarise what they say in English.

Reading. Students choose one of the letter writers and translate into English what they say. Ask them to present the translation to the class so that everyone hears each one translated.

Le détective

Indirect object pronouns. Look at the examples given and ask students to find these examples and any

others in the texts above. Practise with some other examples.

2a Listen. Copy and complete the grid.

Listening (1–5). Students listen to the speakers talking about their pocket money and complete the grid.

Tapescript

1 *Je suis Jacques. Je reçois €6.85 par semaine de mes parents. Avec mon argent, j'achète des jeux électroniques et des billets de cinéma. J'ai assez d'argent, moi.*
2 *Je m'appelle Feyrouze. Toutes les semaines, je reçois €9.15 de mon père. C'est généreux, n'est-ce pas? Mais je dois acheter tous mes vêtements et mes affaires pour le collège – cahiers, stylos, crayons – avec cet argent.*
3 *Je suis Luc. Je ne reçois pas d'argent de poche, mais je travaille dans le jardin de mon grand-père, et il me donne €15.20 par mois. Je n'achète pas grand-chose: du chewing-gum, des magazines de temps en temps. Il me reste assez pour faire des économies pour une mobylette.*
4 *Je suis Louise, et j'ai €4.60 par semaine, mais je dois les gagner en aidant à la maison. C'est mon père qui me les donne. J'achète de la bijouterie et des cadeaux. J'aimerais avoir un peu plus d'argent à moi, pour être un peu plus libre.*
5 *Je m'appelle Boris. Je ne reçois pas d'argent de poche. Mes parents m'achètent ce dont j'ai besoin, et c'est tout. Ça va très bien comme ça.*

Answers

	how much	when	from whom	buys
1	€6.85	weekly	parents	electronic games/cinema tickets
2	€9.15	weekly	dad	clothes, things for school
3	€15.20	monthly	granddad	chewing-gum, magazines; saves for moped
4	€4.60	weekly	dad	jewellery and presents
5	none	n/a	n/a	n/a

AUX MAGASINS

Before moving on to **2b**, look at the statements in the key language box. How many students would agree with each one?

2b Carry out a pocket money survey.

Speaking. Students interview others about their pocket money, using the questions given. To keep this manageable, each student could choose to interview five others. They then collate their results in order to do **2c**.

2c Write up the results of your survey.

Writing. Students write up the survey results using the format given.

Tip box

Recycling language. This is a very important aspect of learning a language and students should frequently be reminded to do this.

3 Write approximately 150 words about pocket money.

Writing. Students write about their pocket money. Encourage them to use the template given. This could be used as a writing piece for the exam or as exam practice.

Further practice of the language and vocabulary of this spread is provided as follows:

À l'oral, page 107: Conversation 1

MODULE 6

4 À la poste et à la banque

(Student's Book pages 102–103)

Main topics and objectives

- Sending letters and parcels
- Exchanging money

Key language

Est-ce qu'il y a une boîte aux lettres/une poste/une cabine téléphonique près d'ici?
Je voudrais envoyer une carte postale/une lettre/un paquet (en Écosse).
C'est combien pour envoyer (une lettre) (en Écosse)?
Voici mon passeport. J'ai oublié mon passeport.

Donnez-moi des billets de (€50).
Le taux est à combien en ce moment?
Est-ce que je peux avoir quelques pièces de dix cents?
Je voudrais (quatre) timbres à (€0,40).
Je voudrais une télécarte.
Je voudrais changer des chèques de voyage/ 50 livres sterling.

Resources

Cassette C side 1
Cahier d'exercices, page 48 (ex. 11)

Start by introducing key language and a typical transaction. What phrases will they need? Build up a dialogue using the language in the key language box.

1a Listen. Who is speaking?

Listening (1–6). Students listen and note the name of the speaker in each transaction.

Tapescript

1 *Est-ce qu'il y a une cabine téléphonique près d'ici, s'il vous plaît?*
2 *J'aimerais envoyer ce paquet en Écosse, s'il vous plaît.*
3 *Je voudrais envoyer cette lettre en Irlande.*
4 *C'est combien pour envoyer ces cartes postales au pays de Galles, s'il vous plaît?*
5 *Donnez-moi cinq timbres à 46 cents, s'il vous plaît.*
6 *Où est la boîte aux lettres?*

Answers

1 Boris	**2** Thomas	**3** Marie-Claire
4 Juliette	**5** Anna	**6** Yann

1b In pairs. Practise these conversations.

Speaking. Students practise the transactions according to the pictures.

2 Listen. Copy and complete the grid.

Listening (1–6). Students listen and note what each person wants and what the problem is. It does not contain actual language they have just met, but they should be able to understand enough.

Tapescript

1 – *Bonjour, madame. Je voudrais des timbres, s'il vous plaît.*
  – *Je suis désolée, mais on ne vend pas de timbres ici. Il faut aller dans un tabac.*
2 – *Je voudrais changer des chèques de voyages, s'il vous plaît.*
  – *Avez-vous une pièce d'identité?*
  – *Ah zut, j'ai laissé mon passeport à la maison.*
3 – *Est-ce qu'il y a un téléphone ici?*
  – *Oui, il y a une cabine téléphonique, mais ça ne marche pas en ce moment. Le téléphone est cassé.*

4 – *Bonjour, mademoiselle. Je voudrais envoyer ce paquet en Angleterre, s'il vous plaît.*
  – *Oui, ça fait €6.50.*
  – *Ah non, je n'ai pas assez d'argent.*
5 – *Je veux téléphoner en Angleterre, mais le téléphone n'accepte pas mes pièces.*
  – *Il faut une télécarte pour téléphoner de cette cabine, mademoiselle.*
6 – *Bonjour, monsieur. Je voudrais 10 timbres à 46 cents, s'il vous plaît.*
  – *Excusez-moi, mais je n'ai pas de timbres ici. Il faut aller à la caisse numéro 4.*

Answers

	wants	**problem**
1	stamps	don't sell stamps
2	change traveller's cheques	left passport at home
3	know if there's a phone	there is but it's broken
4	send a parcel to England	not enough money
5	telephone England	phone won't accept money, only phone cards
6	buy 10 stamps	no stamps, go to till 4

Introduce the key language from the box on page 103 before doing activity **3a**.

3a You are in a bank. Match the questions and answers.

Reading (1–5). Students match the questions with the answers given in the speech bubbles.

Answers

1 d	**2** b	**3** a	**4** c	**5** e

3b In pairs. Practise this conversation in French.

Speaking. With a partner, students recreate a transaction following the English instructions.

Further practice of the language and vocabulary of this spread is provided as follows:

Cahier d'exercices, page 48 (ex. 11)

5 Je suis perdue!

(Student's Book pages 104–105)

Main topics and objectives
● Reporting a loss

Key language

J'ai perdu mon appareil-photo/sac/porte-monnaie/parapluie/ma montre.
Je l'ai laissé …
J'étais (dans le metro).
(Le sac) était …
Il y avait … dedans.

Grammar
● Perfect and imperfect tenses (revision)

Skills/Strategies
● Using different tenses

Resources
Cassette C side 1

It may be useful to introduce this reading exercise without too much support, to encourage students to cope independently with new language. Remind them to read through the text quickly for gist, then to re-read, guessing new language where they can and identifying key words they will have to look up. Remind them that they may not have to understand everything in order to answer the questions. After students have completed the exercise, go over it with them, checking how effective their strategies were.

1 Listen and read. Find the French for the expressions below.

Listening. Students listen and read the story at the same time. They then find the French in the text for the English expressions given. You may prefer to play the recording first and see if they can pick out a few things that they understand.

Tapescript

– *Super, la Tour Eiffel, je m'en vais maintenant visiter l'Arc de triomphe.*
Génial, l'Arc de triomphe. J'ai faim, je vais déjeuner dans un resto très chic et très cher!
Délicieuse, cette soupe de poisson très chic et très chère!
Sensass, l'art moderne, c'est très chic et très cher!
– *Plus tard …*
– *Alors, qu'est-ce que vous avez perdu?*
– *D'abord, j'ai perdu ma valise, puis mon appareil-photo et mon bonnet. Tout était très chic et très cher.*
– *À quelle heure?*
– *Ce matin vers dix heures.*
– *Où étiez-vous?*
– *J'étais dans le métro, puis dans le bus. Ensuite j'ai perdu mon sac à main et mon portable. Le sac était en cuir, noir, très chic et très cher. Je l'ai laissé au Centre Pompidou. Il y avait tout dedans – mon porte-monnaie, ma pièce d'identité, mon agenda. Tout était très chic et très cher. Et j'ai oublié mon parapluie dans un restaurant – quelle idiote!*
– *Le parapluie était de quelle couleur?*
– *J'ai perdu mon identité et vous me posez des questions sur la couleur de mon parapluie. Décidément je suis perdue!*

Answers

1 Où étiez-vous?   2 Il y avait tout dedans.
3 Je l'ai laissé … 4 Le parapluie était de quelle couleur?
5 Ce matin vers dix heures.   6 J'étais dans le métro.
7 Qu'est-ce que vous avez perdu?
8 J'ai perdu mon sac à main et mon portable.
9 J'ai perdu ma valise, puis mon appareil-photo.
10 J'ai oublié mon parapluie dans un restaurant.

2 In pairs. Practise the conversation. Then use the pictures below and change the underlined words to make 3 new conversations.

Speaking. Students practise the example conversation and then use the pictures to create three new conversations. Model alternatives with the class first.

Tip box

Tenses. You may have to allow some time to revise this with oral and/or written exercises, depending on students' competence.

3 Write approximately 100 words about an item you have lost. (You could adapt the long speech bubble in the story.)

Writing. Students could use this as a writing piece for their exam or as exam practice.

All the key vocabulary and structures from this module are listed on the **Mots** pages 108–109. These can be used for revision by covering up either the English or the French. Students can check here to see how much they remember from the module and use them to prepare for the assessments.

Assessment materials for Modules 5 and 6 and an end-of-year ssessment are available in the separate Assessment Pack.

Further speaking and grammar practice on the whole module is provided on **Cahier d'exercices** pages 49–50.

Entraînez-vous: À l'oral

(Student's Book pages 106–107)

Speaking practice: Modules 5 & 6

These spreads give regular practice in the three types of speaking activity required for the internally assessed speaking elements of the Standard Grade and Intermediate courses: conversations, transactions and prepared talks.

The activities on the speaking pages are designed to allow students to build up their speaking skills while working with a partner independently of teacher support. They also include handy hints on how students can improve their speaking grades.

Page 106 provides speaking activities for Module 5: conversations on where you live and what you can do to help the environment, a transaction on finding information at a tourist office and a prepared talk on life in the town versus life in the country.

Page 107 provides speaking activities for Module 6: a conversation on pocket money, a transaction in a shoe shop and a prepared talk on a recent shopping trip.

À toi! A & B

(Student's Book pages 190–191)

Self-access reading and writing at two levels

These pages are designed to give students extra practice in reading and structured writing. There are two differentiated pages relating to each chapter: A and B. Page A is at an easier level and page B more challenging. You may wish students to work on the page most appropriate to their level or work through both pages. You may feel it is useful to work with students on the activities, but it should be possible for most students to work on them independently. The most appropriate time to use each page is indicated within the relevant teaching notes.

À Toi! A, page 190

This page is best used after pages 98–99 of the Student's Book.

1 Read the texts, then copy and complete the sentences in French below.

Answers

1 Printemps de la Mode	2 Montredon	3 22h
4 Halle aux Chaussures	5 La Bastide	
6 Épicerie La Rondelle	7 jours	8 Saint-Laurent
9 Charras, de Provence	10 Havre-Caumartin	

2 You have bought this article. Write to complain about it.

Tip box

This reminds students how to begin and end letters correctly.

À toi! B, page 191

This page is best used after pages 96–97 of the Student's Book.

1a Read the texts and answer the questions in English.

Answers

1 Céline	2 Victor	3 Yolande	4 Jean-Pierre	5 Max

1b Choose 2 passages and summarise in English what the people say.

Answers

Victor: Likes big shops because there is a lot of choice. Hates small shops.
Yolande: Likes markets and small shops where you know people. Thinks there is not the quality in big shops and hates packaging.
Jean-Pierre: Is for Sunday shopping – good to shop on a Sunday – practical.
Max: Very busy so is liberated by Internet shopping.
Céline: Against Sunday shopping as it's a day of rest.

2 What do you think about Sunday trading? Write approximately 150 words to give your views.

Cahier d'exercices, page 44

1 (writing task)

2
Answers

> 2 bottles of white wine / biscuits / beef / cereals / coffee / beer / 3 baguettes / potatoes / cherries / green beans

3
Answers

> **a** a hypermarket
> **b** every day except Sunday
> **c** annual holiday

Cahier d'exercices, page 45

4
Answers

> **a** in the basement
> **b** second floor
> **c** on the ground floor
> **d** Menswear, ladieswear, childrenswear, toys, bookshop, card shop
> **e** 09:00 to 19:00
> **f** Sunday
> **g** lift

5
Answers

> Mum and Dad: a beautiful coat
> Bertrand: a green cap
> Aunt Amélie: a hooded sweatshirt
> Grandma: money to buy what I want
> Madeleine: a navy blue V neck jumper

Cahier d'exercices, page 46

6a
Answers

> **a** une grande surface
> **b** on peut tout y trouver
> **c** son copain est très dépensier
> **d** à la mode, mais pas chers
> **e** nous n'avons rien acheté
> **f** des gants de moto en cuir
> **g** nous mettons de l'argent de côté
> **h** je le mérite bien

6b
Answers

> a, b, c, f, h

Cahier d'exercices, page 47

6 Aux magasins

(pp. 98–99)

7 Put this conversation into the correct order. Number the phrases.

a D'accord. Et de quelle couleur? ____
b En 45. ____
c Je peux vous aider, Monsieur? ____
d Elles me vont. Merci! C'est combien? ____
e Au revoir. ____
f Elles sont malheureusement trop petites. ____
g En quelle pointure? ____
h En noir, s'il vous plaît. ____
i Et celles-là? ____
j Voilà, Madame. Au revoir! ____
k Que pensez-vous de celles-ci? ____
l Je voudrais une paire de chaussures, s'il vous plaît. ____
m 35 euros. ____

8 Read these promotions and complete the grid in English.

1 pull noir en soie, du 1 au 3 €53
2 pantalon blanc en coton, du 36 au 42 €35
3 sandales en cuir bleu marine, du 36 au 41 €46
4 chemisier en viscose beige, du 40 au 46 €76
5 gants violets en laine, S au XL €18

item	material	colour	sizes available	price
1				
2				
3				
4				
5				

9 Find the correct answer for each question.

1 Vous l'avez en rouge?
 a Nous l'avons essayé.
 b Oui, en rouge et dans toutes les tailles.
 c C'est un beau pull rouge.

2 Ça coûte combien?
 a C'est trop cher.
 b Par chèque ou carte de crédit.
 c Douze euros, Monsieur.

3 Est-ce que je peux l'essayer?
 a Ça coûte 28 euros.
 b Oui, la cabine d'essayage est par ici.
 c C'est très cher.

4 C'est en solde?
 a Oui, c'est vendu.
 b Oui, c'est beau.
 c Oui, c'est tarif réduit.

5 Vous êtes plutôt économe ou dépensier?
 a Économique.
 b Beaucoup d'argent de poche.
 c Ah! Malheureusement, dépensier!

6 Pouvez-vous me rembourser?
 a Ce n'est pas de ma faute.
 b Il me faut le reçu.
 c Je voudrais parler au gérant.

Métro pour l'Écosse © Heinemann Educational 2002

47

Cahier d'exercices, page 48

6 Aux magasins

(pp. 98–99)

10 Read this e-mail from Cassandre and answer the questions in English.

Salut Camille,
Hier j'ai invité mon patron et sa femme à manger: CATASTROPHE!
J'avais préparé une bonne soupe aux pommes de terre mais j'ai mis du sucre au lieu du sel dedans. C'était AFFREUX! En plus, mon patron a fait tomber sa cravate dans sa soupe!
Sa femme portait des vêtements ridicules: un pantalon jaune, des bottes rouges et un t-shirt à fleurs! Ha ha ha!!! Moi, j'avais mal aux pieds parce que mes chaussures étaient trop serrées ...
Ils sont partis à 20h30!!! Je crois que je vais perdre mon job. Au revoir, argent de poche!!!
Réponds-moi dès que tu auras ce message!
Bisous,
Cassandre

a Who did Cassandre invite for supper last night? (1) _____
b What was the soup made of? (1) _____
c What mistake did she make? (1) _____
d What happened to the man? (1) _____
e How was the lady dressed? (3) _____
f Which part of Cassandre's body was hurting and why? (2) _____
g What does she say goodbye to? (1) _____

(pp. 102–103)

11 Read these phrases and work out if it is a customer (C) or an employee (E) who is speaking.

a Je voudrais envoyer ce paquet en Écosse, s'il vous plaît. ____
b Cinq timbres pour les États-Unis, ça fait quatre euros, s'il vous plaît. ____
c Une télécarte, s'il vous plaît. ____
d Il est possible de changer des chèques de voyage ici? ____
e L'euro est à combien, s'il vous plaît? ____
f Non, désolé, je n'ai pas de monnaie pour la cabine téléphonique. ____
g Servez-vous du minitel sur votre droite, vous trouverez toutes les informations nécessaires. ____
h C'est combien, un timbre pour l'Angleterre? ____

Métro pour l'Écosse © Heinemann Educational 2002

48

7
Answers

a 5	b 4	c 1	d 10	e 13	f 8	g 3	h 6	i 9
j 12	k 7	l 2	m 11					

8
Answers

item	material	colour	sizes available	price
1 jumper	silk	black	1 to 3	€53
2 trousers	cotton	white	36 to 42	€35
3 sandals	leather	navy blue	36 to 41	€46
4 blouse	viscose	beige	40 to 46	€76
5 gloves	wool	purple	small to extra large	€18

9
Answers

1 b	2 c	3 b	4 c	5 c	6 b

10
Answers

a her boss and his wife   b potato
c She put sugar in the soup instead of salt.
d His tie fell in the soup.
e yellow trousers, red boots and a t-shirt with flowers
f her feet – her shoes were too tight.
g her pocket money

11
Answers

a C	b E	c C	d C	e C	f E	g E	h C

Cahier d'exercices, page 49

6 Aux magasins

Grammaire

1 Complete the phrases with a suitable adjective from the box below.

a un short _____
b une chemise _____
c des chaussettes _____
d des manteaux _____
e un pantalon _____
f une jupe _____

violette bleu noirs gris vertes rouge

2 Translate these French phrases into English.

Rappel

	masc.sing.	fem.sing.	masc.pl.	fem.pl.
this/these	celui/cet	cette	ces	ces
this one/these ones	celui-ci	celle-ci	ceux-ci	celles-ci
that one/those ones	celui-là	celle-là	ceux-là	celles-là

a ce pull _____
b cette cravate _____
c celle-ci, la jaune! _____
d celui-là, le jaune! _____
e ces cravates _____
f ces pulls _____
g celles-ci, les bleues! _____
h ceux-ci, les bleus! _____

3 Replace the underlined words with the correct pronoun.

a Je prends le sac. _____
b J'aime ces baskets. _____
c Je voudrais le gâteau. _____
d Je cherche les parapluies. _____
e Il adore le chocolat. _____
f Elle aime beaucoup la musique pop. _____
g Il préfère le pantalon noir. _____
h Nous aimons la cravate à rayures. _____

Rappel
Instead of always repeating nouns, we use pronouns meaning 'it'/'them'.

| | masc. sing. | fem. sing. | plural |
| | le | la | les |

Example: Je bois le café. » Je le bois. (I drink it.)
Je mange les bonbons. » Je les mange. (I eat them.)

49

Cahier d'exercices, page 50

6 Aux magasins

Bilan

1 Qu'est-ce qu'il y a comme magasins près de chez toi?

2 Quel est ton magasin préféré et pourquoi?

3 Tu aimes faire les courses? Qu'est-ce que tu aimes acheter?

4 As-tu fait du shopping récemment? Décris la journée.

5 Tu préfères les supermarchés ou les petits magasins? Pourquoi?

6 Que penses-tu des grandes surfaces? Pourquoi?

7 Tu reçois de l'argent de poche? Combien? De qui? C'est assez?

8 Tu le dépenses comment? Tu fais des économies?

9 Qu'est-ce que tes parents t'achètent?

10 Décris quelque chose que tu as perdu.

50

1
Answers

a bleu/gris/rouge
b violette/rouge
c vertes
d noirs/gris
e bleu/gris/rouge
f violette/rouge

2
Answers

a this jumper
b this tie
c this one, the yellow one!
d that one, the yellow one!
e these ties
f these jumpers
g these, the blue ones!
h these, the blue ones!

3
Answers

a Je le prends.
b Je les aime.
c Je le voudrais.
d Je les cherche.
e Il l'adore.
f Elle l'aime beaucoup.
g Il le préfère.
h Nous l'aimons.

En vacances

(Student's Book pages 110–127)

Topic area	Key language	Grammar	Skills/Strategies
Déjà vu (pp. 110–113) Talking about different countries Talking about the weather Understanding the weather forecast Talking about what you will do in different weathers	*Je passe mes vacances en Grande-Bretagne/Allemagne/Espagne/France/ Grèce/Italie/Hollande/Suisse/Finlande/Suède/Afrique/Australie/Thaïlande/ au Portugal/Japon/Canada aux États-Unis/Canaries* Nationalities *la plupart du temps/normalement/d'habitude/souvent/de temps en temps/rarement en été/automne/hiver/au printemps Il fait beau/chaud/mauvais/froid/du vent. Il pleut/neige. Il y a du brouillard/du soleil/des nuages. Il fera beau/mauvais/chaud/froid. Il fera du vent. Il pleuvra. Il y aura du brouillard/des nuages/des éclaircies/des averses/des orages. Le temps sera … nuageux/brumeux/variable/pluvieux/ensoleillé/couvert/frais. S'il fait beau/mauvais … on ira/j'irai au centre sportif/à la plage/aux magasins. On fera/Je ferai du ski/des courses/une promenade. On jouera/Je jouerai au tennis/football. On visitera/Je visiterai un château/musée.*	*en/au/aux* + countries Future tense	Learning weather expressions Listening skills Using *on* to vary writing
1 L'année dernière (pp. 114–115) Saying what you did on holiday last year	*L'année dernière je suis allé(e) (en France). J'ai passé mes vacances (dans un gîte/hôtel/camping/appartement, chez mon/ma correspondant(e)). Je suis parti(e) avec (ma famille, mes copains, mes camarades de classe). J'ai voyagé (en voiture/avion/bateau). Le voyage a duré (5 heures). C'était affreux/génial/super/nul. Il faisait beau/mauvais/froid/chaud.*	Perfect tense (revision) Imperfect	Essay skills: opinions, linking words and tenses
2 Au syndicat d'initiative (pp. 116–117) Asking for information at the tourist office	*On peut … louer des vélos/pédalos/canoës-kayaks/visiter le lac/la cathédrale/le château faire une promenade en bateau/aller à la plage/à la patinoire/au bowling/au parc Astérix jouer au volley/au ping-pong faire du camping/du ski nautique/de la planche à voile Je voudrais … s'il vous plaît. un dépliant/une carte/une liste des distractions/de restaurants une liste d'hôtels/un plan de la ville/un horaire des bus/trains*	*on peut* + infinitive	Using IT for research and to produce a guide Ideas for producing a guide

Topic area	Key language	Grammar	Skills/Strategies
3 À l'hôtel (pp. 118–119) Booking in at a hotel	*Je voudrais une chambre pour 2 personnes avec un grand lit/deux petits lits. avec salle de bains/douche/W-C/vue sur la mer/balcon pour trois nuits/une semaine C'est combien par nuit? Le (petit déjeuner) est à quelle heure? Est-ce qu'il y a (un restaurant/une piscine/un parking/un ascenseur)?*		Writing a formal letter
4 Ça ne marche pas! (pp. 120–121) Talking about accommodation problems	*Il n'y a pas de cintres/serviettes/savon/assez de couvertures. Le mini-bar est vide. La chambre est sale. Les W-C ne marchent pas. La douche/La lampe/Le bidet/Le téléphone ne marche pas. Il y a un problème avec le robinet. Il y a de l'eau par terre dans la salle de bains. Il y a trop de bruit. La chambre donne sur la rue.*	Imperfect tense (revision)	Writing a formal letter Adapting a letter
5 Découverte vacances (pp. 122–123) Discussing different types of holiday	*J'aime les visites guidées. J'aime voyager en autocar. Je suis à la recherche des choses différentes. Je veux apprendre à connaître une culture différente. J'aime rester sur place. J'aime faire des croisières. J'aime les grandes aventures. J'aime me bronzer. J'ai horreur des vacances à la plage. J'aime rester dans des auberges de jeunesse. J'aime rencontrer des gens.*		Tips for writing essays
Entraînez-vous: À l'écrit (pp. 124–125) Les grandes vacances	Language from Module 7		Extended writing using the 3rd person Structure, opinions and accuracy
À toi! A and B (pp.192–193)	Language from Module 7		Reading and writing skills

The vocabulary and structures taught in Module 7 are summarised on the **Mots** pages of the Student's Book, pages 126–127.
Further speaking practice on the language of the module is provided on À l'oral, page 142.
Assessment tasks for Modules 7 and 8 combined are provided in the separate Assessment Pack.

Déjà vu

(Student's Book pages 110–113)

Main topics and objectives

- Talking about different countries
- Talking about the weather
- Understanding the weather forecast
- Discussing plans for different weathers

Key language

Je passe mes vacances …
en Grande-Bretagne/Allemagne/Espagne/France/
Grèce/Italie/Hollande/Suisse/Finlande/Suède/
Afrique/Australie/Thaïlande
au Portugal/Japon/Canada
aux États-Unis/Canaries
Nationalities
la plupart du temps/normalement/d'habitude/
souvent/de temps en temps/rarement
au printemps/en automne/hiver/été
Il fait beau/mauvais/chaud/froid.
Il fait du vent. Il pleut. Il neige.
Il y a du brouillard. Il y a des nuages. Il y a du soleil.
Il fera beau/mauvais/chaud/froid.
Il fera du vent. Il pleuvra.

Il y aura du brouillard/des nuages/des éclaircies/
des averses/des orages.
Le temps sera nuageux/brumeux/variable/pluvieux/
ensoleillé/couvert/frais.
S'il fait beau/mauvais …
on ira/j'irai au centre sportif/à la plage/aux magasins.
on fera/je ferai du ski/des courses/une promenade.
on jouera/je jouerai au tennis/football.
on visitera/je visiterai un château/musée.

Grammar

- *en/au/aux* + countries
- Future tense
- Using *on* to vary writing

Skills/Strategies

- Learning weather expressions
- Listening skills

Resources

Cassette C side 2
Cahier d'exercices, page 51

Before starting this spread, revise by asking your students in groups to note down as many names of different countries and cities as they can remember in French. Ask if they can remember any cities which are not the same in French as in English (e.g. *Édimbourg, Londres*). Remind them that although the spelling might be the same, the pronunciation rarely is (e.g. Paris, Berlin). Introduce any countries from the key language box which have not been mentioned.

1a Write the French names for all the countries on the map, noting whether they are masculine or feminine.

Writing. Students note the articles and genders, as well as the names of the countries on the map.

Answers

Great Britain = *la Grande-Bretagne*	Finland = *la Finlande*
Canada = *le Canada*	Germany = *l'Allemagne* (f)
USA = *les États-Unis* (m)	Holland = *la Hollande*
France = *la France*	Italy = *l'Italie* (f)
Switzerland = *la Suisse*	Greece = *la Grèce*
Spain = *l'Espagne* (f)	Thailand = *la Thaïlande*
Portugal = *le Portugal*	Japan = *le Japon*
Sweden = *la Suède*	Australia = *l'Australie* (f)
	Also: Africa = *l'Afrique* (f)

Le détective

en/au/aux + countries. Point out that the general rule is *en* + country, and that there are very few masculine countries.

1b Complete the gaps in the following sentences, using a dictionary or the *Mots* (page 126) to find the languages.

Reading (1–10). Students find out the words for the nationalities/languages themselves. This should help them to keep these words separate from the words for the countries.

Answers

1 En Allemagne, on parle allemand.
2 Au Portugal, on parle portugais.
3 Aux États-Unis, on parle anglais.
4 Au Japon, on parle japonais.
5 En Grèce, on parle grec.
6 En Suède, on parle suédois.
7 En Italie, on parle italien.
8 Au Canada, on parle anglais et français.
9 Aux Canaries, on parle espagnol.
10 En Hollande, on parle hollandais.

1c In pairs. Partner A writes a country name in secret. B guesses the country by asking questions. A must only answer *oui* or *non*.

Speaking. Students use the examples and the map from **1a** to help them formulate simple questions.

1d Listen. Note the country/countries mentioned.

Listening (1–10). Students listen once for the countries. They then listen a second time and note down any other details they recognise.

Tapescript

1 *Si je pars en vacances, je préfère passer mes vacances en Allemagne. J'ai beaucoup d'amis là-bas.*
2 *Moi, j'adore les États-Unis. On se promène dans les rues et on se croit dans un film. Génial!*
3 *Moi, j'ai l'habitude de passer mes vacances en Grèce, c'est mon pays préféré. Toutes ces îles parfaites avec leurs petites maisons blanches et la mer émeraude. Magnifique!*
4 *J'aime aller en Espagne. C'est pas loin de la France et la culture m'intéresse beaucoup.*
5 *Moi, j'adore la Suisse. Faire du ski et se balader dans les montagnes – c'est tranquille. Ça me plaît.*
6 *Je veux perfectionner mon anglais, alors quand je pars en vacances, j'aime aller en Grande-Bretagne, car j'aime parler anglais.*
7 *Pour moi, la Hollande. Je trouve les gens très accueillants et il y a beaucoup de choses à faire et à voir.*
8 *Je voudrais visiter le Japon. J'aimerais voir Tokyo, mais le paysage m'intéresse aussi. Les collines, les cerisiers…*
9 *J'ai lu 'La Plage' et j'ai vu le film aussi. Maintenant j'ai envie d'aller en Thaïlande. Mais est-ce qu'il y aura trop de touristes? Je ne sais pas.*
10 *Je voudrais visiter les pays francophones en Afrique. Le Bénin, le Cameroun, le Sénégal. Mais aussi, la Tunisie et le Maroc dans le nord. Je les verrai un jour …*

Answers

1 Germany	2 USA	3 Greece
4 Spain	5 Switzerland	6 GB
7 Holland	8 Japan	9 Thailand
10 (French-speaking countries in) Africa		

2a Read the tourist guide to the weather in the south of France. Which season does the weather map show?

Reading. Students scan the text looking for the weather conditions depicted on the weather map. Revise simple weather expressions first if necessary.

Answer

Spring – the only time of year when storms are mentioned

Tip box

Weather expressions. This reminds students to be well prepared for their final exams by being confident with weather expressions. It is worth spot-checking knowledge of topics like weather, numbers, etc. on a regular basis.

2b Which seasons are being described below, according to the text in **2a**?

Reading (1–6). Students are now asked for a more detailed understanding of the text in **2a**.

Answers

1 Winter *(Il y a rarement du soleil)*
2 Summer *(Dans le sud … il fait souvent trop chaud)*
3 Spring *(Il y a souvent des averses)*
4 Autumn *(Il fait plus frais)*
5 Autumn *(Il fait assez beau)*
6 Winter *(De temps en temps, il neige)*

2c Write a tourist guide to the weather for each season in Scotland. Use the text in **2a** to help you.

Writing. Students write a guide similar to that in **2a**, but for Scotland. Discuss first with them the use of modifiers such as *assez*, *trop* and *très*, and of the negatives *ne … pas*, and *ne … jamais*.

Student's Book pages 112–113

Introduce this spread by asking your students to look up irregular future tense stems in the dictionary. They should record them in context, e.g.

faire	Aujourd'hui il fait froid.	Demain il <u>fera</u> froid.
être	Aujourd'hui le temps est variable.	Demain le temps ____ variable.
avoir	Aujourd'hui il y a du brouillard.	Demain il y ____ du brouillard.
pleuvoir	Aujourd'hui il pleut.	Demain il ____.

3a Read the sentences and match them with the pictures.

Reading (1–8). Students match the pictures to the correct phrases from the key language box.

Answers

1 b	2 e	3 a	4 d	5 f	6 h	7 c	8 g

Tip box

Listening skills. This reminds students not to panic if they don't catch all the details on the first listening. On the second and third listenings they can try to spot more details.

3b Listen to these weather forecasts. Note the region and the weather.

Listening (1–6). Students listen for the region and for the forecast and make notes in English.

Tapescript

Voici les prévisions météorologiques pour demain, vendredi.

Dans la région parisienne, et au centre de la France, il pleuvra pendant la plus grande partie de la journée, et il y aura des nuages présents jusqu'au soir.

Dans le nord, en Bretagne et en Normandie, il fera assez beau, avec un temps ensoleillé pendant la plus grande partie de la journée.

Dans la région des Alpes et le sud-est de la France, le temps sera ensoleillé, avec des températures entre 23 et 25 degrés.

Dans le sud de la France, dans le Midi et sur la Côte d'Azur, attention, le temps sera variable. Il y aura des vents forts avec des averses et un risque de temps orageux. Il ne fera pas beau.

Cependant, en Alsace, dans le nord-est du pays, le temps sera agréable, avec du soleil et un beau ciel.

Et finalement, dans le sud-ouest et la région des Pyrénées, le matin, il y aura du brouillard et il fera mauvais, mais l'après-midi, vous aurez aussi de la chance: il fera beau et chaud, attention aux coups de soleil!

Answers

B – rain, cloudy
A – quite fine and sunny
F – sunny, between 23° and 25°
E – variable, wind and showers with risk of storms, not fine
C – fine with sun and blue skies
D – morning fog and poor weather, afternoon fine and hot

3c Read the weather forecast for Normandy. Translate it into English.

Answer

Cotentin, showers in the north-east at Barfleur, while on the west coast there will be sunny intervals at Carteret. Further down, even more sun at Mortain, but the sun will not reach as far as Granville where the weather will be cloudy and at Mont-Saint-Michel there will be rain too!

Le détective

The future tense. Remind students that the future stem has an 'r' before the end (and is usually the infinitive).

In preparation for the next activities, do some whole-class oral practice on what they might do in different weathers on holiday.

4a Listen to this teenager talking about what her family will do on holiday. Note each type of weather mentioned. Listen again and note the activities.

Listening. Students listen and note in English the different types of weather mentioned, then listen a second time to note the activities.

Tapescript

Quand je serai en vacances, on fera beaucoup de choses. S'il pleut on ira au cinéma et s'il fait froid on fera les magasins. Mais normalement en vacances il fait chaud, alors on ira à la plage pour se baigner. S'il fait beau de toute façon, on sortira. Je n'aime pas rester à l'intérieur.

Answers

weather	activity
raining	cinema
cold	shopping
hot	beach to swim
fine	go out

Tip box

Using *on*. Take the opportunity to stress again to your students that they should try to show off the range of structures they can manipulate.

4b Write suitable activities for what you will do on holiday in each type of weather. Invent answers if you like.

Writing (a–d). Students prepare in written form the answers that they will need in **4c**.

4c In pairs. Take turns to ask and answer the question for each type of weather. Be inventive!

Speaking. Students now practise giving their answers in spoken form.

Further practice of the language and vocabulary of these spreads is provided as follows:

Cahier d'exercices, page 51

1 L'année dernière

(Student's Book pages 114–115)

Main topics and objectives

● Saying what you did on holiday last year

Key language

L'année dernière je suis allé(e) (en France).
J'ai passé mes vacances dans un
  gîte/hôtel/camping/appartement/chez mon/ma
  correspondant(e).
Je suis parti(e) avec (ma famille, mes copains, mes
  camarades de classe).
J'ai voyagé en (voiture/avion/bateau).
Le voyage a duré (5 heures).
C'était affreux/génial/super/nul.
Il faisait beau/mauvais/froid/chaud.

Grammar

● Perfect tense (revision)
● Imperfect tense

Skills/Strategies

● Essay skills: opinions, linking words and tenses

Resources

À l'oral, page 142: Conversation 1 and Prepared talk
À toi! A, page 192
Cassette C side 2
Cahier d'exercices, page 52 (exs 3a–3b)

Before starting this spread, check that students can still use the perfect tense with confidence, with both *avoir* and *être* (including reflexive verbs). Brainstorm some verbs in the perfect tense that they would want to use for holiday activities. Describe a recent holiday you have had (with some props if possible) and write up some key verb phrases on the OHT/board.

1a Read what Luc has written about his holiday and answer the questions in English.

Reading (1–10). Students answer comprehension questions in English as a first step in understanding the passage.

Answers

```
1 last year in August (2)
2 to the seaside – Carnac in Brittany (3)
3 gîte – house in the country (2)
4 15 days (1)
5 dad, mum and 2 sisters (3)
6 friends of his parents with their dog (2)
7 swim (1)
8 sunny and very hot (2)
9 friends (1)
10 boring (1)
```

Le détective

The imperfect tense. Point out that the endings for the imperfect are the same as for the conditional tense (revise these through spelling the endings to the tune of 'This old man'), and that the difference is 'the little 'r' before the end' in the conditional. Ask students to pick out any verbs in the imperfect from the text in **1a**.

1b Copy and complete the grid in English. Listen once and try to complete the first 3 columns. Then listen again and complete the last 3 columns.

Listening (1–6). Students divide up this complicated listening task by listening for different pieces of information each time. Some students may need the task dividing still further.

Tapescript

1 *Je suis allée en Belgique, avec mes copains. On est restés dans un gîte pendant une semaine. Il faisait très beau, et c'était vraiment super.*

2 *L'année dernière, je suis allé en Italie, avec ma famille. On est restés dans un joli petit hôtel, pendant deux semaines. Il faisait très beau tous les jours, et c'était extra.*

3 *J'ai passé mes dernières vacances en Grande-Bretagne. J'y suis allée avec mes camarades de classe, parce que c'était un voyage scolaire. Je suis restée chez ma correspondante, elle s'appelle Joanne et elle était très gentille. On est restés 10 jours en Angleterre. Il n'a pas fait beau: on a eu de la pluie presque tous les jours. Tant pis: c'était absolument fantastique quand même.*

4 *À Noël, on est allés dans un village à la montagne, dans les Pyrénées, pour des vacances de ski. J'y suis allé avec mon père et ma sœur, et on a passé une semaine là-bas, dans un appartement qu'on avait loué. Bien sûr, il y avait beaucoup de neige mais aussi il y avait du soleil. J'ai adoré mes vacances parce que le ski, c'est ma passion.*

5 *L'été dernier, ma famille et moi, nous sommes allés en Suisse. Nous sommes restés dans un camping, parce que nous avons une caravane. On a passé un mois en Suisse, mais le temps n'était pas extra: il faisait beaucoup de vent et un peu froid. C'était pas mal, mais un peu ennuyeux.*

6 *L'année dernière, je suis allé dans le midi de la France, au bord de la Méditerranée. J'y suis allé avec mon petit frère, parce qu'on est resté chez mes grands-parents, qui habitent sur la Côte d'Azur. On y est restés pendant tout le mois d'août. Il faisait super-beau, et on s'est très bien amusés.*

Answers

	where	who with	stayed in	how long	weather	opinion
1	Belgium	friends	gîte/country house	1 week	very nice	brilliant
2	Italy	family	hotel	2 weeks	fine	great
3	Great Britain	classmates	penfriend's home	10 days	rain	fantastic
4	mountains/Pyrenees	dad & sister	flat	1 week	snow and sun	loved it
5	Switzerland	family	caravan	1 month	windy, a bit cold	bit boring
6	Mediterranean	brother	grandparents' house	1 month	very nice	enjoyed it

2a In pairs. Make up some holidays and talk about them. Try to include lots of details.

Speaking. Students take turns to ask and answer the questions, using the diagram to help them. Model this first with some volunteers.

Tip box

Essay skills. Remind students that a range of language and of tenses is necessary to gain high marks in the Speaking and Writing exams.

2b Write about 100 words about your holidays last year. Include details such as accommodation, travel, weather, etc.

Writing. Encourage your students to write well over 100 words and to use the text in **1a**, the diagram in **2a** and the key language box, as well as the advice on tense range. You may wish to model a text with the whole class contributing, if students need more support.

Further practice of the language and vocabulary of this spread is provided as follows:

À l'oral, page 142: Conversation 1 and Prepared talk

À toi! A, page 192

Cahier d'exercices, page 52 (exs 3a–3b)

2 Au syndicat d'initiative

(Student's Book pages 116–117)

Main topics and objectives

● Asking for information at the tourist office

Key language

On peut …
  louer des vélos/des pédalos/des canoës-kayaks.
  visiter le lac/la cathédrale/le château.
  faire une promenade en bateau.
  aller à la plage/à la patinoire/au bowling/au parc Astérix.
  jouer au volley/au ping-pong.
  faire du camping/du ski nautique/de la planche à voile.
Je voudrais … s'il vous plaît.
  un dépliant/une carte

une liste des distractions/une liste de restaurants
une liste d'hôtels/un plan de la ville
un horaire des bus/des trains

Grammar

● *on peut* + infinitive

Skills/Strategies

● Using IT to research and to produce a guide
● Ideas for producing a guide

Resources

Cassette C side 2
Cahier d'exercices, pages 52–53 (exs 4–5)

Introduce the spread by revising the structure *on peut* + infinitive, by brainstorming the question *Qu'est-ce qu'on peut faire ici dans la région/ville?*.

1a Listen. What is there to do in these towns?

Listening (1–5). Students identify which activities are talked about by writing the letters labelling the pictures. Warn them that there may be up to four activities for each town.

Tapescript

1 Voyons, pour les petits, on peut louer des vélos, et visiter le beau lac. Il y a des cygnes et des canards.

2 Dans le parc principal, on peut jouer au volley et au ping-pong, il y a un tournoi une fois par semaine en été – et on peut louer des pédalos.

3 – Qu'est-ce qu'il y a d'intéressant pour les jeunes ici, madame?
  – Si vous voulez aller au bowling, ou faire une promenade en bateau, il y a ça déjà. Il y a la patinoire aussi.

4 Puisque c'est une station balnéaire, on peut louer des canoës-kayaks … aller à la plage. Là il y a toutes sortes d'activités, le ski nautique, la planche à voile…

5 Dans le coin, on peut faire du camping, et visiter les monuments historiques, tels que le château et la cathédrale. Mais il y a le parc Astérix aussi, alors il y a beaucoup de variété.

Answers

1 j, n	2 d, m, g	3 b, l, e	4 k, a, h, o	5 i, f, c, p

1b Write sentences about 10 of the above activities.

Writing (1–10). Students choose 10 activities from **1a** and write the French phrases for them.

Answers

a On peut aller à la plage.
b On peut aller au bowling.
c On peut visiter la cathédrale.
d On peut jouer au volley.
e On peut aller à la patinoire.
f On peut visiter le château.
g On peut louer des pédalos.
h On peut faire du ski nautique.
i On peut faire du camping.
j On peut louer des vélos.
k On peut louer des canoës-kayaks.
l On peut faire une promenade en bateau.
m On peut jouer au ping-pong.
n On peut visiter le lac.
o On peut faire de la planche à voile.
p On peut aller au parc Astérix.

2a Listen to this conversation at the tourist office. Fill in the blanks with the items from the key language box below.

Listening. Students will find the next activity easier if they write or type the whole text out and fill in the gaps. Alternatively, you could provide the whole text with gaps and words to fill the gaps electronically. They copy and paste words to fill the gaps.

Tapescript

– Bonjour, madame. Pouvez-vous me renseigner? Je voudrais un plan de la ville, s'il vous plaît.
– Oui, voilà. C'est gratuit. Je vous donne un dépliant sur notre ville, aussi, et une carte de la région.
– Qu'est-ce qu'il faut voir?
– Il ne faut pas manquer le château – il est merveilleux.
– Avez-vous une liste d'hôtels, madame? Et pouvez-vous recommander un bon restaurant?
– Oui, voilà. Il y a une liste de restaurants là-dedans aussi.
– Merci beaucoup, madame. Qu'est-ce qu'on peut faire ici?
– Il y a une liste des distractions dans cette brochure.

– Est-ce qu'on peut faire des excursions dans la région?
– Bien sûr, je vais vous donner une liste.
– Et … est-ce qu'on peut jouer au golf?
– Oui, il y a un terrain de golf à 5 kilomètres!
– Qu'est-ce qu'on peut faire le soir?
– Eh bien, il y a le casino et beaucoup de boîtes aussi.
– Ah, oui, j'ai failli oublier, avez-vous un horaire des bus et des trains?
– Voilà. Bonnes vacances!

Answers

a un plan de la ville
b un dépliant
c une carte
d une liste d'hôtels
e une liste de restaurants
f une liste des distractions
g un horaire des bus et des trains

2b In pairs. Practise the conversation in **2a**, then try changing any details you can.

Speaking. Students practise the conversation given and change details when they feel confident.

3a Read the tourist guide to Royan and answer these questions.

Reading (1–8). Students read the brochure and answer comprehension questions in English. Remind them that they do not have to understand every word. They should read for gist, read the questions and then look for the details they need.

Answers

1 small fishing port which bordered the estuary of the Gironde (3)
2 the railway (1)
3 was bombed by the allies (1)
4 Tuesday–Friday, 2–6 (2)
5 tennis, squash, swimming, golf, horse-riding, diving, parachuting, flying, windsurfing (9)
6 Sundays and bank holidays (2)
7 no, you can hire it on site (1)
8 from 1st April–30th September, 9am–7pm (2)

3b Listen to these tourists in Royan. Answer *oui* or *non* to their questions.

Listening (1–8). Students listen to tourists' questions about opening times, etc. and use the tourist guide to Royan in **3a** to say whether or not things are available/possible.

Tapescript

1 Est-ce que le musée est ouvert le lundi?
2 Est-ce qu'on peut jouer aux boules?
3 Est-ce qu'on peut faire des promenades en bateau?
4 Est-ce que le Centre Marin est ouvert le 14 juillet?
5 Est-ce que le zoo ferme à 19 heures?
6 Est-ce que je peux faire du cheval quelque part?
7 Est-ce que le musée est ouvert le matin?
8 Est-ce qu'on peut louer une planche à voile?

Answers

1 non	**2** non	**3** non	**4** non
5 oui	**6** oui	**7** non	**8** oui

Write a tourist guide to your town or the nearest big town. Use the Internet to research its tourist attractions and any sports facilities it has. What is there in your region: *des lochs, des distilleries, des châteaux, des montagnes?* Use the example below, changing the underlined words, but add further details if you can.

Writing. Students should be encouraged to write as much as possible, as accurately as possible. If they use language they are familiar and comfortable with, they should be able to learn their pieces of writing and reproduce them under controlled conditions.

Encourage them to find information about their region in French on the Internet.

Further practice of the language and vocabulary of this spread is provided as follows:

Cahier d'exercices, pages 52–53 (exs 4–5)

3 À l'hôtel

(Student's Book pages 118–119)

Main topics and objectives

● Booking in at a hotel

Key language

Je voudrais…
  une chambre pour 2 personnes
  avec un grand lit/deux petits lits/salle de bains/
  douche/W-C/vue sur la mer/balcon
  pour trois nuits/une semaine
C'est combien par nuit?
Le (petit déjeuner) est à quelle heure?

Est-ce qu'il y a (un restaurant/une piscine/
un parking/un ascenseur)?

Skills/Strategies

● Writing a formal letter

Resources

À l'oral, page 142: Transaction 2
Cassette C side 2
Cahier d'exercices, pages 53–54 (exs 6–7)

Introduce the spread by revising the vocabulary for hotel rooms. Put some of the icons from **1b** onto an OHT and ask students to tell you they would like a room with some of these things.

1a Read and listen to the conversation below and find the French for the following phrases.

Reading (1–6). Students find the equivalents for English phrases they would use themselves if booking a room in France. You may wish to play the recording first before students see the text, and see if they can understand a few facts.

Tapescript

– *Avez-vous une chambre de libre, s'il vous plaît?*
– *Ah non, je regrette, nous sommes complets … Attendez, quelle sorte de chambre voulez-vous?*
– *Je voudrais une chambre pour deux personnes avec salle de bains et un grand lit. Il nous faut un grand lit.*
– *C'est pour combien de nuits?*
– *C'est pour trois nuits.*
– *Ah non, je regrette. Je peux vous offrir deux nuits et c'est tout.*
– *Ah, je ne sais pas. On peut voir la chambre?*
– *Avec plaisir.*
– *Et … c'est combien par nuit?*
– *C'est €28,70 par nuit.*
– *Très bien. C'est bon. Est-ce qu'il y a un restaurant?*
– *Oui, au rez-de-chaussée.*
– *S'il vous plaît, le petit déjeuner est à quelle heure?*
– *Le petit déjeuner est servi au restaurant à partir de 7h30 jusqu'à 10h.*
– *D'accord.*

Answers

1 On peut voir la chambre?	**5** Le petit déjeuner est à quelle heure?
2 Est-ce qu'il y a un restaurant?	
3 C'est combien par nuit?	**6** Je voudrais une chambre pour deux personnes avec salle de bains.
4 Avez-vous une chambre de libre?	

1b Listen. Note the correct details for each conversation.

Listening (1–4). Students listen, and for each category (type of room, facilities in room, length of stay, hotel facilities) choose one item mentioned on the recording.

Tapescript

1 *Bonjour madame, je voudrais une chambre double avec une douche, pour trois nuits, s'il vous plaît. Est-ce qu'il y a un restaurant?*

2 *Bonjour, monsieur. J'ai réservé une chambre de famille, avec salle de bains dans la chambre, et balcon. C'est réservé pour une semaine. Est-ce qu'il y a une piscine à l'hôtel?*

3 *Allô, bonjour madame – ah, pardon, monsieur. Je téléphone pour réserver une chambre pour une personne avec W-C dans la chambre, et avec balcon si possible. Je voudrais rester pour deux nuits. Ah, est-ce qu'il y a un parking, s'il vous plaît?*

4 *Bonjour, mademoiselle. Avez-vous une chambre de libre pour une nuit? Je voudrais une chambre pour deux personnes avec deux petits lits, et vue sur la mer si possible. Est-ce qu'il y a un ascenseur, s'il vous plaît?*

Answers

1 c, f, m, n	**2** d, e or h, k, q	**3** a, g or h, l, o	**4** b, i, j, p

1c In pairs. Use conversation **1a** as a model for these conversations.

Speaking. Students change a few details from the model conversation in **1a** to create four new conversations using the picture cues. Show the class how to do this first using a student volunteer to play the role of the *Employé* (this role does not change).

2 Write two letters to reserve rooms, changing the underlined words in the letter to fit the details in the pictures below.

Writing. Students use the model text to ensure that their writing is idiomatic, accurate and suitable for the context.

> Further practice of the language and vocabulary of this spread is provided as follows:
>
> À l'oral, page 142: Transaction 2
>
> Cahier d'exercices, pages 53–54 (exs 6–7)

4 Ça ne marche pas!

(Student's Book pages 120–121)

Main topics and objectives

● Talking about accommodation problems

Key language

Il n'y a pas de cintres/serviettes/savon/assez de couvertures.
Le mini-bar est vide.
La chambre est sale.
Les W-C ne marchent pas.
La douche/La lampe/Le bidet/Le téléphone ne marche pas.
Il y a un problème avec le robinet.
Il y a de l'eau par terre dans la salle de bains.
Il y a trop de bruit.
La chambre donne sur la rue.

Grammar

● Imperfect tense (revision)

Skills/Strategies

● Writing a formal letter
● Adapting a letter

Resources

À toi! B, page 193
Cassette C side 2
Cahier d'exercices, page 54 (ex. 8)

Introduce the spread by asking what sort of accommodation problems students have had or have heard about. How many of these could they express in French? They may need help with structuring their complaints, in which case provide the following structures on an OHT:

il n'y a pas de…
il n'y a pas assez de…
il y a trop de…
le/la _____ ne marche pas
les _____ ne marchent pas
le/la _____ est _____
les _____ sont _____

1a Match the problems to the numbered details in the picture.

Reading (a–o). Students find the French for many of the expressions they have identified.

Answers

1 Il y a trop de bruit.
2 La chambre donne sur la rue.
3 Il y a un problème avec le robinet.
4 La douche ne marche pas.
5 Il n'y a pas de serviettes.
6 Il n'y a pas de cintres.
7 Il n'y a pas de savon.
8 Le bidet ne marche pas.
9 Le mini-bar est vide.
10 La lampe ne marche pas.
11 La chambre est sale.
12 Les W-C ne marchent pas.
13 Il y a de l'eau par terre dans la salle de bains.
14 Le téléphone ne marche pas.
15 Il n'y a pas assez de couvertures.

1b Listen to this hotel guest's complaints. Write the picture numbers in the right order.

Listening. Students listen to the same complaints being made, this time in spoken form, and write the numbers of the complaints as they hear them.

Tapescript

J'ai jamais vu ça! C'est l'enfer, cet hôtel, je ne m'attendais pas à ça! D'abord, la chambre est sale, la lampe ne marche pas et le téléphone ne marche pas non plus!

Ensuite, je vais dans la salle de bains, les W-C ne marchent pas, la douche ne marche pas, le bidet ne marche pas, il n'y a pas de savon et le comble, il y a de l'eau par terre! En plus, il y a un problème avec le robinet et il n'y a pas de serviettes!

J'ouvre le placard dans la chambre, il n'y a pas de cintres.

Je regarde le lit de plus près – j'ai failli m'évanouir! Il n'y a pas assez de couvertures et je suis allergique aux plumes…

C'est vraiment incroyable, votre hôtel!
Pour terminer, le mini-bar est vide, la chambre donne sur la rue et il y a beaucoup trop de bruit. Mais c'est extraordinaire! Je téléphone tout de suite au syndicat d'initiative. Vous êtes censé être un hôtel de luxe. Pas possible!

Answers

11, 10, 14, 12, 4, 8, 7, 13, 3, 5, 6, 15, 9, 2, 1

Before asking your students to use this language themselves, you may wish to give them more structured practice in saying these things. One way of getting students to repeat language is to put it into a song, or better still to ask your students to write or continue a song using a list of ready-made phrases. The song below contains only two rhyming lines, and can be continued by giving the students examples of rhyming words so that they can continue the song themselves (e.g. *savon/bon/télévision, serviettes/inquiète/fourchette, rue/jus/bu/lu*, etc, *sale/animal/journal, lit/bruit, robinet/bidet/télé, pas/cinéma/tas, placard/cafard/mini-bar*). Remind students that mute -e can be silent (*la douche*) or sounded in a song/poem (*ne marche pas*).

(To the tune of 'The Grand old Duke of York')
Oh, la chambre est trop sale
Il n'y a pas de ceintres
Le téléphone ne marche pas, et
Je veux porter plainte.

Oh, je voudrais porter plainte.
La douche ne marche pas.
Y a de l'eau par terre dans la salle de bains, et
Je viens de voir un rat.

Oh, je voudrais porter plainte …

1c In pairs. Complete this conversation, making as many complaints as possible.

Speaking. Students practise using the complaints, but also using pacifying expressions, and the phrase *en plus*.

2a Read the letter and choose the right answers.

Reading (1–5). Multiple-choice questions in French like these allow students not only to demonstrate understanding but also to expand their vocabulary.

Answers

1 a	**2** b	**3** b	**4** c	**5** a

Rappel

The imperfect tense. Remind your students of the use of the imperfect for describing things in the past (e.g. the weather).

Tip box

Writing/adapting a letter. Encourage your students to use as much of the original letter as they can.

2b Write a letter complaining about your stay in a hotel. Use the letter in **2a** as a model.

Writing. Students can be as imaginative as they like, provided that they use the original letter as a model to retain as much accuracy as possible.

Further practice of the language and vocabulary of this spread is provided as follows:

À toi! B, page 193

Cahier d'exercices, page 54 (ex. 8)

5 Découverte vacances

(Student's Book pages 122–123)

Main topics and objectives

● Discussing different types of holiday

Key language

J'aime les visites guidées.
J'aime voyager en autocar.
Je suis à la recherche d'expériences différentes.
Je veux apprendre à connaître une culture différente.
J'aime rester sur place.
J'aime faire des croisières.
J'aime les grandes aventures.
J'aime me bronzer.
J'ai horreur des vacances à la plage.
J'aime rester dans des auberges de jeunesse.
J'aime rencontrer des gens.

Grammar

Skills/Strategies

● Tips for writing essays

Resources

Cassette C side 2
Cahier d'exercices, page 55

Start by asking where your students have been on holiday and where their ideal holiday destinations would be. Make sure they know how to say these places before starting the spread. Introduce the expressions from the key language box on page 123.

1a Read these 3 holiday adverts and complete the sentences with one of the places.

Reading (1–3). Students demonstrate understanding and increase their vocabulary by filling in the gaps with the correct destination.

Answers

1 Allemagne	2 Suisse	3 Inde

1b Answer these questions in English.

Reading (1–5). Students demonstrate a higher level of comprehension of the text by answering more detailed questions in English, using a dictionary where necessary.

Answers

1 make the most of its history, tradition, culture, delicious food, arts and crafts and its hospitality (5)
2 9 days/7 nights visiting Delhi, Agra and Jaïpur (4)
3 by train; you would see fabulous landscapes of mountains and glaciers, lots of bridges and go through several tunnels (4)
4 a river cruise (1)
5 castles and medieval villages, the site of the Lorelei (3)

2 Listen and note the sort of holiday each person likes. Note any reasons if you can.

Listening (1–5). Students listen and note types of holiday. They can listen again to note the reasons. Make sure they have found out what the words in the key language box mean before they listen.

Tapescript

1 *Moi, j'adore apprendre des choses quand je suis en vacances. J'aime bien les visites guidées. Je sais qu'il y a des gens qui ont horreur de ça, mais moi, j'aime bien. J'aime bien aussi voyager en autocar avec un guide. Je trouve ça très reposant.*

2 *Moi, j'aime bien rester dans des auberges de jeunesse. Ça permet de rencontrer des gens, d'autres jeunes. C'est sympa. Souvent dans des auberges de jeunesse, il y a des activités sportives organisées et des visites différentes. C'est bien fait.*

3 *Moi, je n'aime pas les vacances. Je préfère rester sur place et me reposer. J'aime lire et regarder la télé. J'essaie de rendre visite à des amis aussi.*

4 *Moi, j'aime les grandes aventures, des choses dangereuses – le défi! L'alpinisme, l'escalade – c'est oui! Me bronzer au bord de la mer, à la plage tous les jours comme une sardine grillée – non merci.*

5 *Plutôt que de partir à la campagne ou à la montagne, moi, j'aime faire des croisières. C'est très intéressant, on voit beaucoup de choses et j'aime bien voyager au fil de l'eau – c'est très agréable.*

Answers

1 guided tours (likes travelling by coach, finds it relaxing)
2 youth hostels (can meet other people and often there are sporting activities and outings)
3 doesn't like holidays (prefers staying at home, relaxing, reading, watching TV, visiting friends)
4 likes adventures and dangerous things (mountaineering, climbing)
5 likes cruises (you see a lot of things)

3 Read what Pierre says about the holidays he likes and answer the questions in English.

Reading (1–9). Students show understanding by answering English comprehension questions about the text. Make sure they are aware of the need to find enough facts to get maximum marks (e.g. 4 facts for question 3).

Answers

1 in Europe (1)
2 big towns (1)
3 likes to relax which is not possible in a town – too much traffic, people and noise. (4)
4 likes nature – mountains, rivers and valleys and pretty villages (4)
5 peace and tranquillity (2)
6 likes meeting people from other cultures who have had different experiences (2)
7 hates them – prefers to decide himself where he goes and when (2)
8 isolated/deserted (1)
9 he has so many places to see nearer home (2)

Tip Box

Tips for writing essays. Encourage students to write as accurately and as much as they can. Demonstrate, on an OHT, how to structure an essay and how to plan to include opinion phrases, different tenses and time phrase and impressive sentences. Above all, show students that the text in **3** contains lots of very impressive, very accurate language which they can lift or adapt.

4a Write about 150 words on the sort of holiday you prefer. Remember to give opinions and reasons for them – and to make comments!

Writing. Encourage students to try to write well over 150 words and to use all the advice from the tip box.

4b Learn what you have written and give a presentation, either to your group or on a tape. You may use short notes to remind you of your talk.

Speaking. Once students have had their writing corrected, they should learn it to give a presentation. Any notes should be reminders of content, not whole sentences, as this would make the talk more stilted.

Further practice of the language and vocabulary of this spread is provided as follows:

Cahier d'exercices, page 55

All the key vocabulary and structures from this module are listed on the **Mots** pages 126–127. These can be used for revision by covering up either the English or the French. Students can check here to see how much they remember from the module and use them to prepare for the assessments.

Assessment materials for Modules 7 and 8 are available in the separate Assessment Pack.

Further speaking and grammar practice on the whole module is provided on **Cahier d'exercices** pages 56–57.

Writing practice: Les grandes vacances

The **À l'écrit** spreads give regular, guided practice in preparing for the writing sections of Standard Grade and Intermediate examinations. Each double-page spread always starts with a model text which acts as a stimulus to give students ideas about what they might include in their ownwriting. Students are encouraged to look at the detail of the text through the structured reading activities, and are guided gradually towards producing their own sentences in French, in preparation for the final task in which they are asked to produce an extended piece of writing. The **Au Secours!** panel is a feature on all of the À l'écrit spreads. It presents language and structures that students can include in their writing, and reminds them of general points which will enable them to get a better grade.

To qualify for the writing components at Standard Grade or Intermediate writing N.A.B.s, final versions must be produced under controlled conditions. Students should be encouraged to use the language they understand and are familiar with so as to learn what they have written with a high degree of accuracy. They should be warned about the dangers of copying. At Standard Grade, students should be guided to write over 25 words at Foundation level, 50 words at General level and 100 words at Credit level.

Students should be encouraged to see that they can get Credit marks at Standard Grade and A grades at Intermediate 2 in Writing! Remind them of the following tips to help them get a better grade.

Handy tips for students

1 Structure your writing: a good beginning and ending, and 3 distinct paragraphs!

   Choose formats which structure themselves, e.g. a letter.

2 Focus your writing on one aspect of a module.

3 Choose aspects which give you opportunities to write about your opinions.

4 Choose aspects which allow you to use impressive vocabulary and phrases.

5 Make sure you include examples of different tenses in your writing.

6 It is very important to write accurate French! Make sure the language you choose for your writing is memorable for **you**. Only you can know how much new and impressive French you can learn to write out accurately in exam conditions!

This spread guides students towards producing an extended piece of writing on the topic of **holidays**. It helps them to structure their writing, using phrases to describe the weather, the time and past activities. Students should be encouraged to write as accurately and as much as they can.

1 Each week, Danielle writes about the weather (in yellow in the text). Match the pictures to the descriptions of the weather for each week.

Answers

> **a** week 6: *Il faisait mauvais.*
> **b** weeks 3 and 4: *Il faisait très chaud.*
> **c** week 1: *Il faisait froid et il pleuvait.*
> **d** week 2: *Il faisait toujours assez froid mais il faisait soleil.*
> **e** week 5: *Il faisait soleil.*

2 Each paragraph starts with a time phrase (in blue). Find out what each phrase means and write it out in French and English.

Answers

> **1** *Pendant la première semaine des grandes vacances* – In the first week of the summer holidays
> **2** *Lundi après-midi* – On Monday afternoon
> **3** *Nous avons passé quinze jours en Espagne* – We spent 2 weeks in Spain
> **4** *Toute la semaine* – The whole week
> **5** *Pendant la dernière semaine de mes vacances* – During the last week of my holidays

3 What does Danielle say she did in each paragraph? The verb phrases are in green. Write them in French and English.

Answers

> **week 1:** *Je suis restée à la maison* (I stayed at home), *j'ai regardé beaucoup de télé* (I watched a lot of TV), *j'ai lu* (I read), *j'ai rangé ma chambre* (I tidied my room)
> **week 2:** *J'ai joué au tennis* (I played tennis)
> **weeks 3 and 4:** *J'ai fait de la natation* (I went swimming), *j'ai joué au volley* (I played volleyball), *j'ai fait du shopping* (I went shopping), *j'ai acheté des vêtements* (I bought some clothes), *j'ai trouvé des t-shirts marrants* (I found some funny T-shirts)
> **week 5:** *j'ai travaillé* (I worked), *j'ai répondu au téléphone* (I answered the telephone), *j'ai parlé aux clients* (I talked to the customers), *j'ai fait des litres de café* (I made litres of coffee).
> **week 6:** *j'ai essayé de réviser* (I tried to revise), *j'ai fait un effort* (I made an effort).

4 What does she say other people did? Look for other pronouns (*nous, on, il*) as well as for actual people (*mes copains, mon petit frère*). Write these verb phrases in French and in English.

Answers

> *Mes copains Sophie et Marc étaient en vacances* – My friends Sophie and Marc were on holiday
> *Sophie et Marc sont revenus* – Sophie and Marc came back
> *Nous avons fait un pique-nique* – We had a picnic
> *Nous avons passé quinze jours en Espagne* – We spent 2 weeks in Spain
> *Nous sommes allés* – We went
> *On est allé* – We went
> *Mon petit frère était un peu casse-pieds* – My little brother was a little silly
> *il avait peur, il avait faim, il avait chaud* – he was frightened, he was hungry, he was hot
> *il m'a bien payé* – he paid me well

5 Write an account of your summer holidays. They can be holidays you have actually experienced, or you can make them, up! Use the *Au secours!* panel to help you.

Au secours!
This section reminds students of the following points:
● structure
● talking about what other people did
● When you write your accounts, try to say things about when, what, the weather and a comment!
● opinions
● accuracy

MODULE 7 EN VACANCES — *À toi! A & B*
(Student's Book pages 192–193)

Self-access reading and writing at two levels

These pages are designed to give students extra practice in reading and structured writing. There are two differentiated pages relating to each chapter: A and B. Page A is at an easier level and page B more challenging. You may wish students to work on the page most appropriate to their level or work through both pages. You may feel it is useful to work with students on the activities, but it should be possible for most students to work on them independently. The most appropriate time to use each page is indicated within the relevant teaching notes.

À toi! A, page 192

This page is best used after pages 114–115 of the Student's Book.

1 Choose the best alternative in each case to make your own holiday letter. Write it out as a complete letter.

2 Try to make up your own DIY holiday letter – use your imagination!

À toi! B, page 193

This page is best used after pages 120–121 of the Student's Book.

1 Read the text, then answer these questions in English.

Answers

> **1** Top quality. (1)
> **2** Electricity points, grills next to the tents and impeccable toilet blocks. (3)
> **3** No noise after 22h, dogs forbidden near the swimming pool, no washing-up in the toilet block, showers limited to 3 minutes, no fires. (5)
> **4** He went jogging on the cycle track and played boules on the volleyball court. (2)
> **5** Because a fox has destroyed the rubbish bag he had put in front of his tent. (3)
> **6** Went to a hotel. (1)

2a Make up 5 more rules for this campsite. They don't have to be sensible!

2b You have spent a holiday at this campsite. Write a letter (about 100 words) to a French friend saying what it was like. Use words and phrases from the text to help you.

Cahier d'exercices, page 51

1
Answers

a Il est français.   **b** Il est anglais.   **c** Elle est espagnole.   **d** Il est portugais.   **e** Elle est américaine.

2
Answers

Lundi = c   **Mardi** = e   **Mercredi** = f   **Jeudi** = d   **Vendredi** = a   **Samedi** = g   **Dimanche** = b

Cahier d'exercices, page 52

3a
Answers

a a week ago
b in the Black Forest, in the South of the country
c snows a lot
d skied, went on outings in the region, bought some souvenirs
e at his penfriend's house

3b (writing task)

4
Answers

1 c   **2** g   **3** f   **4** h   **5** b   **6** a   **7** d   **8** e

Cahier d'exercices, page 53

5
Answers

1 b   **2** a   **3** c   **4** d

6
Answers

a deux personnes	**b** un grand lit	**c** une douche
d rester	**e** trois août	**f** dix août
g ascenseur	**h** chiens	**i** petit déjeuner

Cahier d'exercices, page 54

7
Answers

a America	**b** one day

c hot-dogs and ice-creams
d she had a sea view and a double bed
e breakfast was served too early at 6.30 am
f very hot (30ºc) **g** with her friends when she is older

8 (writing task)

Cahier d'exercices, page 55

(pp. 122–123)
9a In the text, circle or highlight the French for each phrase and
write the letter of the English phrase next to it:

Bienvenue à Bavay, cité antique vieille de 2000 ans!

Bavay est le plus grand site gallo-romain au nord de Paris. Cette petite ville se situe
dans le département du Nord à environ quatre-vingts kilomètres de Lille.

Bavay, dont le nom vient du latin Bagacum, se distingue par son originalité historique.

À voir:
■ Le musée archéologique et le site.
■ Le musée de la bataille de Malplaquet du 11/09/1709. Cette bataille a eu lieu entre les Français d'un côté et les Anglais et les Espagnols de l'autre.
■ Le beffroi et l'hôtel de ville datant du XVIIème siècle et de style espagnol.

Sports et loisirs:
Il y a deux salles de sport et un stade. Vous pouvez pratiquer le football, le tennis, le tir à l'arc ou encore la gymnastique et la danse.

Spécialités:
Bavay doit sa renommée à ses célèbres bonbons 'les chiques'. La bière 'La Bavaisienne' est aussi très appréciée.

a	the biggest Gallo-Roman site	e	this battle took place
b	about 80km	f	dating from the 17th century
c	the name comes from the Latin	g	you can play football
d	its historic originality	h	its famous sweets

9b Tick (✓) the six correct sentences about the text from 9a in the grid below.

	Example: Bavay est une ville du nord de la France.	✓
a	Bavay est une vieille ville touristique.	
b	Ce sont les Romains qui ont créé le site.	
c	Bavay est une ville moyenne.	
d	Paris est à 80 kilomètres de Lille.	
e	La bataille de Malplaquet a eu lieu au printemps.	
f	Les Français se sont battus contre les Anglais dans cette bataille.	
g	Le beffroi n'est pas typiquement français.	
h	On peut pratiquer la natation à Bavay.	
i	Il y a deux grandes spécialités bavaisiennes.	
j	'Les chiques' sont des sucreries très appréciées.	

55

9a
Answers

le plus grand site gallo-romain = a
environ quatre-vingts kilomètres = b
le nom vient du latin = c
son originalité historique = d
cette bataille a eu lieu = e
datant du XVIIième siècle = f
vous pouvez pratiquer le football = g
ses célèbres bonbons = h

9b
Answers

a, b, d, f, g, i, j

Cahier d'exercices, page 56

Grammaire

1 The perfect tense with *être*. Translate the phrases below.

You must use the auxiliary *être* (to be) with the following verbs in the perfect tense:
naître (to be born)   monter (to go up)   sortir (to go out)
arriver (to arrive)   partir (to leave)   aller (to go)
venir (to come)   entrer (to go in)   rester (to stay)
revenir (to come back)   retourner (to go back)   tomber (to fall)
devenir (to become)   mourir (to die)   descendre (to go down)

Example: We (masc.) arrived. = *Nous sommes arrivés.*

a He fell. = _____
b I (masc.) became. = _____
c They (masc.) went. = _____
d They (fem.) came back. = _____
e We (fem.) went up. = _____
f I (fem.) went out. = _____
g You (tu/masc.) went in. = _____
h I (fem.) stayed. = _____
i She went down. = _____

Rappel
je suis
tu es
il/elle/on est
nous sommes
vous êtes
ils/elles sont
+ past participle
Remember to make the past participle agree with the subject.

2 Identify the tense: perfect (Pe), imperfect (Im), present (Pr) or future (Fu).
a Il fait beau. _____   f Il fera froid. _____
b Il a neigé. _____   g Il pleuvait. _____
c Il y aura des nuages. _____   h Il y a du brouillard. _____
d Il neigera. _____   i Il pleut. _____
e Il fait mauvais. _____   j Il a fait chaud. _____

3 Put these sentences into the imperfect tense.
a Le téléphone ne marche pas. = _____
b Nous avons froid. = _____
c Il y a du bruit. = _____
d J'entends les voisins tous les soirs. = _____
e Les serveurs sont impolis. = _____

To form the imperfect, take the nous form of the present tense, remove the -ons ending and add:
for *je*: ais
for *tu*: ais
for *il/elle*: ait
for *nous*: ions
for *vous*: iez
for *ils/elles*: aient
*être is irregular, so check it first!

56

1
Answers

a Il est tombé. **b** Je suis devenu. **c** Ils sont allés.
d Elles sont revenues. **e** Nous sommes montées.
f Je suis sortie. **g** Tu es entré. **h** Je suis restée.
i Elle est descendue.

2
Answers

a Pr **b** Pe **c** Fu **d** Fu **e** Pr **f** Fu **g** Im **h** Pr
i Pr **j** Pe

3
Answers

a Le téléphone ne marchait pas. **b** Nous avions froid.
c Il y avait du bruit.
d J'entendais les voisins tous les soirs.
e Les serveurs étaient impolis.

Cahier d'exercices, page 57

Bilan

1 Où aimes-tu passer tes vacances normalement? Pourquoi?

2 Tu préfères aller à l'étranger ou rester en Grande-Bretagne? Pourquoi?

3 Qu'est-ce que tu fais normalement pendant les vacances?

4 Où est-ce que tu préfères loger et comment aimes-tu voyager?

5 Où es-tu allé(e) l'année dernière? Qu'est-ce que tu as fait? C'était bien?

6 Quel temps faisait-il?

7 Où aimerais-tu aller l'année prochaine et pourquoi?

8 Quel type de vacances n'aimes-tu pas et pourquoi?

9 Es-tu déjà allé(e) en France? Si oui, parle-moi de ta visite.

10 Tu as déjà logé à l'hôtel/dans un camping? C'était bien? Pourquoi/Pourquoi pas?

57

145

Bienvenue en France!

(Student's Book pages 128–145)

Topic area	Key language	Grammar	Skills/Strategies
Déjà vu (pp. 128–131) Exchanging greetings Talking about your house or flat Giving details about rooms in a house	Bon séjour! Bonnes vacances! Bon week-end! Bonne année! Bon anniversaire! Bonne chance! Bon voyage! Bonne journée! As-tu faim? Entre, et assieds-toi! Es-tu fatigué(e)? Voici ta chambre. Bonne nuit! As-tu soif? As-tu besoin d'une serviette, de savon, ou de dentifrice? Bonjour et bienvenue en France! Le voyage s'est bien passé? Je te présente ma (mère) et mon (père). J'habite à ... J'habite une maison/un appartement. Il y a (7) pièces. Au rez-de-chaussée, il y a le salon/la salle de séjour/la salle à manger/la cuisine/les W-C. Au premier étage, il y a (3) chambres et une salle de bains. une maison individuelle/un bungalow/un appartement/un vieux bâtiment/un immeuble en banlieue/en ville/au bord de la mer En haut/En bas, il y a ... Dehors il y a ... un jardin, une pelouse, des arbres, des fleurs. Dans ... il y a ... de la moquette, un canapé, un frigo/congélateur, une cuisinière à gaz, un lave-vaisselle, un lavabo, une douche, une machine à laver, une télévision, le buffet, la baignoire, un miroir, une chaîne hi-fi, un fauteuil, un four à micro-ondes.	près de/loin de depuis + present tense	
1 Voici ma chambre (pp. 132–133) Describing your room	Ma chambre est (très) grande/petite. En face de/À côté de/À gauche/droite ... il y a ... une chaîne hi-fi/un magnétoscope/un lit/une lampe/des posters aux murs. La moquette est (verte) et les rideaux sont (bleus). Je trouve ça (génial). Je partage ma chambre avec ... J'ai une chambre à moi ...	Prepositions	Using more sophisticated expressions
2 On sort manger? (pp. 134–135) Eating out with friends and colleagues	Comme hors-d'œuvre/plat principal/dessert/boisson, je voudrais/je prends ... C'est quoi exactement? C'est du poisson/de la viande/de la volaille/un légume. Dans une sauce/en croûte/garni. C'est une spécialité écossaise/anglaise. C'est un dessert ... C'est une sorte de ... avec ... servi(e) avec ...		Explaining a menu in French
3 On se plaint (pp. 136–137) Complaining at a restaurant	Je n'ai pas de (fourchette). Ma cuillère/Ma fourchette/Mon couteau est sale. L'addition n'est pas juste. Mon potage est froid. On n'a pas de sel ou de poivre. Je n'ai pas de verre. Je regrette ... il n'y a pas de réservation/le restaurant est complet/il n'y a plus de (poulet)/il y a une erreur ici. Ça ne va pas! Je voudrais parler au gérant. C'est incroyable! Il y a une erreur ici. Il y a une mouche dans mon potage! Ce poisson est avarié! Les fruits sont pourris. Le potage est trop salé. Le garçon/La serveuse est impoli(e). C'est la dernière fois que je dîne ici! Je suis vraiment désolé(e). Ça ne m'est jamais arrivé avant.		Writing a formal letter

Topic area	Key language	Grammar	Skills/Strategies
4 Les médias (pp. 138–139) Talking about books, magazines and films	C'est un roman d'aventures/un roman policier/une bande dessinée/ une histoire de guerre/un livre de science-fiction. C'est triste/super/génial/intéressant. Le héros/L'héroïne est/était cool/courageux (-euse)/comique. Le dernier livre que j'ai lu était … Il s'agit de … Le héros/L'héroïne était … Il s'agit de … Je l'ai trouvé … Je peux le recommander/l'envoyer. Ça ne vaut pas la peine. J'ai vu … C'était très émouvant/très romantique/nul/impressionnant. C'est une comédie/un drame psychologique/un film de science-fiction/un western/une histoire d'amour. Il s'agit d'un homme qui … C'est un film qui m'a touché/qui ne m'a fait aucun effet. L'histoire était … Les acteurs étaient superbes/bons/nuls. La réalisation était parfaite/ennuyeuse. J'aime les films qui me font rire/pleurer/peur.	Relative pronouns: qui/que Perfect tense/imperfect tense	Using tenses Linking words
5 La télé (pp. 140–141) Discussing TV	J'aime/J'aime beaucoup/Je n'aime pas tellement/Je déteste … les informations/les documentaires/les dessins animés/les jeux/le télé-journal/les émissions de musique/les émissions de sport/les films d'horreur/de science-fiction/d'amour/les séries/les feuilletons/la publicité. parce que c'est … intéressant/amusant/passionnant/barbant/bête/ennuyeux. Ça me fait rire. Il s'agit de la vie personnelle de … C'est (une série) qui existe depuis … ans. Il/Elle a lieu (en Australie). Le présentateur est … Les acteurs sont … C'est très populaire. J'aime cette émission parce que …		Using common sense! Using ICT for research
Entraînez-vous: À l'oral (pp. 142–143)	Language from Modules 7 and 8		Practice for the speaking exam Using different tenses Presentation skills
À toi! A and B (pp. 194–195)	Language from Module 8		Reading and writing skills

The vocabulary and structures taught in Module 8 are summarised on the **Mots** pages of the Student's Book, pages 144–145.
Further writing practice on the language of the module is provided on **À l'écrit**, pages 160–161.
Assessment tasks for Modules 7 and 8 combined are provided in the separate Assessment Pack.

Déjà vu
(Student's Book pages 128–131)

Main topics and objectives

- Exchanging greetings
- Talking about your house or flat
- Giving details about rooms in a house

Key language

Bon séjour! Bonnes vacances! Bon week-end! Bonne année! Bon anniversaire! Bonne chance! Bon voyage! Bonne journée!
As-tu faim? Entre, et assieds-toi! Es-tu fatigué(e)?
Voici ta chambre. Bonne nuit! As-tu soif? As-tu besoin d'une serviette, de savon, ou de dentifrice? Bonjour et bienvenue en France! Le voyage s'est bien passé? Je te présente ma (mère) et mon (père).
J'habite à …
J'habite une maison/un appartement.
Il y a (7) pièces.
Au rez-de-chaussée, il y a le salon/la salle de séjour/ la salle à manger/la cuisine/les W-C.
Au premier étage, il y a (3) chambres et une salle de bains.
une maison individuelle/un bungalow/un appartement

un vieux bâtiment/un immeuble
en banlieue/en ville/au bord de la mer
En haut/En bas, il y a …
Dehors il y a un jardin, une pelouse, des arbres, des fleurs.
Dans le salon/la cuisine, il y a de la moquette, un canapé, un frigo/congélateur, une cuisinière à gaz, un lave-vaisselle, un lavabo, une douche, une machine à laver, une télévision, le buffet, la baignoire, un miroir, une chaîne hi-fi, un fauteuil, un four à micro-ondes.

Grammar

- *près/loin de*
- *depuis* + present tense (revision)

Resources

Cassette D side 1
À l'oral, page 143 : Conversation 1
Cahier d'exercices, pages 58–59

Start by revising/brainstorming the language of meeting and greeting – *bonjour/salut/ça va*, etc., and the greetings which are in **1a**.

1a Which bubble belongs to each situation?

Reading (1–8). Students identify which speech bubble belongs with each situation.

Answers

1 e	2 c	3 b	4 g	5 a	6 h	7 d	8 f

1b Listen. Put the speech bubbles below in the right order, then match each one to a picture.

Listening. Students listen and put the speech bubbles in the correct order before matching them to the appropriate picture. In order to emphasise language for future use, it may be useful to ask students to change the speech bubbles to the *vous* form. When would they use each?

Tapescript

Bonjour, et bienvenue en France! Le voyage s'est bien passé?
Je te présente ma mère, Catherine, et mon père, René.
Entre, et assieds-toi! Es-tu fatiguée?
As-tu soif?
As-tu faim?
As-tu besoin d'une serviette, de savon ou de dentifrice?
Voici ta chambre. Bonne nuit!

Answers

f, g, b, d, a, e, c						
a 5	b 3	c 7	d 4	e 6	f 1	g 2

Before moving on to **2a**, introduce/revise rooms in a house with pictures or by describing what you do in each room. Introduce the other expressions in the key language box.

2a Copy and complete the letter with the words in the box.

Reading. Students complete the letter using the words given. Make sure they look very carefully at the gapped sentences and work out whether a verb, noun or adjective is needed in each gap.

Answers

1 bonjour	2 Lyon	3 maison	4 pièces	5 manger
6 cuisine	7 premier	8 trois	9 salle	

2b Using the letter in **2a** as a model, write approximately 50 words about your house or flat.

Writing. Students now write about their own house or flat. Remind them that they do not need to tell the truth! Encourage them to use the language and structures in the key language box as a guide. Are there any words they need to add?

3 In pairs. Practise this conversation, then replace the underlined words with your own details to make a new conversation.

Speaking. Students should practise the example conversation first, perhaps trying to learn it by heart, before replacing the underlined words with their own details. Point out to them how very useful it is to be able to spell your address quickly and correctly.

Before students attempt activity **4**, introduce types of housing as listed in the key language box. Can they work out what each is in English?

4a Listen. Put the pictures in the right order.

Listening (1–5). Students listen and put the pictures of the types of housing in the correct order.

Tapescript

1 *J'habite une maison qui est assez grande. Elle est toute neuve. Elle se trouve dans un village dans l'est. On a un grand jardin avec beaucoup de fleurs et d'arbres. J'aime bien habiter là.*

2 *On habite en banlieue dans un vieux bâtiment un peu moche. J'aime pas trop pour vous dire la vérité. Je préférerais habiter à la campagne ou à la montagne.*

3 *Nous habitons en ville, en plein centre – c'est très animé, j'adore ça. Il y a toujours des gens qui passent. Nous habitons un grand immeuble à vingt étages. C'est très moderne. Nous sommes au cinquième étage. C'est moyen, notre appart. On a un balcon aussi. J'aime bien chez moi.*

4 *J'habite avec mes grands-parents dans une petite maison rose au bord de la mer. C'est un bungalow – il y a un seul étage. C'est super cool – j'adore entendre la mer le soir.*

5 *J'habite dans une maison individuelle près d'un parc. Tous les jours après le collège, je rentre en courant pour aller jouer au foot avec mes copains.*

Answers

1 b	2 c	3 a	4 e	5 d

Rappel

loin de/près de. This reminds students how useful these words are. Put your town name on the board and make a list of places that are near and far.

4b Listen again. Copy and complete the grid. Note any extra details.

Listening (1–5). Students listen to the recording for **4a** again and complete the grid.

Answers

where	likes (✓/✗)	other detail(s)
1 village	✓	big garden, house quite big
2 suburbs	✗	would prefer country or mountains

Answers/continued …

where	likes (✓/✗)	other detail(s)
3 town centre	✓	very lively, always people passing, 5th floor flat, medium size with balcony
4 seaside	✓	with grandparents, bungalow (1 floor), likes hearing the sea
5 near to a park	✓	detached house, plays football with friends

Student's Book pages 130–131

Rappel

depuis + present tense. Ask students to write a list of their own sentences using *depuis*, e.g. *j'habite ici depuis dix ans, je fais du judo depuis un an, j'apprends le français depuis quatre ans, je joue de la guitare depuis deux ans.*

4c In pairs. Practise these conversations. Change the underlined words to make a new conversation.

Speaking. Students practise the example conversations, which use *depuis*, then change the words underlined to make a new conversation.

5a Listen. Copy and complete the grid.

Listening (1–5). Students listen to the estate agent describing different flats, and complete the grid.

Tapescript

1 *C'est un très joli appartement. Il y a un salon et une belle salle à manger. La cuisine est assez grande, il y a trois chambres. Il y a aussi une assez grande salle de bains.*

2 *Vous allez sûrement aimer cet appartement très moderne. C'est un appartement à deux chambres, avec cuisine, salle de séjour, et salle de bains.*

3 *Je suis sûre que cet appartement va vous plaire, mademoiselle. Il y a une cuisine et une jolie salle de bains. La cuisine et le salon sont assez grands, et il y a des W-C séparés aussi. Il y a trois chambres.*

4 *C'est un autre appartement à trois chambres qui est très bien aménagé. Il y a une petite cuisine, un salon, et une salle de bains. L'appartement n'est pas grand, mais il est très confortable.*

5 *Voici un de nos appartements de luxe, qui se trouve dans un immeuble neuf. Il y a une cuisine, une salle de séjour et la salle à manger, bien sûr. Mais on vous offre aussi deux salles de bains, des W-C, et quatre chambres.*

Answers

no. of bedrooms	no. of bathrooms	other details
1 3	1	lounge, dining room, big kitchen
2 2	1	modern, kitchen and sitting room

Answers/continued …

	no. of bedrooms	no. of bathrooms	other details
3	3	1	kitchen and lounge quite big, separate W-C
4	3	1	well equipped, small kitchen, lounge, not big but comfortable
5	4	2	luxury appt., new building, kitchen, sitting room, dining room, W-C

5b You are an estate agent. Describe each of these properties to your partner.

Speaking. Students take it in turns to describe to a partner the properties shown. Model this first with the class if necessary.

Before moving on to **6a**, brainstorm the language of furniture and appliances. Draw pictures of empty rooms – what would you need to fill them? Give students cards which they fill in with the name of a piece of furniture (from the dictionary if required) and then stick on to the empty room. Introduce the word for any item of furniture from the key language box which is not known. It may be useful to draw a house on the board or have a picture on an OHT to demonstrate *en haut, en bas, dehors.*

6a Read Émilie's letter. Make a list of all the rooms and furniture/appliances mentioned.

Reading. Students list all the rooms, furniture and appliances mentioned in the letter in French. They should check that they understand them all.

Answers

Pièces: le salon, la salle à manger, la cuisine, des W-C, un bureau, la salle de bains, quatre chambres, cave
Meubles: un canapé, une télévision, un lavabo, lave-vaisselle, la cuisinière à gaz, le congélateur

6b Write a summary of Émilie's letter in English (about 50 words).

Reading. Students summarise the letter in English. Remind them that a summary is not a word for word translation but must include all the relevant details.

Answers

All well in Scotland. Family kind.
House: medium size in quiet road near the town centre. 2 floors, 9 rooms: lounge, dining room, kitchen, toilet, office, bathroom and 4 bedrooms.
Carpet everywhere but no cellar or dishwasher.
Pretty garden – lawn, flowers and trees. Too cold to eat outdoors. Garage with freezer.

7a Make a note of what is in each picture. Then listen. Which item in each room does the speaker not mention?

Listening. Firstly, ask students to note in French what they can see in each picture. They then listen and identify what item(s) are not mentioned for each picture.

Tapescript

Oui, voici le salon, pièce très importante pour nous, on aime bien se reposer devant la télé à discuter. On a un grand canapé. La télé au milieu bien sûr. La chaîne stéréo sur le buffet là-bas et de l'autre côté, toutes les photos de famille – y en a qui sont pénibles…

Ensuite, voici la cuisine. Mes parents font la cuisine tous les deux. On a une cuisinière à gaz – mon père préfère ça. On a un frigo tout neuf là – style années cinquante – c'est chouette, non? Le congélateur est en haut, je viens piquer de la glace quand je regarde les films tard le soir! Mes parents ne s'en rendent pas compte. Il faut pas leur dire, hein! Oui, lave-vaisselle, indispensable! Et la machine à laver. Quand tu auras de la lessive, tu me diras, d'accord?

On va monter et je vais te montrer ta chambre et la salle de bains. C'est normal quoi, la baignoire, le lavabo, attention aux jouets de mon petit frère qui traînent sur cette jolie moquette bleue. Je n'aime pas ça la moquette dans la salle de bains, mais mes parents pensent que ça fait luxe! Joli petit miroir pour te regarder.

Dans ta chambre tu as une belle vue sur notre petit jardin. On dirait la campagne, non? Ma mère adore faire le jardinage. Regarde ses jolies fleurs et sa pelouse. Elle pique une crise si on marche là-dessus! En été, on fait des grillades sur la terrasse – j'aime bien être dehors, c'est sympa.

Answers

a the chairs	**b** the microwave		
c the shower	**d** the tree		

7b Describe one of these pictures to your partner. Your partner says which one you are describing.

Speaking. Students choose one of the pictures and describe it to a partner who must guess which one it is. You could extend this by giving students other pictures of properties. (Information on houses for sale in France can be downloaded off the Internet.)

Further practice of the language and vocabulary of this spread is provided as follows:

À l'oral, page 143: Conversation 1

Cahier d'exercices, pages 58–59

1 Voici ma chambre

(Student's Book pages 132–133)

Main topics and objectives

● Describing your room

Key language

Ma chambre est (très) grande/petite.
En face de/À côté de/À gauche/ À droite de …
il y a ….
   une chaîne hi-fi/lampe
   un magnétoscope/lit
   des posters aux murs
La moquette est (verte).
Les rideaux sont (bleus).
Je trouve ça (génial).
Je partage ma chambre avec …
J'ai une chambre à moi.

Grammar

● Prepositions

Skills/Strategies

● Using more sophisticated expressions

Resources

Cassette D side 1
Cahier d'exercices, page 60

Introduce the spread by brainstorming the language of furniture and appliances in a bedroom. Introduce any not known.

1a Read what Alain says about his room. Draw a plan and mark the position of the different items.

Reading. Students read the text, then draw a plan marking the various items mentioned.

Answers

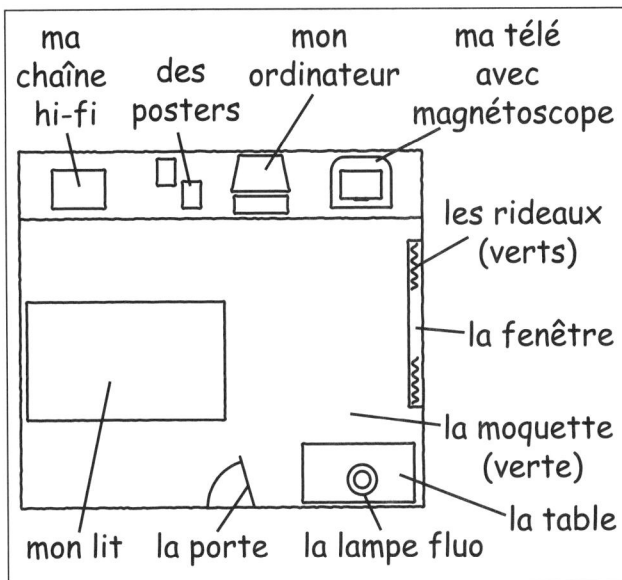

1b True or false?

Reading (1–5). Students read the text again and say whether the statements are true or false.

Answers

1 ✗	2 ✗	3 ✓	4 ✗	5 ✗

Rappel

Prepositions. This reminds students of some prepositions which will be useful in this context. Practise some sentences using them.

2a Listen. Choose the right answers.

Listening (1–5). Students listen and select the correct answers. First, get them to look at the sentences and work out what they mean. Impress on them the importance of preparing before listening.

Tapescript

– *Tu as une chambre à toi, Max?*
– *Oui, j'ai une chambre à moi. Je n'aimerais pas partager ma chambre. Je pense que ce serait difficile de partager, surtout à mon âge.*
– *Et toi, Josette, est-ce que tu dois partager ta chambre?*
– *Oui, je partage ma chambre avec ma sœur, mais je ne suis pas d'accord avec Max. Ma sœur et moi, on s'entend très, très bien, on aime bien être ensemble. On aime la même musique, alors c'est bien – j'ai une chaîne hi-fi dans la chambre.*
– *Et toi, Mohammed, tu as une chambre pour toi?*
– *Oui, j'ai beaucoup de chance, j'ai ma propre chambre et j'aime bien. J'ai une télé dans ma chambre. Je peux regarder ce que je veux quand je veux. J'ai accès à Internet – j'ai tout ce qu'il faut.*
– *Carmen, tu as une chambre pour toi?*
– *Non, je dois partager ma chambre avec ma petite sœur. C'est pénible. Elle est tout le temps en train de papoter – ça m'énerve. Je suis impatiente de quitter la maison et de m'installer dans un petit appart.*
– *Et toi, Tristan, tu as ta propre chambre?*
– *Carmen me fait pitié. Chez moi, tout est permis, personne n'a le droit d'entrer. Mes parents respectent ma chambre comme ma chambre. Je ne pourrais pas partager. Non, impossible…*

Answers

1 b	2 c	3 c	4 b	5 a

2b Read these statements from the listening in **2a**. Choose 3 which apply to you and your room, and explain what they mean in English.

Reading (a–i). Students choose 3 statements which apply to them and translate them.

Answers

a I share my room with my sister.
b I have my own room.
c I have my own room/a room to myself.
d No one is allowed to come in.
e I would not like to share my room.
f I have a stereo in my room.
g I have a TV in my room.
h I am impatient to leave home.
i My parents respect my room as my own.
j I have to share my room. It's terrible.

2c Listen again. Which 2 sentences does each person say?

Listening. Students listen to the recording for **2a** again and note which two of the sentences in **2b** each person says.

Answers

Max: c, e
Josette: a, f
Mohammed: b, g
Carmen: j, h
Tristan: d, i

3 In pairs. Practise this conversation. Change the underlined words to make a new conversation.

Speaking. With a partner, students practise the example conversation then change the underlined words to make a new conversation.

Tip box

Using more sophisticated phrases. This asks students to look again at Alain's letter to help them create more interesting sentences. Write two or three simple sentences on the board and brainstorm how they could be made more sophisticated.

4a Describe your room in approximately 100 words, showing how the items in it reflect your personality and interests.

Writing. Students write about their room using the key language box for support. Point out to them how important it is to personalise it by giving reasons and opinions, e.g. *j'ai une chaîne hi-fi car j'adore la musique, surtout la musique pop. Mon groupe préféré est …*

4b Make a presentation of approximately 2 minutes to your group/class about your bedroom.

Speaking. Encourage students to use the language from all the activities they have just done to put together their presentation – which should include personal details, opinions and some sophisticated sentences! They can then add this to their prepared speaking tape.

Further practice of the language and vocabulary of this spread is provided as follows:

Cahier d'exercices, page 60

2 On sort manger

(Student's Book pages 134–135)

Main topics and objectives

● Eating out with friends and colleagues

Key language

Comme hors-d'œuvre/plat principal/dessert/boisson, je voudrais/je prends ...
C'est quoi exactement?
C'est de la viande/volaille.
C'est du poisson. C'est un légume.
dans une sauce/en croûte/garni
C'est une spécialité écossaise/anglaise.

C'est un dessert ... C'est une sorte de ... avec ... servi(e) avec ...

Skills/Strategies

● Translating

Resources

Cassette D side 1

To underline the importance of language learning for **future** use, point out to students that eating out in France (or in Britain, but speaking French) is something they may have to do in a business context, as well as on holiday. Brainstorm the kind of language they might need. You may also wish to take time here to talk about typical French dishes and perhaps show some real menus. Look at the menu on page 134 and discuss the items on it.

1a Listen. Note each person's order from the menu below, in English.

Listening (1–5). Students listen and note down each order in English.

Tapescript

1 *Comme hors-d'œuvre, je voudrais des crudités. Comme plat principal, je voudrais le poulet rôti et des haricots verts, et comme dessert, je voudrais une glace, s'il vous plaît. Comme boisson, apportez-moi une bière.*
2 *– Vous avez choisi?*
   – Oui, quel est le plat du jour?
   – C'est une omelette aux fines herbes, madame.
   – D'accord. Je vais prendre l'omelette comme plat principal. Comme entrée, je vais prendre les fruits de mer, et comme dessert, la mousse au chocolat.
   – Oui. Vous voulez quelque chose à boire, madame?
   – Oui, une carafe de vin blanc, s'il vous plaît.
   – Tout de suite.
3 *– Pour moi, ça sera des crudités pour commencer, et après, le bœuf bourguignon. Quelle est la pâtisserie maison?*
   – C'est une tarte aux pommes.
   – Mmm, délicieux. Une pâtisserie maison, donc, et de l'eau, s'il vous plaît.
4 *Moi, je voudrais des crudités, le poulet rôti, et une glace. Je vais boire de l'eau aussi.*
5 *– Et vous, mademoiselle?*
   – Je vais essayer l'assiette de saucisson sec comme hors-d'œuvre.
   – Oui. Et comme plat principal?
   – Je voudrais le bœuf bourguignon. Comme dessert, une glace, s'il vous plaît.

– Oui. Qu'est-ce que vous voulez boire?
– De l'eau minérale, s'il vous plaît.

Answers

> **1** crudités (mixed, raw vegetables), roast chicken with green beans, ice-cream and beer
> **2** sea food, omelette, chocolate mousse, white wine
> **3** crudités, beef, apple tart and water
> **4** crudités, roast chicken, ice-cream and water
> **5** sausage/salami, beef, ice-cream and mineral water

1b In pairs. Practise this conversation. Change the underlined words to order what you would like from the menu.

Speaking. Students practise the example transaction and then choose their own meal from the menu given.

2a Match the questions and answers.

Reading (1–6). Students match the questions to the answers. Check that students know what they all mean.

Answers

| 1 c | 2 f | 3 a | 4 d | 5 e | 6 b |

2b Listen. Which dish is it? Listen again and note any details.

Listening (1–6). Students listen and note the dish of the day. They then listen again and note any extra details.

Tapescript

1 *– Quel est le plat du jour?*
   – C'est du bœuf bourguignon.
   – C'est quoi exactement?
   – C'est du bœuf, donc de la viande, avec des légumes comme des carottes et des oignons, dans une sauce.
2 *– Quel est le plat du jour?*
   – Aujourd'hui, c'est le colin aux épinards.
   – C'est quoi exactement?
   – C'est du poisson avec des épinards. Des épinards,

c'est un légume vert. C'est le légume préféré de Popeye, vous savez!

3 – *Quel est le plat du jour?*
  – *C'est la blanquette de poulet.*
  – *C'est quoi exactement?*
  – *C'est du poulet dans une sauce à la crème. C'est très bon.*

4 – *Quel est le plat du jour?*
  – *C'est une spécialité de notre région, c'est la quiche lorraine.*
  – *C'est quoi exactement?*
  – *Alors, c'est une sorte de tarte, faite avec des œufs, du lait et des lardons dedans.*

5 – *Quel est le plat du jour, s'il vous plaît?*
  – *C'est des poivrons farcis.*
  – *Et c'est quoi exactement?*
  – *Alors, des poivrons rouges, des poivrons verts, avec, à l'intérieur, du riz et des légumes, le tout dans une sauce tomate.*

6 – *S'il vous plaît, quel est le plat du jour?*
  – *Alors aujourd'hui, le plat du jour, c'est le steak haché.*
  – *Ah, et c'est quoi exactement?*
  – *Oh, ça ressemble à un hamburger, mais c'est très bon.*

Answers

> **1** d: beef with vegetables like carrots and onions in a sauce
> **2** e: fish with spinach – the favourite vegetable of Popeye!
> **3** b: chicken in cream sauce
> **4** c: sort of tart made with eggs, milk and bacon
> **5** f: red and green peppers stuffed with rice and vegetables in a tomato sauce.
> **6** a: like a hamburger

3a In pairs. Practise and learn this conversation.

Speaking. Students practise and learn the example conversation. Discuss why it is useful to learn a conversation like this. As extension, they could change various details in the conversation.

3b You are in a Scottish restaurant with a colleague who doesn't speak English. Explain the menu on the right to them in French. Use the words below and the key language to help you.

Speaking. Students explain the Scottish menu in French, using the notes and the key language box to help them. You may wish to model this with the class first to give them a clear idea of how the language is used.

3 On se plaint

(Student's Book pages 136–137)

Main topics and objectives

● Complaining at a restaurant

Key language

Je n'ai pas de (fourchette).
Ma cuillère/Ma fourchette/Mon couteau est sale.
L'addition n'est pas juste.
Mon potage est froid.
On n'a pas de sel ou de poivre.
Je n'ai pas de verre.
Je regrette … il n'y a pas de réservation/le restaurant est complet/il n'y a plus de (poulet)/il y a une erreur ici.
Ça ne va pas!
Je voudrais parler au gérant.
C'est incroyable!
Il y a une erreur ici.
Il y a une mouche dans mon potage!
Ce poisson est avarié!

Les fruits sont pourris.
Le potage est trop salé.
Le garçon/La serveuse est impoli(e).
C'est la dernière fois que je dîne ici!
Je suis vraiment désolé(e).
Ça ne m'est jamais arrivé avant.

Grammar

Skills/Strategies

● Writing a formal letter

Resources

Cassette D side 1
À l'oral, page 143: Transaction 2
Cahier d'exercices, page 61

Introduce the spread by brainstorming the kind of things you may have to complain about. Compare the results with the language in the key language box, adding to it if necessary.

1 Match each situation to a sentence in the key language.

Reading. Students match each picture to a sentence in the key language box.

Answers

> **1** L'addition n'est pas juste.
> **2** Je n'ai pas de verre.
> **3** Ma cuillère est sale.
> **4** Mon potage est froid.
> **5** Je n'ai pas de fourchette.
> **6** Ce couteau n'est pas propre.
> **7** On n'a pas de sel ou de poivre sur cette table.

Tip box

Listening skills. Remind students not to panic when they don't understand everything on tape. They should concentrate on what they do understand and also think in advance of the vocabulary they might hear.

2a Listen and note the problem.

Listening (1–4). Students listen to these restaurant complaints and note the problems.

Tapescript

1 – *Bonjour, monsieur, j'ai réservé une table pour huit heures, pour deux personnes.*
  – *Pour huit heures. À quel nom?*
  – *C'est au nom de Gourbeault.*
  – *Gourbeault, Gourbeault… ah non, non, je regrette, madame, il n'y a pas de réservation au nom de Gourbeault pour ce soir, et le restaurant est complet.*
  – *Le restaurant est complet? Ah non, ça va pas.*
2 – *Monsieur? Vous avez bien commandé le poulet rôti?*
  – *Oui, c'est ça, j'adore le poulet rôti, c'est mon plat préféré.*
  – *Ah oui, mais je… je regrette, monsieur, il n'y a plus de poulet.*
  – *Il n'y en a plus? Ça alors! Un restaurant sans poulet? Non, mais c'est quelque chose, ça…*
3 – *Garçon! Garçon!*
  – *Oui, mademoiselle?*
  – *J'aimerais bien commencer à manger mon omelette et mes frites, mais je n'ai pas de fourchette.*
  – *Oh, excusez-moi, mademoiselle, je vais vous en chercher une tout de suite.*
4 – *Garçon! Je voudrais l'addition, s'il vous plaît.*
  – *Oui, monsieur. Un moment, s'il vous plaît… La voilà.*
  – *Mais ça ne va pas! Il y a une erreur ici, cette addition n'est pas juste. Je n'ai pas bu trois bouteilles de vin, moi !*

Answers

> **1** No reservation made, restaurant full.
> **2** No more roast chicken.
> **3** No fork – wants to start eating omelette.
> **4** Mistake in the bill – has not drunk 3 bottles of wine!

2b Explain these sentences in English.

Reading (1–12). Students explain the sentences in English. It may be useful to do these round the class.

Answers

1 It's not all right!
2 I would like to speak to the manager.
3 It's unbelievable.
4 There is a mistake here.
5 There is a fly in my soup.
6 This fish is off.
7 The fruit is bad.
8 The waiter/waitress is impolite/rude.
9 It's the last time I eat here.
10 I am really sorry.
11 The soup is too salty.
12 It has never happened to me before.

2c In groups. Devise a sketch using some of the phrases in **1**, **2a** and **2b**. Practise using the model first.

Speaking. Students write their own sketch using the model for support. Is there any language they can use from the last time they learned about complaining, in Module 6? Encourage them to have fun with this!

3 You have had an unfortunate experience while dining with colleagues in a French restaurant. Changing the underlined words, write a letter of complaint to the manager.

Writing. Students write a letter of complaint using the sample letter for support. Point out that this is something they may need to do in a business context.

Further practice of the language and vocabulary of this spread is provided as follows:

À l'oral, page 143: Transaction 2

Cahier d'exercices, page 61

4 Les médias

(Student's Book pages 138–139)

Main topics and objectives

● Talking about books, magazines and films

Key language

C'est …
  un roman d'aventures/policier
  une bande dessinée
  une histoire de guerre
  un livre de science-fiction
C'est triste/super/génial/intéressant.
Le héros/L'héroïne est/était cool/courageux(-euse)/
  comique.
Le dernier livre que j'ai lu était …
Il s'agit de …
Je l'ai trouvé …
Je peux le recommander/l'envoyer.
Ça ne vaut pas la peine.
J'ai vu …
C'était très émouvant/romantique/nul/impressionnant.
C'est une comédie/un drame psychologique/un film de
science-fiction/un western/une histoire d'amour.
Il s'agit d'un homme qui …
C'est un film qui m'a touché/qui ne m'a fait aucun effet.
L'histoire était …
Les acteurs étaient superbes/bons/nuls.
La réalisation était parfaite/ennuyeuse.
J'aime les films qui me font rire/pleurer/peur.

Grammar

● Relative pronouns: *qui* and *que*

Skills/Strategies

● Using tenses
● Using linking words

Resources

Cassette D side 1
Cahier d'exercices, page 62 (ex. 10)

Begin with a class discussion of the types of books they like. What was the last book they read? What words do they already know in French to describe it and what words do they need to learn? Introduce the language from the key language boxes on page 138.

1a Andrew and Alice have written about the last books they read. Write a summary in English of what they say.

Reading. Students read and summarise the texts using the key language boxes for support.

Answers

Alice: I read 'Angela's Ashes' by Frank McCourt. It was about a boy's youth in Ireland and the USA. It was interesting and sad. Can recommend – can send you my copy.
Andrew: I read 'Lord of the Rings' by Tolkien. Great but very long. Was about a hobbit who has to conquer the forces of evil. Can recommend it but in French as the language is quite complex.

1b Listen. Copy and complete the grid.

Listening (1–5). Students listen and complete the grid in English.

Tapescript

1 *Le dernier livre que j'ai lu était un roman d'aventures, avec un héros génial. Il s'agit d'un jeune garçon qui part à la mer et qui voyage autour du monde avec une bande de pirates – mais c'est triste à la fin.*
2 *Le dernier livre que j'ai lu était une BD, une bande dessinée. J'adore les bandes dessinées. C'est très populaire en France. Quand on va à la Fnac, il y a toujours des gens en train de bouquiner dans la section BD.*

Eh bien, dans ce livre, il s'agit d'un héros très sympa, mais qui était un peu bête. Il doit sauver son ami de sa mère cruelle. Je l'ai trouvé super. Il faut le lire.
3 *Le dernier livre que j'ai lu était un polar, un roman policier de Raymond Chandler. Le héros était Philip Marlowe et il était super cool. Il s'agit d'une femme qui veut retrouver une pièce de monnaie très rare … Il faut le lire pour savoir la suite. Je l'ai trouvé génial. Je le recommande à tous.*
4 *Récemment, j'ai lu un roman super bien: 'La vague noire' de Michèle Kahn. C'est une histoire de guerre. Les protagonistes sont la famille Bernstein. L'histoire est inspirée du récit d'une rescapée des camps de concentration. Il y a beaucoup de tension et c'est triste par moments, mais j'ai beaucoup aimé cette histoire d'une famille courageuse.*
5 *Le dernier livre que j'ai lu était un livre de science-fiction. L'héroïne était une extra-terrestre très comique qui a beaucoup d'aventures différentes. Je l'ai trouvé très intéressant.*

Answers

	genre	hero(es)/heroine(s)	opinion
1	adventure	young boy – nice	sad
2	cartoon	very kind but a bit silly	great
3	police story	Philip Marlowe – cool	good
4	war novel	Bernstein family – brave	liked it
5	science fiction	funny extra-terrestrial	interesting

1c Write an e-mail in French to a friend about a book you have read recently. Write approximately 50 words.

Writing. Students type an e-mail on a book they have read recently, using the key language boxes and **1b** for support. Encourage them to write more than 50 words if they can – it could be used as practice for their writing exam.

2 Use the information in this graph to complete the text on the next page.

Reading. Look at the headings on the graph with students first. How many can they guess? They then use the information in the bar chart to complete the English text below.

Answers

1 football articles	**7** beauty advice
2 music pages	**8** horoscopes
3 surveys	**9** skateboarding articles
4 crosswords	**10** info on the stars
5 games/quizzes	**11** fashion pages
6 problem pages	

➕ A class survey could be carried out and the results written up.

Before going on to **3a**, brainstorm types of films. Describe a film you saw recently, using the language from the key language box. Write up the key phrases, then ask questions to get students to talk about films they have recently seen.

3a Listen to these people talking about a visit to the cinema. Copy and complete the grid.

Listening (1–5). Students listen to the tape and complete the grid as fully as they can.

Tapescript

1 – *Quel est le dernier film que vous avez vu?*
– *J'ai vu 'Billy Elliot'. C'était une comédie très émouvante et très impressionnante. Les acteurs étaient superbes et la réalisation était parfaite. J'aime les films qui me font rire.*

2 – *Quel est le dernier film que vous avez vu, madame?*
– *Le dernier film que j'ai vu, c'était 'La minute de vérité' avec Jean Gabin. C'était un drame psychologique. Je n'ai pas aimé. J'ai trouvé la réalisation ennuyeuse et l'histoire n'était pas intéressante. Les acteurs ont bien joué par contre.*

3 – *Excusez-moi, quel est le dernier film que vous avez vu?*
– *Le dernier film que j'ai vu était 'Le visionnaire', un film de science-fiction. Je n'ai pas aimé. Je ne me rappelle plus de l'histoire, je préfère les westerns, moi.*

4 – *Dites-moi monsieur, quel est le dernier film que vous avez vu?*
– *Le dernier film que j'ai vu? Voyons, c'était une histoire d'amour avec Juliette Binoche, c'était bien. Binoche est une très bonne actrice, mais j'ai oublié le nom du film. C'était bien quand même.*

5 – *Quel est le dernier film que vous avez vu, mademoiselle?*
– *C'était un dessin animé. Je suis allée au cinéma avec mon papa. C'était super.*

Answers

	genre	opinion	other detail(s)
1	comedy	moving, impressive, funny	great actors, good direction
2	psychological drama	did not like: boring production and story not interesting	actors good
3	science fiction	did not like	prefers westerns
4	love story	good	Juliette Binoche – good actress
5	cartoon	great	went with dad

3b In pairs, take turns to ask and answer the questions. Use the phrases in the key language box.

Speaking. Students work with a partner, asking and answering the questions as fully as they can, using the key language box for support. Model this first with the class if necessary.

Tip box

Linking words and past tenses. This reminds students to use linking words whenever they can, and to use the perfect and imperfect when talking about the past. Talk about the importance of linking words. Can they think of any more which would be useful? Encourage them to use as many as they can in activity **3c**.

3c Imagine you are a film critic. Write an article about the last film you saw (about 100 words). Write about the genre, the story, the actors, the location and – very importantly – your opinion.

Writing. Using the key language box for support, students write about the last film they saw. This could be used as one of their exam writing pieces.

Rappel

qui and *que*. Remind students of times when they have already met this: *j'ai un frère qui s'appelle …*, and *le dernier film que j'ai vu …* Practise with an exercise where the *qui* and *que* are missed out.

➕ Students could use the language they have learnt in this spread to describe a pop video they have recently seen.

Further practice of the language and vocabulary of this spread is provided as follows:

Cahier d'exercices, page 62 (ex. 10)

MODULE 8 · BIENVENUE EN FRANCE!

5 La télé

(Student's Book, pages 140–141)

Main topics and objectives

● Discussing TV

Key language

J'aime/J'aime beaucoup/Je n'aime pas tellement/
Je déteste ...
  les informations/les documentaires
  les dessins animés/les jeux
  le télé-journal/les émissions de musique/sport
  les films d'horreur/de science-fiction/d'amour
  les séries/les feuilletons/la publicité
parce que c'est...
  intéressant/amusant.
  passionnant/barbant.
  bête/ennuyeux.
Ça me fait rire.
Il s'agit de la vie personnelle de ...
C'est (une série) qui existe depuis ... ans.

Il/Elle a lieu (en Australie).
Le présentateur est ...
Les acteurs sont ...
C'est très populaire.
J'aime cette émission parce que ...

Skills/Strategies

● Using IT for research
● Using common sense!

Resources

Cassette D side 1
À toi! A and B, pages 194–195
Cahier d'exercices, pages 62–63 (exs 11–14)
À l'oral, page 143: Prepared talk

Introduce the spread by brainstorming favourite TV programmes. What kind of programmes are they in French? Introduce any types of programme not known.

1a List in French all the kinds of programmes mentioned in the text. Find a British example for each kind.

Reading. Students list the programme types mentioned and note a British example for each.

Answers

> **Programmes mentioned are:** les émissions de musique, les documentaires sur la nature, la publicité, les dessins animés, les films policiers, les films d'horreur et de science-fiction, les informations, le télé-journal, les films d'amour, les séries américaines et anglaises, les émissions de sport, les jeux télévisés, les feuilletons

1b Answer these questions.

Reading (1–9). Students read the text and answer the questions in English. Remind them that the points after each question indicate how many pieces of information they need to find.

Answers

> **1** Musical programmes and documentaries about nature (2)
> **2** She thinks they're silly. (1)
> **3** It makes him laugh. (1)
> **4** Detective films, cartoons, horror and science fiction films (any 2)
> **5** The news or perhaps a film (2)
> **6** American and English series (1)
> **7** Listening to classical music on the radio (2)
> **8** No, because there are no sports programmes on (2)
> **9** Game shows and soaps (2)

1c Listen. Identify the British TV programmes.

Listening (1–6). Students listen to the descriptions and identify the TV programmes. Remind them that, although they will not understand every word, they should be able to find the answer from the parts they do understand.

Tapescript

1 *C'est une série policière, qui a lieu à Glasgow. Il s'agit d'un détective et de ses collègues. Ils se livrent à des investigations sur des crimes souvent violents. L'acteur qui était la vedette est mort.*

2 *C'est une émission pour les jeunes, qui a lieu dans un collège à Londres. Il s'agit de la vie scolaire, et des vies personnelles des élèves et des profs.*

3 *C'est un dessin animé très populaire. Il s'agit d'une famille américaine. Le père adore manger, la mère a les cheveux très bizarres, le fils est très méchant, et la fille joue du saxophone.*

4 *C'est un feuilleton qui existe depuis plus de 25 ans. Il s'agit de la vie des habitants d'une rue dans le nord de l'Angleterre. C'est un programme qui est amusant mais qui peut être aussi tragique.*

5 *C'est un jeu télévisé, où on peut gagner beaucoup d'argent, jusqu'à un million de livres Sterling. Le présentateur crée beaucoup de tension pendant le jeu.*

6 *C'est une émission de sport qu'on peut voir le samedi après-midi. On y voit des matchs de rugby, des courses de chevaux, des concours d'athlétisme, et les résultats des matchs de foot joués ce jour-là.*

Answers

> **1** Taggart   **2** Grange Hill
> **3** The Simpsons **4** Coronation Street
> **5** Who wants to be a millionaire?   **6** Grandstand

What do young people watch in France? Find out and then ask your French assistant or penpal what he/she thinks of the programmes.

Students use the Internet to find out what some current TV programmes are. They can then ask a penfriend or assistant what they think of these programmes.

2a Do we watch too much TV? Read the opinions below and decide whether you agree, disagree or don't know.

Reading (1–6). Students note whether they agree, disagree or don't know. They will need to look carefully at each text – ask them to work in pairs to work out what the bubbles mean, before answering.

2b Summarise in English the opinions you agree with.

Reading. Students summarise the statements they agree with.

Answers

1 People watch too much TV and talk less – they're in front of the TV all the time.
2 TV is dangerous – people go out less. I only watch documentaries.
3 It's terrible watching TV all the time. TV is not good for society or your health.
4 Too many adverts.
5 TV is a form of education. You have to be selective, that's all.
6 Too much violence. Small children watch horrible things.

Tip box

Using common sense. This reminds students of the importance of this elusive quality when doing an exam!

3 Read the article. Answer the questions below in English.

Reading (1–4). Students read the text and answer the questions in English. They will not understand every word, but encourage them to read it through quickly first for gist. They should then look at the questions and go back and read the text a second time in more detail.

Answers

1 It has a lot of influence; they want to sell their products (1)
2 The agencies (1)
3 Alcohol and tobacco (2)
4 For the designer labels (1)

4 Prepare a presentation about your favourite TV programme.

Speaking. Students use the framework given to prepare a presentation on their favourite programme. This could be used as an on-going speaking assessment and can be recorded onto their prepared speaking cassette.

Further practice of the language and vocabulary of this spread is provided as follows:

À l'oral, page 143: Prepared talk

À toi! A and B, pages 194–195

Cahier d'exercices, pages 62–63 (exs 11–14)

All the key vocabulary and structures from this module are listed on the **Mots** pages 144–145. These can be used for revision by covering up either the English or the French. Students can check here to see how much they remember from the module and use them to prepare for the assessments.

Assessment materials for Modules 7 and 8 are available in the separate Assessment Pack.

Further speaking and grammar practice on the whole module is provided on **Cahier d'exercices** pages 64–65.

Entraînez-vous: À l'oral

(Student's Book pages 142–143)

Speaking practice: Modules 7 & 8

These spreads give regular practice in the three types of speaking activity required for the internally assessed speaking elements of the Standard Grade and Intermediate courses: conversations, transactions and prepared talks.

The activities on the speaking pages are designed to allow students to build up their speaking skills while working with a partner independently of teacher support. They also include handy hints on how students can improve their speaking grades.

Page 142 provides speaking activities for Module 7: a conversation about holidays generally, a transaction in a hotel and a prepared talk on last year's holidays.

Page 143 provides speaking activities for Module 8: a conversation introducing business colleagues, a transaction in a restaurant and a prepared talk on TV and the media.

Self-access reading and writing at two levels

These pages are designed to give students extra practice in reading and structured writing. There are two differentiated pages relating to each module: A and B. Page A is at an easier level and page B more challenging. You may wish students to work on the page most appropriate to their level or work through both pages. You may feel it is useful to work with students on the activities, but it should be possible for most students to work on them independently. The most appropriate time to use each page is indicated within the relevant teaching notes.

À toi! A, page 194

This page is best used after pages 140–141 of the Student's Book.

1a Read the text and answer the questions. Who …

Answers

1 Anonyme	2 Julia	3 Laura	4 Flore

1b Find the French for the following.

Answers

1 c'est débile   2 ça fait peur   3 je fais des cauchemars
4 se ronger les ongles   5 un bon film d'épouvante
6 avec un coussin devant les yeux   7 j'ai horreur de ça!
8 il y a beaucoup trop de violence
9 seul sur son canapé

2 What do you like watching on TV/video? Write approximately 100 words about your viewing habits.

À toi! B, page 195

This page is best used after pages 140–141 of the Student's Book.

1a Read the text and answer the questions in English.

Answers

1 He is a lawyer. (1)
2 3 days a week in the Paris office and 2 days a week in Edinburgh. (2)
3 He has an appartment in Edinburgh and he rents a small flat in Paris. (2)
4 His speaking French. (1)
5 At school and he spent 2 months living with a French family. (2)
6 He has to meet French colleagues, speak on the telephone and communicate by e-mail. (any 2)
7 Went to the Pyrenees with 2 friends from the Paris office. (2)
8 You get to know new people, new places and a completely different culture. (3)

1b Choose one of the 3 paragraphs and summarise it in English (30–35 words).

Answers

Possible answers:
Has worked in France for 2 years as a lawyer – divides his time between Paris and Edinburgh – has flats in both places.
Speaks French – learnt French at school and by spending 2 months with a French family. Speaks French both in Paris and in Edinburgh.
Now has good friends in France. Last year went on holiday with 2 friends from the Paris office. Lots of advantages of working abroad: getting to know new people, places and a new culture.

2 What do you think are the advantages of learning a foreign language? Write approximately 150 words.

Cahier d'exercices, page 58

1
Answers

a Fr	**b** Fr	**c** Sc	**d** Fr	**e** Sc	**f** Fr	**g** Fr
h Fr	**i** Sc	**j** Sc				

2 (writing task)

3
Answers

a 7	**b** 6	**c** 4	**d** 8	**e** 2	**f** 3	**g** 1	**h** 5

Cahier d'exercices, page 59

4 (writing task)

5
Answers

SCOTLAND	FRANCE
not many blocks of flats	many blocks of flats
gardens smaller but prettier	gardens larger but fewer flowers
carpets everywhere	floors wooden or tiled
eat in the lounge, watching TV	eat in the dining room or kitchen
eat less bread	bread with every meal
evening meal at about 6pm	evening meal at about 8pm
pupils wear a uniform	pupils wear jeans and trainers
drive on the left	drive on the right

Cahier d'exercices, page 60

6
Answers

a, c, f

7 (writing task)

Cahier d'exercices, page 61

8

Answers

intérieur – faim – menu – recommander – légumes – comme – glace – cuillère – entrée – désolé

9 (writing task)

Cahier d'exercices, page 62

10

Answers

a 7	**b** 6	**c** 4	**d** 1	**e** 9
f 8	**g** 3	**h** 10	**i** 2	**j** 5

11

Answers

1 f	**2** d	**3** j	**4** h	**5** a
6 g	**7** i	**8** b	**9** e	**10** c

Cahier d'exercices, page 63

12

Answers

a Jurassic Park	**b** Friends	**c** Digimon
d Elizabeth	**e** Stade 2	**f** Hit machine
g Astérix et Obélix		

13 (writing task)

14 (writing task)

Cahier d'exercices, page 64

1

Answers

a J'apprends le français depuis trois ans.
b J'habite ici depuis deux semaines.
c On regarde la télé depuis cinq heures.
d Elle travaille dans la cuisine depuis l'après-midi.
e Je fais mes devoirs depuis quatre heures.

2
Answers

a Je mangeais du chocolat.
b Michel regardait le film.
c Sonia et Raphaël écoutaient leurs CD préférés.
d Je jouais au foot toute la matinée.
e Le chien buvait beaucoup d'eau.

3
Answers

a des	b du	c de la	d des	e de l'
f du	g de la	h du	i de la	j du

Cahier d'exercices, page 65

8 Bienvenue en France!

Bilan

1 Dans quelle sorte de maison habites-tu?

2 Comment est ta maison/ton appartement?

3 Quelle est ta pièce préférée? Pourquoi?

4 Parle-moi de ta chambre.

5 Comment serait ta maison idéale?

6 Tu as déjà mangé au restaurant? Si oui, où et quand? Décris le repas.

7 Parle-moi d'un livre que tu as lu récemment.

8 Parle-moi d'un film que tu as aimé.

9 Qu'est-ce que tu aimes regarder à la télé? Pourquoi?

10 Qu'est-ce que tu as regardé hier soir?

Métro pour l'Écosse © Heinemann Educational 2002

65

Topic area	Key language	Grammar	Skills/Strategies
Déjà vu (pp. 146–149) Talking about meal times Talking about daily routine in the present and the past	*Je prends le petit déjeuner/déjeuner/goûter/dîner (à sept heures).* *Je me lève à … Je me lave. Je me brosse les dents.* *Je quitte la maison à … Je vais au collège en …* *J'arrive au collège à … Je rentre à la maison à …* *Je me couche à … Je me suis levé(e) à …* *Je me suis lavé(e). Je me suis brossé les dents.* *J'ai quitté la maison. Je suis allé(e) au collège en … Je suis arrivé(e) au collège à …* *Je suis rentré(e) à la maison à …* *Je me suis couché(e) à …*	Reflexive verbs: present and perfect	
1 Avez-vous la pêche? (pp. 150–151) Talking about healthy eating	*le pain/le beurre/la confiture/la salade/les crudités/le bifteck/le poisson/ les haricots verts/les pommes de terre/un yaourt/une glace/du potage/ des pâtes/un chocolat chaud/un Coca/un hamburger/des frites/une pizza/ des chips/une omelette/un gâteau/le sel/des œufs* *C'est sain/malsain.* *Il faut manger plus/moins/beaucoup de …*	*il faut* + infinitive	ICT: preparing a website
2 La cuisine et les habitudes (pp. 152–153) Talking about food preferences	*La nourriture est bonne/affreuse.* *Il y a beaucoup de choix/Il n'y a pas de choix.* *C'est cher/Ce n'est pas cher.* *C'est rapide. Il faut attendre.* *J'aime manger à la cantine. Je ne mange jamais à la cantine.* *Il faut faire la queue/attendre longtemps.* *Il n'y a que des frites. On mange tous ensemble. Je préfère apporter un casse-croûte. Il y a trop de monde.* *la cuisine chinoise/italienne/marocaine/thaïlandaise/indienne/française* *C'est facile à faire. J'aime les sauces différentes.* *C'est piquant et épicé. C'est très sucré.* *C'est différent et ça change de la cuisine française.*	Negatives: *ne … jamais, ne … que* The pluperfect tense	Tips for writing: tenses, opinions and linking words

Topic area	Key language	Grammar	Skills/Strategies
3 Ça ne va pas (pp. 154–155) Talking about illnesses and accidents	*J'ai très chaud/froid. Je n'ai pas faim. Je suis malade. J'ai mal au cœur. J'ai la grippe. Je suis enrhumé(e). J'ai vomi. Je me sens très fatigué(e). Je me suis blessé(e) à la jambe. Il/Elle est blessé(e). J'ai pris un coup de soleil. J'ai de la fièvre. Je tousse. Prenez ces comprimés/pastilles/ce sirop. Reposez-vous. Prenez rendez-vous chez le médecin. Buvez beaucoup d'eau. J'ai mal à la gorge/à la tête/au ventre/au dos/au cou/aux oreilles.*	Expressions with *avoir*	
4 Ça vaut le risque? (pp. 156–157) Talking about smoking and alcohol	*Je suis pour/contre les cigarettes. On a l'air plus adulte. Le tabac sent mauvais. On risque le cancer et les maladies cardiaques. Ça me détend. Si on s'habitue au tabac, on ne peut pas s'arrêter. Les cigarettes coûtent très cher. J'ai plus de confiance en moi. L'odeur du tabac cause des problèmes pour les autres.*	Using *on* Imperfect tense (revision)	Tips for a presentation
5 Vivre sainement (pp. 158–159) Discussing healthy lifestyles	Language from the whole module	Question words	Recycling vocabulary from other modules Using ICT to e-mail
Entraînez-vous: À l'écrit (pp. 160–161) En bonne forme	Language from Modules 8 and 9		Extended writing Using longer sentences Using comments and exclamations.
À toi! A and B (pp. 196–197)	Language from Module 9		Reading and writing skills

The vocabulary and structures taught in Module 9 are summarised on the **Mots** pages of the Student's Book, pages 162–163.
Further speaking practice on the language of the module is provided on **À l'oral**, page 176.
Assessment tasks for Modules 9 and 10 combined are provided in the separate Assessment Pack.

Déjà vu

(Student's Book pages 146–149)

Main topics and objectives

- Talking about meal times and your daily routine
- Talking about daily routine in the present and the past

Key language

Je prends le petit déjeuner/le déjeuner/le dîner (à sept heures).
Je me lève à …
Je me lave.
Je me brosse les dents.
Je quitte la maison à …
Je vais au collège en …
J'arrive au collège.
Je rentre à la maison à …
Je me couche à …
Je me suis levé(e) à …
Je me suis lavé(e).

Je me suis brossé les dents.
J'ai quitté la maison.
Je suis allé(e) au collège en …
Je suis arrivé(e) au collège à …
Je suis rentré(e) à la maison à …
Je me suis couché(e) à …

Grammar

- Reflexive verbs in the present and perfect

Resources

Cassette D side 2
À l'oral, page 176: Conversation 2
Cahier d'exercices, pages 66–67 (exs 1–4)

Start with a discussion of the differences in eating routines of the French and the British. Hopefully most General, Credit and Intermediate 2 students would be able by this point in the course to sustain much if not all of the discussion in French. Some students may have been to France – ask them about their experiences regarding meal times. Draw their attention to the key language box and the fact that the French use *prendre* for 'to have' a meal. Make sure they know the names for different meals and ask *À quelle heure est-ce que tu prends le petit déjeuner?*, etc.

1 Read the article and answer the questions below in as much detail as you can.

Reading (1–4). Students read the text and answer the questions in English.

Answers

> **1** Usually taken early, consists of buttered bread, croissants or chocolate pastry with coffee, tea or hot chocolate.
> **2** Lunch between 12–2pm and dinner between 7–9pm.
> **3** Biscuits, buttered bread, hot chocolate.
> **4** French people live in order to eat.

2a Listen. Who's speaking?

Listening (1–8). This gives practice in meals and meal times. Students listen and identify who is speaking from the information given.

Tapescript

1 Je prends le dîner à vingt heures.
2 Je prends le déjeuner à douze heures quarante-cinq.
3 Je prends le petit déjeuner à six heures trente.
4 Je prends le dîner à vingt heures quarante-cinq.
5 Je prends le repas de midi à treize heures quinze.

6 Je prends le petit déjeuner à sept heures quinze.
7 Je prends le repas du soir à dix-neuf heures trente.
8 Je prends le petit déjeuner à huit heures.

Answers

1 Laure	**2** Marie	**3** Laure	**4** Suzanne
5 Laure	**6** Suzanne	**7** Marie	**8** Marie

2b In pairs. Take the part of one of the people in **2a** and say when you have your meals. Your partner says who you are.

Speaking. Students assume the identity of one of the speakers in **2a** and say when they have their meals. Their partner works out who they are. They then swap roles.

Before moving on to **3a**, introduce/revise all the daily routine expressions form the key language box on page 147. Practise orally round the class, asking at what time students do all the activities.

Rappel

Reflexive verbs in the present tense. Point out the pattern which they have already met in a previous module. Practise this – *Tu te laves à quelle heure? / Je me lave à …* / Ask third person – *Il/Elle se lave à quelle heure?* Then go on to remind them of other reflexive verbs. A short written exercise, perhaps as homework, may be useful.

3a Read the text and answer the questions below in French.

Reading. This practises 3rd person singular forms of the verbs. Students read the comic strip and then answer the questions that follow in French.

Answers

> 1 Il se lève à six heures et demie.
> 2 Il se lave dans la salle de bains.
> 3 Il quitte la maison vers sept heures et demie.
> 4 Il va au collège en car.
> 5 Il prend son déjeuner à la cantine.
> 6 Il préfère dormir l'après-midi.
> 7 Il se couche à vingt-deux heures.

3b Use the model above to describe your daily routine. Write 100–150 words.

Writing. Students use **3a** and the key language box to help them write about their daily routine.

Student's Book pages 148–149

4a Listen. Copy and complete the sentences about this French Olympic athlete.

Listening (1–8). Students listen and complete the sentences in French.

Tapescript

Je fais de la natation depuis l'âge de quatre ans, et mon rêve, c'est de gagner une médaille aux jeux Olympiques.

Je me lève tous les jours à six heures. Après avoir pris un petit déjeuner léger – un jus de fruits, un yaourt – je vais à la piscine vers six heures et demie. À la piscine, je m'entraîne avec le club de natation jusqu'à huit heures et demie, quand je rentre à la maison.

Je me douche et je mange encore un peu, puis, à neuf heures, je quitte la maison pour aller au travail. J'ai un emploi dans une banque locale, où je commence à neuf heures et quart et finis à six heures moins le quart.

Directement après le travail, vers six heures du soir, je pars pour la piscine: et oui, il faut faire encore un peu d'entraînement … on s'entraîne pendant deux heures et demie, puis, vers huit heures trente, je me douche et je vais chez moi.

Je me couche tôt, vers dix heures, parce que je dois me lever de bonne heure le lendemain matin.

Answers

> 1 À 6h, elle se lève.
> 2 À 6h30, elle va à la piscine.
> 3 À 8h30, elle rentre à la maison.
> 4 À 9h, elle quitte la maison.
> 5 Elle travaille de 9h15 à 5h45.
> 6 À 18h, elle part pour la piscine/fait de l'entraînement.
> 7 À 20h30, elle se douche/va chez elle.
> 8 Vers 22h, elle se couche.

4b Read this text about Fabien Barthez. Choose the correct ending for each sentence.

Reading (1–11). This is a more complex reading text. Remind students to read the text first for gist, then to look at the questions before reading the text again for more detail. You may wish to exploit the text further by asking them to pick out the French expressions for some English ones you give. As a follow-up, you could introduce some more football vocabulary if your students are keen on the subject.

Answers

> 1 française   2 gardien de but   3 Monaco   4 2000
> 5 7h45   6 en voiture   7 à la maison   8 s'entraîner
> 9 3 heures   10 se lave   11 minuit

➕ 🖳 Students could find out some more about Barthez or other French footballers.

5a Listen and answer the questions in English.

Listening (1–10). Students listen and answer the questions in English. Remind students that the points indicate the number of pieces of information they are looking for. This activity builds on the vocabulary met so far and recycles some vocabulary from other modules.

Tapescript

– *Je suis Thomas. Moi, j'habite loin du lycée. Mon père m'emmène en voiture, mais on doit quitter la maison à sept heures pile. C'est trop tôt. J'arrive au lycée à huit heures moins cinq et les cours commencent à huit heures. Parfois je me demande si je devrais être interne …*

– *Je m'appelle Gilles. Je mets cinq minutes pour aller au collège. C'est pratique. J'habite juste à coté, j'y vais donc à pied. Je quitte la maison à huit heures dix pour arriver à huit heures quinze.*

– *Je m'appelle Benoît. Je prends le bus pour aller au lycée. Normalement, je mets une demi-heure pour y aller, mais ça dépend de la circulation. Je pars de chez moi à sept heures vingt-cinq et j'arrive avant huit heures.*

– *Liliane, c'est moi. Je prends mon vélo pour aller au collège – c'est bien pour l'environnement, c'est pas cher, et c'est le moyen de transport le plus rapide en plus! J'en ai pour vingt minutes. Je quitte la maison à huit heures moins vingt et j'arrive à huit heures pour le premier cours.*

– *Je m'appelle Maude. J'habite Paris alors je dois prendre le métro pour aller au collège. Je n'aime pas ça – c'est sale et il y a trop de monde. C'est long aussi. Je n'ai que quatre arrêts, mais normalement je mets au moins une demi-heure. Les cours commencent à huit heures et quart, alors je quitte la maison à sept heures et demie au plus tard.*

Answers

> 1 by car 2 7am 3 5 minutes 4 on foot 5 bus
> 6 the traffic
> 7 it's good for the environment, it's not expensive and it's the quickest way (3)
> 8 metro
> 9 it's dirty, there are too many people and it takes a long time (3)
> 10 7.30

5b In pairs. Interview each other.

Speaking. Students use the example conversation to interview one another about their daily routine. This practises some language from the recording in **5a**.

5c Write up the results of your interview.

Writing. Students write up the results of their interview, using the 3rd person singular.

Rappel

Reflexive verbs in the perfect tense. This reminds students that reflexive verbs conjugate with *être* in the perfect tense. Their past participle will therefore have to agree in gender and number with the subject. Ask them round the class what they did yesterday: *Tu t'es levé(e) à quelle heure hier?*, etc.

6a In pairs. Read this interview about what someone did yesterday, then change the details to talk about yourself.

Speaking. Students work in pairs, using the example conversation to support them in talking about what they did yesterday.

6b Using the perfect tense, describe what you did yesterday. Remember the rules for *être* verbs!

Writing. Students write about what they did yesterday, using their work from **6a** and the key language box as support. Remind them that not all verbs will be *être* verbs!

6c Describe what Luc did yesterday, using the perfect tense. Use the information given in activity **3a**.

Writing. Students change **3a** to the perfect tense, giving practice in the 3rd person singular. You may prefer to go over this with the whole class orally or on the board/OHP first.

Answer

> Il s'est levé à six heures et demie. Il s'est lavé et s'est brossé les dents à 6.45. Il a pris le petit déjeuner dans la cuisine. Il a quitté la maison vers 7h30 et il est allé au collège en car. Il est arrivé au collège à 7h45. Il a eu cours de 8h à 12h. À l'heure du déjeuner, il a mangé à la cantine. L'après-midi, il a passé son temps à dormir en classe. Il est rentré à la maison vers 16h30. Il s'est couché à 22h.

Further practice of the language and vocabulary of these spreads is provided as follows:

À l'oral, page 176: Conversation 2

Cahier d'exercices, pages 66–67 (exs 1–4)

1 Avez-vous la pêche?

(Student's Book pages 150–151)

Main topics and objectives

● Talking about healthy eating

Key language

le pain/le beurre/la confiture/la salade
les crudités/le bifteck/le poisson
les haricots verts/les pommes de terre
un yaourt/une glace/du potage/des pâtes
un chocolat chaud/un Coca
un hamburger/des frites/une pizza
des chips/une omelette/un gâteau
le sel/des œufs
C'est sain/malsain.
Il faut manger plus/moins/beaucoup de …

Grammar

● il faut + infinitive

Skills/Strategies

● ICT: preparing a website

Resources

Cassette D side 2
Cahier d'exercices, pages 67–68 (exs 5–6b)

Introduce the spread by brainstorming foods. *Qu'est-ce que vous aimez manger? Qu'est-ce que vous n'aimez pas manger? Quel est votre plat préféré? Êtes-vous allergique à certains produits?* Then go over the language in the key language box and decide with your students whether you need to add to it.

1a What are these food groups? Match the pictures with the names.

Reading (1–6). Students match the names to the pictures.

Answers

1 d	2 f	3 b	4 e	5 a	6 c

1b Match each food group with its functions.

Reading. Students match the food groups and functions.

Answers

a 3	b 6	c 4	d 2	e 1	f 5

1c Listen and check your answers to **1b**.

Listening. Students listen and check their answers to **1b**.

Tapescript

Eh bien, le lait, le fromage, le yaourt, ce sont des exemples de produits laitiers, et il nous faut les produits laitiers, parce qu'ils apportent des protéines et des vitamines, bien sûr, et aussi le calcium, ce qui est très important pour les dents et les os.

Le pain et les céréales donnent des vitamines, des fibres et de l'énergie, et il faut en manger. Pour avoir de l'énergie qui dure, le pain et les céréales sont vraiment efficaces.

Les fruits et les légumes, on le sait, contiennent des fibres et des vitamines, surtout la vitamine C. Il faut en manger 4 ou 5 fois par jour.

Les produits sucrés, tels que le chocolat, les biscuits et les bonbons, contiennent beaucoup de calories. Ils donnent de l'énergie mais ça ne dure pas.

La nourriture grasse, il faut l'éviter autant que possible, parce que le cholesterol là-dedans est très mauvais pour la santé.

Quant à la viande et au poisson, ces aliments sont une source de protéines et de vitamines, mais il faut faire attention aussi parce qu'ils contiennent beaucoup de matières grasses.

1d Give 2 items in French which belong to each food group.

Writing. Students write 2 items in French for each food group.

2a Copy the grid. Listen and note what Sarah and Thomas have for each meal. Is their diet healthy or unhealthy?

Listening. Students listen and note what the speakers eat. Make sure they leave enough space in their grids to write all the information.

Tapescript

– Eh bien moi, je trouve qu'en général je ne mange pas trop mal. Le matin, je prends du pain pour le petit déjeuner, avec du beurre et de la confiture à la fraise. Je bois un bol de café.
À midi, je mange à la cantine. Comme hors-d'œuvre, il y a souvent de la salade ou des crudités, qui sont très bonnes pour la santé. Normalement on a le choix entre deux plats: un bifteck, peut-être, ou du poisson, avec des haricots verts ou parfois des pommes de terre. Comme dessert, il y a un yaourt ou une petite glace.
Le soir, à la maison, on prend souvent du potage et puis des pâtes ou de la salade. On mange légèrement le soir. Je ne bois que de l'eau, parce que c'est bon pour la peau, n'est-ce pas?

– *Le matin, je ne mange rien, parce que je n'ai pas le temps: je suis toujours en retard pour le car … quelquefois mon père me force à boire un peu de chocolat chaud, et c'est tout.*
À midi, je vais en ville avec mes copains au lieu d'aller à la cantine. On va au fast-food, où on prend un hamburger et des frites, et on boit toujours un grand Coca. Parfois on prend une glace ou un gâteau avant de retourner au collège.
Le soir, je mange devant la télé. Je n'aime pas ce que mes parents préparent. Je préfère manger une pizza surgelée et un paquet de chips. C'est rapide et c'est très bon. Mais je sais bien que ce n'est pas très sain.

Answers

	breakfast
Sarah	bread with butter and strawberry jam, bowl of coffee
Thomas	nothing – sometimes a bowl of chocolate
	lunch
Sarah	salad or chopped raw vegetables, steak or fish with green beans or potatoes, yoghurt or ice-cream
Thomas	hamburger and chips, Coke, sometimes ice-cream or cake
	dinner
Sarah	often soup, then pasta and salad, drinks water
Thomas	frozen pizza, packet of crisps
	healthy? (✓/✗)
Sarah	✓
Thomas	✗

2b Try the test!

Reading. Students complete the test and check their answers. They could work in pairs, if you prefer, taking it in turns to read out the questions and the possible answers in the style of 'Who wants to be a millionaire?'.

Answers

1 a	**2** c	**3** b	**4** a	**5** c	**6** c

Rappel

il faut + infinitive. Remind students that this is an extremely useful expression to know and use. Brainstorm different examples – *il faut faire les devoirs, il faut apprendre les verbes irréguliers, il faut écouter le prof, il faut arriver à l'heure*, etc.

3 Prepare a radio advert to encourage people to eat healthily. Use the phrases on the right.

Speaking. Students prepare a radio advert for healthy eating. You may need to brainstorm some ideas first. Go over the phrases given and add more if possible.

Use what you have done in **3** to prepare a website encouraging people to eat more healthily.

Students can show off their IT skills in this activity.

4 What are the advantages and disadvantages of fast food? Give your opinion in 75–100 words.

Writing. Students give their opinions of fast food. Go over the expressions on the notepad first and add more if necessary. This could be used as preparation for an exam piece of writing. If so, remind students to include other tenses, e.g. *Hier, j'ai mangé chez McDonalds, c'était délicieux mais très cher.*

Further practice of the language and vocabulary of this spread is provided as follows:

Cahier d'exercices, pages 67–68 (exs 5–6b)

2 La cuisine et les habitudes

(Student's Book pages 152–153)

Main topics and objectives

● Talking about food preferences

Key language

La nourriture est bonne/affreuse.
Il y a beaucoup de choix. Il n'y a pas de choix.
C'est cher. Ce n'est pas cher.
C'est rapide. Il faut attendre.
J'aime manger à la cantine. Je ne mange jamais à la cantine.
Il faut faire la queue/attendre longtemps.
Il n'y a que des frites. On mange tous ensemble.
Je préfère apporter un casse-croûte.
Il y a trop de monde.
la cuisine chinoise/italienne/marocaine/thaïlandaise/ indienne/française
C'est facile à faire.
J'aime les sauces différentes.
C'est piquant et épicé.
C'est très sucré.
C'est différent et ça change de la cuisine française.

Grammar

● Negatives other than *ne ... pas*
● The pluperfect tense

Skills/Strategies

● Tips for writing

Resources

Cassette D side 2
À l'oral, page 176: Conversation 1
Cahier d'exercices, page 68 (exs 7–8)

Begin by discussing in French what students do for lunch. Ask how many eat in the school canteen and ask them what they think of it. Write the expressions from the key language box on the OHT/board and ask questions about them, e.g. *Il y a beaucoup de choix?*, etc.

1a Listen and read, then note the key points these young people mention about school meals.

Listening (1–4). Students listen to and read the text and note the key points each person makes. You may wish to play the recording first before looking at the text, to see if students can pick out key facts or whether each speaker likes the canteen food or not. Then listen and read again for more detail.

Tapescript

1 *Je ne mange jamais à la cantine – j'ai horreur de ça. Il faut faire la queue et attendre longtemps, et il n'y a que des frites! Le café à côté est meilleur.*
2 *Moi, je trouve sympa de manger à la cantine. On mange tous ensemble en famille et la nourriture est bonne. J'aime bien.*
3 *Je n'aime pas manger à la cantine. Il n'y a pas beaucoup de choix – je préfère apporter un casse-croûte.*
4 *Je n'aime pas manger à la cantine, il y a trop de monde. Je préfère apporter des sandwichs. Je les prépare le soir avant de me coucher, comme ça ils sont faits. Je n'aime pas la bouffe à la cantine.*

Answers

1 Never eats in the canteen, hates it, you have to queue and there's only chips. The café next door is better.
2 Likes eating in the canteen, eating together as a family and the food is good.
3 Doesn't like it – not a lot of choice, prefers to bring a snack.
4 Doesn't like it – too many people, prefers to bring sandwiches, doesn't like the food there.

1b Look at the opinions in the key language box. Write them out in two lists: for and against school meals.

Reading. Students divide the language in the key language box into categories for and against school meals.

Answers

For:
La nourriture est bonne.
Il y a beaucoup de choix.
Ce n'est pas cher.
C'est rapide.
J'aime manger à la cantine.
On mange tous ensemble.
Against:
Il y a trop de monde.
Je préfère apporter un casse-croûte.
Il faut faire la queue.
Il faut attendre.
La nourriture est affreuse.
Il n'y a pas de choix.
C'est cher.
Je ne mange jamais à la cantine.
Il n'y a que des frites.

Rappel

Negatives. This reminds students to use a range of negatives. Give them phrases and ask them to try to put them into as many negatives as possible, e.g. *je vois: je ne vois pas, je ne vois jamais, je ne vois personne, je ne vois rien*, etc.

Before tackling **2a**, introduce the expressions from the key language box at the bottom of the page. Say what sort of cuisine you like and give one of the reasons. Ask students whether they agree with you.

2a Listen. Note in French the type of food these people like. Then listen again and select a phrase from the key language below for each person.

Listening (1–5). Using the key language box as support, students listen and note the type of food the speakers like. They then add a phrase from the key language box for each person.

Tapescript

1 Moi, j'adore la cuisine indienne. C'est piquant, épicé. En plus, c'est bon pour la santé.

2 Moi, je suis fanatique de la cuisine thaïlandaise. C'est délicieux et c'est très facile à faire. C'est simple, quoi! Ma maman adore quand je lui fais des nouilles ou un curry.

3 Ma mère vient du Maroc et c'est vrai que la cuisine marocaine est très bonne, le couscous et les desserts aussi, très sucrés – délicieux!

4 J'aime beaucoup la cuisine chinoise – le canard laqué, le riz, les calamars, les coquilles St Jacques au piment. C'est différent et ça change de la cuisine française.

5 Moi, j'adore les pizzas et les pâtes, la cuisine italienne. J'aime les tomates et le fromage. J'aime aussi les sauces différentes, bolognaise ou carbonara.

Answers

1 indienne – C'est piquant et épicé.
2 thaïlandaise – C'est facile à faire.
3 marocaine – C'est très sucré.
4 chinoise – C'est différent et ça change de la cuisine française.
5 italienne – J'aime les sauces différentes.

2b In pairs. What kind of food do you prefer and why?

Speaking. Students discuss with a partner, comparing the kind of food they like and why. Listen to answers round the class.

3 Read this article and answer the questions below in English.

Reading. Students read the article and answer the questions in English. Afterwards, discuss as a class whether students agree with the descriptions of the eating habits of Scottish and French people. Discuss stereotypes if students are able.

Answers

1 They like fish and chips, they eat jam with lamb and their bread is like a piece of plastic.
2 Fish, oysters and vegetables
3 Snails, frogs legs and raw meat – don't like spicy things.

Le détective

The pluperfect tense. Point out to students that the pluperfect works the same way in French as in English, so it is really not difficult. Ask them to work out why it is *elle était allée*. Practise other examples. They will mainly need this tense for recognition purposes only.

Tip box

Writing tips. Remind students to check that their final piece of exam writing reflects this advice on including a range of tenses, opinions, and linking and qualifying words.

4 Write an article on food (100 words or more). Use the model below (on the right) to help.

Writing. Students use the model to write about food. They should include a variety of tenses, linking words, opinions and sophisticated sentences. You may wish to create a poster or wall display highlighting what makes a good piece of writing.

Further practice of the language and vocabulary of this spread is provided as follows:

À l'oral, page 176: Conversation 1

Cahier d'exercices, page 68 (exs 7–8)

3 Ça ne va pas

(Student's Book pages 154–155)

Main topics and objectives

● Talking about illnesses and accidents

Key language

J'ai très chaud/froid. Je n'ai pas faim.
Je suis malade. J'ai mal au cœur.
J'ai la grippe. Je suis enrhumé(e).
J'ai vomi. Je me sens très fatigué(e).
Je me suis blessé(e) à la jambe. Il/Elle est blessé(e).
J'ai pris un coup de soleil.
J'ai de la fièvre. Je tousse.
Prenez ces comprimés/pastilles.
Prenez ce sirop.

Reposez-vous.
Prenez rendez-vous chez le médecin.
Buvez beaucoup d'eau.
J'ai mal à la gorge/tête.
J'ai mal au ventre/dos/cou/aux oreilles.

Grammar

● Expressions with *avoir*

Resources

Cassette D side 2
Cahier d'exercices, pages 69–70 (exs 9–12)

To introduce this spread, you may wish to briefly revise parts of the body and then go on to talk about illnesses and the construction *j'ai mal …* Go over the language in the key language box. Most are in the 1st person. Practise adapting them to other parts of the verb. Check students know what they all mean, perhaps by asking them to mime, e.g. *J'ai vomi, qu'est-ce que c'est?*!

1a Match the pictures to the problems in the key language box.

Reading (a–n). Students match the pictures to the language in the key language box.

Answers

a J'ai très froid.	**b** J'ai vomi.
c Je tousse.	**d** J'ai très chaud.
e J'ai mal au cœur.	**f** J'ai la grippe.
g Je suis enrhumé.	**h** Je me suis blessé à la jambe.
i J'ai de la fièvre.	**j** J'ai pris un coup de soleil.
k Je suis malade.	**l** Il est blessé.
m Je me sens très fatiguée.	**n** Je n'ai pas faim.

Before moving on to **1b**, introduce the advice phrases from the key language box at the bottom of page 154. Say a piece of advice and students must say an illness/problem which matches.

1b Listen to these conversations in a chemist's. Note the problem (use your answers for **1a** a–n) and the action suggested – there may be more than one!

Listening (1–6). Students listen to the conversations in the chemist's and note the problem and the remedy in French. Point out to students that they can take rough notes while listening and then tidy up their spelling using the key language box.

Tapescript

1 – Oh là là, je me suis blessé à la jambe ce matin en descendant de l'escalier. Aïe, ça fait mal. Qu'est-ce que je devrais faire?
 – Reposez-vous un peu au lit, et prenez ces comprimés.
2 – Bonjour, j'ai mal au cœur depuis ce matin, et ce n'est pas normal.
 – Eh bien non, mademoiselle. Vous avez sûrement mangé quelque chose qui ne vous réussit pas. S'il vous plaît, buvez beaucoup d'eau et reposez-vous au lit.
3 – Salut, je me sens très fatigué tout le temps, même si je me couche de très bonne heure. Qu'est-ce que j'ai?
 – Prenez rendez-vous chez le médecin, monsieur.
4 – J'ai vomi ce matin, et plusieurs fois. Et maintenant, je n'ai pas du tout faim. Qu'est-ce que vous pouvez me conseiller?
 – Je vous conseille de prendre ce sirop. Il est très efficace contre le mal de ventre.
5 – Je suis vraiment enrhumée depuis deux jours. Je crois que j'ai la grippe. La nuit, j'ai très très chaud et je ne peux pas dormir.
 – Vous devriez vous reposer au lit. Prenez ces comprimés et ces pastilles deux fois par jour aussi.
6 – Je ne sais pas ce que j'ai, mais je me sens vraiment malade. J'ai froid tout le temps et ce matin j'ai vomi.
 – Mmm. Pour être sûr, monsieur, il faut prendre rendez-vous chez le médecin.

Answers

	problem	action
1	h	Reposez-vous. Prenez ces comprimés.
2	e	Buvez beaucoup d'eau. Reposez-vous.
3	m	Prenez rendez-vous chez le médecin.
4	b, n	Prenez ce sirop.
5	g, f, d	Reposez-vous. Prenez ces comprimés et ces pastilles.
6	k, a, b	Prenez rendez-vous chez le médecin.

Rappel

Expressions with *avoir*. Practise this for other parts of the verb and for other *avoir* expressions. How many other expressions which use *avoir* can students remember?

2a Copy and complete this conversation with the words on the right.

Reading. Students complete the conversation at the doctor's using the words given. Remind them to look carefully to see whether there should be a noun, adjective or verb in each gap.

Answers

1 asseyez-vous	**2** vais	**3** gorge	**4** enrhumé	**5** soif
6 dormir	**7** examiner	**8** bouche	**9** grippe	**10** sirop
11 pastilles	**12** lit	**13** jours	**14** revoir	

2b Listen. Copy and complete the grid.

Listening (1–4). Students listen and complete the grid in English.

Tapescript

1 – *Bonjour madame. Comment allez-vous aujourd'hui?*
  – *Oh, vous savez, docteur … j'ai mal aux oreilles et à la gorge depuis une semaine.*
  – *Aux oreilles et à la gorge … vous permettez? … Mmm … Dites 'ahh' …*
  – *Aah …*
  – *Ah oui, oui, ce n'est pas grave. Je vais vous donner du sirop. Il faut prendre ce sirop trois fois par jour, après les repas. Vous avez compris?*
  – *Oui, merci docteur.*
2 – *Ah, monsieur Pinaud. Est-ce que vous allez mieux?*
  – *Ah non, docteur. J'ai toujours très mal au ventre, et hier soir, j'ai vomi. J'ai mal au cœur ce matin encore une fois. Ça devient pénible.*
  – *Bon, je vais vous prendre rendez-vous à l'hôpital.*
3 – *Bonjour madame.*
  – *Bonjour docteur. C'est mon fils. Il s'est blessé à la tête ce matin, en jouant dans le jardin. Maintenant, il a très mal à la tête.*
  – *Oh mon pauvre… attends… je peux regarder? … Ne pleure pas… ah oui. Madame, je vous donne ces comprimés pour votre fils. Il doit prendre un comprimé toutes les deux heures. D'accord?*
  – *Un comprimé toutes les deux heures. Merci, docteur.*
4 – *Ah docteur, bonjour.*
  – *Bonjour madame. Qu'est-ce qui ne va pas?*
  – *J'ai mal au dos depuis deux semaines maintenant.*
  – *Je peux vous examiner? Vous avez mal au cou aussi?*
  – *Oui, oui, j'ai mal au cou – surtout la nuit.*
  – *Bon, je vous conseille de rester au lit pendant deux ou trois jours, pour voir si ça vous aide. Revenez me voir dans une semaine, s'il vous plaît. Fixez un rendez-vous maintenant avec la réceptionniste.*
  – *OK, merci docteur.*

Answers

	symptoms	doctor's advice
1	earache/sore throat	take cough mixture 3 times a day
2	tummy ache/been sick, feel sick	go to hospital
3	injured head	1 tablet every 2 hours
4	bad back and neck	stay in bed for 2 or 3 days, come back in a week

2c In pairs. Practise the conversation in **2a** three times, changing the problem and the doctor's advice each time.

Speaking. Students adapt the conversation in **2a** to create three new conversations using different problems and remedies.

3a Listen and read the text, then answer the questions.

Reading (1–4). This text introduces a few pieces of new language which students should be able to understand quite easily. Students read the text and then answer the questions in English.

Answers

1 There has been an accident. His friend is injured. (2)
2 He doesn't know. He is bleeding. (2)
3 In the garden opposite. (2)
4 Rings for an ambulance. (1)

3b Find the French for …

Reading (1–4). Students find the French for the expressions in the text.

Answers

1 Mon ami est blessé.
2 C'est grave?
3 Je vais téléphoner pour une ambulance.
4 Va le rejoindre.

➕ Students adapt the details in the conversation in **3a** to make new conversations.

Further practice of the language and vocabulary of this spread is provided as follows:

Cahier d'exercices, pages 69–70 (exs 9–12)

4 Ça vaut le risque?

MODULE **9** EN BONNE FORME

(Student's Book pages 156–157)

Main topics and objectives

● Talking about smoking and alcohol

Key language

Je suis pour/contre les cigarettes.
On a l'air plus adulte.
Le tabac sent mauvais.
On risque le cancer et les maladies cardiaques.
Ça me détend.
Si on s'habitue au tabac, on ne peut pas s'arrêter.
Les cigarettes coûtent très cher.
J'ai plus de confiance en moi.
L'odeur du tabac cause des problèmes pour les autres.

Grammar

● Using *on* (revision)
● Imperfect tense (revision)

Skills/Strategies

● Tips for a presentation

Resources

Cassette D side 2
À l'oral, page 176: Prepared talk
À toi! A and B, pages 196–197
Cahier d'exercices, pages 70–71 (exs 13a–14)

Introduce the spread by brainstorming the health problems facing young people. What language do they need? Introduce the topic of smoking. Put the expressions from the key language box on the board/OHT. How many can they work out? Do they agree with them?

1a Read the speech bubbles and write them in 2 lists – positive and negative.

Reading. Students divide the speech bubbles into two categories, positive and negative.

Answers

Positive: Ahmed, Hervé, Sabrina, Yolande
Negative: Alicia, Sylvie, Élodie, François, Elsa

1b Listen to these young people's opinions and decide who from **1a** is speaking.

Listening (1–9). Students listen and decide who is speaking based on what they say. Warn them that they will need to listen carefully, as what they will hear is not word for word what they see in the speech bubbles in 1a.

Tapescript

1 *Alors, moi, je pense que si on fume, on a l'air plus adulte.*
2 *Ah non, je ne suis pas d'accord, et en plus, le tabac sent mauvais.*
3 *Et puis, on risque le cancer et des maladies cardiaques.*
4 *Non, moi, j'aime bien fumer – c'est reposant de fumer une cigarette et ça me détend.*
5 *Oui, mais le problème c'est que si on s'habitue au tabac, on ne peut pas s'arrêter.*
6 *Et elles coûtent très cher, les cigarettes.*
7 *Moi, je veux faire la même chose que mes copains, donc je fume. C'est pour ça que je fume en effet.*
8 *Pour moi, c'est une question de confiance, si j'ai une cigarette à la main, j'ai plus de confiance en moi.*
9 *Mais, c'est égoïste! L'odeur du tabac cause des problèmes pour les autres, y compris les petits enfants.*

Answers

1 Ahmed	2 Alicia	3 Elsa	4 Hervé	5 François
6 Élodie	7 Yolande	8 Sabrina	9 Sylvie	

Rappel

Using *on*. This reminds students how often *on* is used in French. Look at different phrases with *on* and how they can be translated each time.

Tip box

Tips for a presentation. Remind students – again! – of the importance of using different tenses, link words, opinions and varied vocabulary. Writing and speaking give them their opportunities to show off!

1c Do you smoke? Why/why not? Prepare a short talk for your class.

Speaking. Students give their opinion on smoking. This could be used as an on-going speaking assessment and recorded onto their speaking cassette.

1d You have seen these pictures in a magazine. What do you think? Write to the magazine in French. Answer these questions.

Writing. Students write a letter to the magazine, based on the questions given. Prepare this with the class first if necessary,

2a Listen to these radio adverts. Match each one with a campaign poster.

Listening (1–4). Students listen to the adverts and match each one to a poster. Remind them that they will not understand everything, but should understand enough if they listen out for key phrases. They could work with a partner before they listen and try to predict some of the language they might hear for each poster.

Tapescript

1 – Allez, juste un petit verre de vin avant de partir…
– C'est gentil, mais j'ai la voiture. Et je ne bois rien quand je conduis ma voiture.
– Un tout petit peu de vin rouge, ça peut pas vous causer de problème …
– Non, vraiment, non merci. Un jus de fruits, peut-être?
– Mais écoutez, moi, j'ai bu six verres de vin ce soir, et regardez comme je suis.
– Oui, exactement. Je vous laisse. Merci de votre hospitalité.

2 – Ah, quelle jolie photo! C'est votre fille? Quel âge a-t-elle? Elle va à quel collège?
– C'était ma fille. Elle avait 15 ans. Elle allait au collège dans notre village.
– Elle avait 15 ans? Elle allait à notre collège local? Mais … ?
– Oui, elle est morte il y a sept mois et quatre jours. Elle allait aussi en boîte … et elle se droguait. Elle croyait ça cool … mais plus maintenant …
– Surveillez vos enfants, qu'ils ne vivent pas leur vie à l'imparfait.

3 – Tu as de beaux yeux, tu sais …
– Merci.
– J'adore tes cheveux longs …
– C'est gentil.
– Ta bouche est belle.
– Je te remercie.
– Et tes mains sont des mains de princesse …
– Mmm … euh … oui, merci beaucoup …
– Est-ce que tu veux sortir en boîte avec moi ce soir?
– Non merci, les doigts marron, les dents jaunes, la bouche qui pue et une gorge comme un homme de 65 ans, curieusement, ça ne me plaît pas. Et en plus, l'odeur me donne mal au cœur.

4 – Tu n'as pas faim? Tu n'as pas envie de manger? Ou tu as envie de manger trop? Tu te trouves trop mince? Tu te trouves trop grosse? On est là pour toi, n'hésite pas à nous contacter: numéro vert 08 00 81 68 16.

Answers

1 d	2 a	3 c	4 b

Rappel

The imperfect tense. Remind students of when to use and how to form the imperfect tense. In this instance, it is used to mean 'used to'. Ask students the question *Que faisais-tu quand tu avais 10 ans?*, etc.

2b Read the text and answer the questions.

Reading (1–6). Students read the text and answer the questions which follow in English. Remind them of reading strategies: read for gist first, look at the questions, then read again for more detail.

Answers

1 Marie-Jo	2 Daniel	3 Ludo	4 Manon
5 Ludo	6 Manon		

2c Choose 2 letters and summarise their points in English.

Reading. Students write a summary of any two of the letters. This practises understanding more detail. They could work in pairs if you prefer.

Answers

Manon: Young people know the risk of smoking, but they don't care because it's cool. She thinks it's stupid.
Ludo: He thinks alcohol is dangerous. Everyone drinks, even parents. You don't know what you're doing when you have drunk too much.
Daniel: When he was 16 he smoked and drank to impress others. He realised he had to stop to avoid lung cancer.
Marie-Jo: Eating disorders amongst young people are a risk. The media make people feel you must be slim, and make young people suffer.

Further practice of the language and vocabulary of this spread is provided as follows:

À l'oral, page 176: Prepared talk

À toi! A and B, pages 196–197

Cahier d'exercices, pages 70–71 (exs 13–14)

5 Vivre sainement

MODULE 9 EN BONNE FORME

(Student's Book pages 158–159)

Main topics and objectives

- Discussing healthy lifestyles

Key language

Language from the whole module

Grammar

- Question words

Skills/Strategies

- Recycling vocabulary from other chapters
- Using ICT to e-mail

Resources

Cassette D side 2

This spread brings together and extends the language of the chapter. Brainstorm ideas for healthy living. There is no key language box on this page. What might it contain if there were? Recap on language met throughout the chapter.

1 Which sites could these people visit? There may be more than one!

Reading (1–5). Students identify the site(s) these people might visit.

Answers

1 À comme Active, Bodyplanet, Castaing Jean-Marie, Forme et santé
2 Sécurité Solaire
3 À comme Active, Bodyplanet, Castaing Jean-Marie, Condition physique et santé, Forme et santé, Objectif forme
4 Bodyplanet, Castaing Jean-Marie, Condition physique et santé, Objectif forme
5 Estheweb

2 Work out what these sentences mean. Then listen and correct any that are wrong.

Listening (1–10). Students work out what the sentences mean (in pairs if you wish), and then listen to see if any are wrong.

Tapescript

Chacun d'entre nous désire et recherche le bonheur. On parle beaucoup aujourd'hui des médecines douces et des produits bio. Mais comment protéger l'organisme qui est notre corps?
Pour vivre longtemps en pleine forme avec beaucoup d'énergie, il suffit de suivre quelques règles très simples et pas trop difficiles.
Les dix commandements pour la santé sont les suivants:
1 – Il ne faut pas fumer trop de cigarettes.
2 – Il ne faut pas boire trop d'alcool.
3 – Il faut éviter de boire trop de caféine.
4 – Il faut boire deux litres d'eau par jour.
5 – Il faut éviter la drogue.
6 – Il faut éviter les matières grasses – plus de frites, mes enfants!
7 – Il faut faire travailler ses jambes tous les jours – oubliez la voiture et l'ascenseur!

8 – Il faut prendre des vitamines et bien dormir.
9 – Il faut serrer les fesses, rentrer le ventre, sortir la poitrine et marcher tête haute.
10 – Il faut garder la forme – en faisant de l'exercice aérobic deux fois par semaine pendant au moins vingt minutes.
Bref, la modération avant toute chose. Ceci vous assurera une vie longue et heureuse. À vous de jouer!

Answers

1 You must not smoke too many cigarettes.
2 You must drink too much alcohol.
3 You must avoid drinking too much caffeine.
4 You should drink 10 litres of water a day.
5 You must encourage drugs.
6 You must eat lots of fatty foods – eat lots of chips my friends!
7 You must work your legs every day – forget your car and the lift!
8 You must take vitamins and sleep less.
9 You must tighten your bottom, hold in your stomach, push out your chest and walk with your head up.
10 You must keep fit by exercising twice a week for at least 20 minutes.

Corrections:

2 Il ne faut pas boire trop d'alcool.
4 Il faut boire deux litres d'eau par jour.
5 Il faut éviter la drogue.
6 Il faut éviter la matière grasse, plus de frites, mes enfants!
8 Il faut prendre les vitamines et bien dormir.

3 Read the text and answer the questions below in French.

Reading (1–6). This text contains some unknown and more complex language. Before students try to answer, make sure they read the text for gist, choose some words to look up (not too many) and then try the French questions.

Answers

1 Parce que cela remplit et élimine les toxines.
2 Non, ce n'est pas bien.
3 Il faut manger un yaourt nature ou une pomme.
4 Il faut éviter les chips.
5 Il faut prendre le temps de manger.
6 Faites un petit peu d'exercice chaque jour.

Tip box

This advises students to look back to earlier parts of their book where language recurs. Remind them of the importance of drawing together the language they have learned – that no language is peculiar to one topic.

Rappel

Question words. Remind students of the importance of being able to ask questions and of knowing question words accurately. Can they think of any more question words?

4 In pairs. Prepare an interview for a magazine. Use the questions below. (You don't have to tell the truth!)

Speaking. Students use the questions given to prepare an interview about healthy living with a partner.

▣ Prepare a questionnaire on healthy living and e-mail it to a friend.

Students can use some of the questions from activity 4 for this and invent some of their own.

➕ Students could prepare their own website or make a Powerpoint presentation to encourage a healthy lifestyle. This would bring together the language of the module.

All the key vocabulary and structures from this module are listed on the **Mots** pages 162–163. These can be used for revision by covering up either the English or the French. Students can check here to see how much they remember from the module and use them to prepare for the assessments.

Assessment materials for Modules 9 and 10 are available in the separate Assessment Pack.

Further speaking and grammar practice on the whole module is provided on **Cahier d'exercices** pages 72–73.

Writing practice: En bonne forme

The À l'écrit spreads give regular, guided practice in preparing for the writing sections of Standard Grade and Intermediate examinations. Each double-page spread always starts with a model text which acts as a stimulus to give students ideas about what they might include in their ownwriting. Students are encouraged to look at the detail of the text through the structured reading activities, and are guided gradually towards producing their own sentences in French, in preparation for the final task in which they are asked to produce an extended piece of writing. The **Au Secours!** panel is a feature on all of the À l'écrit spreads. It presents language and structures that students can include in their writing, and reminds them of general points which will enable them to get a better grade.

To qualify for the writing components at Standard Grade or Intermediate writing N.A.B.s, final versions must be produced under controlled conditions. Students should be encouraged to use the language they understand and are familiar with so as to learn what they have written with a high degree of accuracy. They should be warned about the dangers of copying. At Standard Grade, students should be guided to write over 25 words at Foundation level, 50 words at General level and 100 words at Credit level.

Students should be encouraged to see that they can get Credit marks at Standard Grade and A grades at Intermediate 2 in Writing! Remind them of the following tips to help them get a better grade.

Handy tips for students

1 Structure your writing: a good beginning and ending, and 3 distinct paragraphs!

   Choose formats which structure themselves, e.g. a letter.

2 Focus your writing on one aspect of a module.

3 Choose aspects which give you opportunities to write about your opinions.

4 Choose aspects which allow you to use impressive vocabulary and phrases.

5 Make sure you include examples of different tenses in your writing.

6 It is very important to write accurate French! Make sure the language you choose for your writing is memorable for you. Only you can know how much new and impressive French you can learn to write out accurately in exam conditions!

This spread guides students towards producing an extended piece of writing on the topic of **healthy living**.

1 Find out what the 9 phrases in blue mean in English.

Answers

> *des tartines* = toast, *plat préféré* = favourite dish/meal, *surtout* = especially/above all, *hors-d'œuvres* = starters, *j'essaie* = I try, *la vache folle* = mad cow disease, *supporter* = to stand, *goût* = taste, *admettre* = to admit, *renoncer* = to give up

2a How does Jean-Luc answer each of John's questions?

Answers

> **Qu'est-ce que tu prends au petit déjeuner?**
> Je prends des tartines: du pain grillé avec du beurre et de la confiture ou parfois je prends des croissants.
> **Qu'est-ce que tu aimes manger?**
> Mon plat préféré, c'est le cassoulet, c'est un plat qui est fait avec des saucisses, du porc, des haricots blancs et des tomates. En plus, j'adore tout ce qui est sucré: les desserts, les gâteaux, le chocolat. J'aime aussi la cuisine chinoise et vietnamienne.
> **Tu aimes le fast-food?**
> Oui, j'aime le fast-food, mais j'essaie de ne pas manger trop d'hamburgers.
> **Tu as des allergies ou est-ce qu'il y a des choses que tu n'aimes pas manger?**
> Je n'ai pas d'allergies mais j'ai horreur des carottes.
> **Est-ce que tu fumes?**
> Je fume de temps en temps.
> **Est-ce que tu bois de l'alcool?**
> Je bois du vin et de la bière. Je n'aime pas trop les alcools plus forts comme le vodka ou le whisky.

2b Answer John's questions with your own information.

3 Now write about 200 words on the subject of food. You can use your answers to John's questions, but make sure you write at least 2 more sentences after each answer. Use the *Au secours!* panel to help you. Try to include:

- a description of a local speciality
- at least 3 different tenses
- lots of comments and exclamations

Au secours!

This section reminds students of the following points
- building long sentences following the pattern: when, what, where/who with, comment
- using the perfect tense
- using the future or conditional
- using comments and exclamations
- asking yourself questions

À toi! A & B

(Student's Book pages 196–197)

Self-access reading and writing at two levels

These pages are designed to give students extra practice in reading and structured writing. There are two differentiated pages relating to each chapter: A and B. Page A is at an easier level and page B more challenging. You may wish students to work on the page most appropriate to their level or work through both pages. You may feel it is useful to work with students on the activities, but it should be possible for most students to work on them independently. The most appropriate time to use each page is indicated within the relevant teaching notes.

À Toi! A, page 196

This page is best used after pages 156–157 of the Student's Book.

1a Read the text and answer the questions in English.

Answers

> **1** 42% men and 27% women
> **2** 47%
> **3** Smoke more than 10 cigarettes a day.
> **4** Smoke at least 1 cigarette a day.
> **5** Smoke more than 10 cigarettes a day.
> **6** It is the average age for starting to smoke.
> **7** Men
> **8** Die prematurely from smoking.
> **9** 79 billion francs

1b Find the French for the following.

Answers

> **1** les chiffres
> **2** plus de
> **3** au moins
> **4** moyen
> **5** première

2 What is your view? Write approximately 100 words about your views on smoking.

À Toi! B, page 197

This page is best used after pages 156–157 of the Student's Book.

1 Read the text and answer the questions in English.

Answers

> **1** Advice for alcohol consumption. (1)
> **2** Drive a car or operate machinery. (2)
> **3** If combined with medicine or drugs. (2)
> **4** Two standard glasses. (1)
> **5** Three standard glasses. (1)
> **6** At least one day a week without alcohol. (1)
> **7** During childhood or pre-adolescence, during pregnancy, when you drive a vehicle or dangerous machinery, when you have responsibilities which require vigilance, when you're taking certain medicines. (any 3)
> **8** Everyone reacts differently to alcohol according to how big they are, their physical and psychological health. If you drink without eating, alcohol passes more quickly into the blood and its effects are greater. (5)

2 What do you think is important in a healthy lifestyle? Write approximately 150 words.

Cahier d'exercices, page 66

Cahier d'exercices, page 67

1
Answers

a *Breakfast* – le petit déjeuner – à sept heures trente – une tartine et du café

b *Lunch* – le déjeuner – à midi – un sandwich au jambon

c *Snack* – le goûter – à seize heures – une pomme et un biscuit

d *Supper* – le dîner – à dix-neuf heures – de la viande et des légumes

2
Answers

1 f: Je me réveille.
2 d: Je me lève.
3 a: Je me lave et je me brosse les dents.
4 i: Je prends mon petit déjeuner.
5 g: Je vais au collège.
6 h: Je rentre du collège.
7 e: Je fais mes devoirs.
8 b: Je prends mon dîner.
9 j: Je regarde un peu la télé avant de me coucher.
10 c: Je me couche.

3
Answers

a Je me lève.
b Je me brosse les dents.
c Je vais au collège.
d Je rentre du collège/Je rentre à la maison à cinq heures.
e Je fais mes devoirs.

4
Answers

a Je me suis levé(e).
b Je me suis brossé(e) les dents.
c Je suis allé(e) au collège.
d Je suis rentré(e) du collège/Je suis rentré(e) à la maison à cinq heures.
e J'ai fait mes devoirs.

5
Answers

a a Coke/un Coca   **b** milk/du lait
c an egg/un œuf – eggs/des œufs
d cigarettes/des cigarettes   **e** sweets/des bonbons

6a
Answers

d, f, h

Cahier d'exercices, page 68

6b (writing task)

7
Answers

Martin: ✗
Géraldine: ✓
Isa: ✓
Mireille: ✗
Immacolata: ✓
Thomas: ✗

8
Answers

cold dishes – preparing meals – don't eat breakfast – restaurants which have opened since 1993 – spend the least time at the dinner table – fat – sugar and alcohol – sitting at a table – more popular than traditional meals – are eaten by more and more people – half – never drink wine.

Cahier d'exercices, page 69

9
Answers

a à la tête	b au nez	c à l'oreille
d à la gorge	e au ventre	f au bras
g aux jambes	h au genou	i aux pieds

10
Answers

	What is the problem?	Appointment on which day?	What time is the appointment?
Conversation a	headache	Monday	10:45
Conversation b	stomach ache	Friday	10:40
Conversation c	sprained knee	Thursday	14:50
Conversation d	baby has toothache	Wednesday	Between 12:00 and 16:00

Cahier d'exercices, page 70

11 (writing task)

12
Answers

1 b	2 b	3 a	4 c	5 c	6 b	7 a	8 c

Cahier d'exercices, page 71

13a
Answers

1 C	**2** A	**3** D	**4** C	**5** B	**6** A	**7** D	**8** B	**9** A	**10** D

13b
Answers

a elle est maigre comme un clou

b qui fume comme un pompier

c Il est nerveux et perd patience très facilement

d il est toujours en colère contre quelque chose

e Mon copain boit depuis quelques années

f je ne sais pas quoi faire

g Presque deux paquets de clopes par jour

h le pire, c'est que ça ne touche pas seulement les filles

14
Answers

anorexic – chocolate – sweets – fish – water – girls

Cahier d'exercices, page 72

1
Answers

a me **b** nous **c** s' **d** vous **e** se **f** s' **g** t' **h** nous

2
Answers

a J'ai chaud.

b Il a froid.

c Elle a dix-huit ans.

d Nous avons faim/On a faim.

e Ils/Elles ont soif.

f Vous avez mal.

g As-tu soif?/Tu as soif?/Est-ce que tu as soif?

h Je n'ai pas froid.

i J'ai peur.

j A-t-elle mal?/Elle a mal?/Est-ce qu'elle a mal?

3
Answers

a Il faut boire beaucoup d'eau.

b Il faut rester en bonne forme.

c Il ne faut pas manger trop de matières grasses.

d Il ne faut pas boire trop de café.

e Il ne faut pas sauter un repas.

Cahier d'exercices, page 73

MODULE 10 LE TRANSPORT

Le transport

(Student's Book pages 164–179)

Topic area	Key language	Grammar	Skills/Strategies
Déjà vu (pp. 164–167) Talking about transport Giving directions Asking for information	en auto/voiture/autobus/car/métro/train/avion/bateau/taxi, à pied/vélo Pour aller …?/Je vais … en France/Angleterre/au camping/collège/cinéma/ château/commissariat/parc/marché/supermarché/syndicat d'initiative/ restaurant/stade/à l'hôpital/à la banque/boulangerie/gare/piscine Prenez la première/deuxième/troisième rue à droite/à gauche. Allez/Continuez tout droit. Montez la rue jusqu'aux feux/jusqu'au carrefour/jusqu'au rond-point. Traversez le pont/les feux. C'est à gauche/à droite/au coin. C'est en face de vous. La cathédrale/Le musée/La plage/La gare routière/L'auberge de jeunesse/L'hôtel … C'est près d'ici? Le trajet dure combien de temps? Prenez le bus (ligne 5). Descendez (au terminus). Je voudrais … Avez-vous …? Est-ce-qu'il y a …? Où est …? Est-ce qu'il faut …? Est-ce qu'on peut …? À quelle heure? C'est combien?	Different ways of saying 'to/to the' Imperative: *vous* form Using *y*	Using key phrases
1 Pardon, madame … (pp. 168–169) Asking about journeys Discussing modes of transport	Je voudrais visiter (la France), qu'est-ce que vous me proposez? Le vol dure combien de temps? Et le prix? C'est moins cher/ennuyeux/plus lent/rapide. C'est pratique/long/rapide/lent. Ça me rend malade. On peut discuter/jouer aux cartes. Il y a des prix raisonnables. Il n'y a pas assez de (parkings). C'est bon/mauvais pour l'environnement.		Agreeing and disagreeing
2 À la gare et ailleurs (pp. 170–171) Buying tickets Getting around at the station	Consigne/Sortie de secours/Réservations/Entrée/Buffet/Guichet/Quais/ Compostage/Salle d'attente/Bagages/Objets trouvés C'est où? C'est … en face/près/à côté du quai numéro 3/de la sortie de secours/des réservations/du bar/de la grande porte Je voudrais un aller simple/aller-retour pour (Londres). En première/deuxième classe, fumeurs/non-fumeurs. Le prochain train part/arrive à quelle heure? Quel est le numéro du quai?	Prepositions quel(le)(s)	Using IT for research

186

Topic area	Key language	Grammar	Skills/Strategies
3 En panne (pp. 172–173) Discussing breakdowns Talking about traffic problems	*Je suis en panne. J'ai un pneu crevé.* *Pouvez-vous m'envoyer quelqu'un?* *Je n'ai pas de roue de secours.* *J'ai un problème avec la batterie/la roue/le volant/les freins/les phares.* *Je suis sur la route nationale 10 à côté d'Auchan.* *À mon avis … Je pense qu'il y a …/il n'y a pas …* *peu de/trop de/beaucoup de/assez de …* *embouteillages/pollution/transports en commun/zones piétonnes/pistes cyclables/circulation*		Giving information Using a range of tenses Using ICT
4 Trop de voitures? (pp. 174–175) Talking about accidents	*Hier/La semaine dernière/Lundi dernier/Hier soir …* *J'ai vu un accident. Il y a eu un accident.* *Il y avait du brouillard, etc.* *La route était glissante. C'était très dangereux.* *Je descendais/traversais la rue … Je roulais lentement …* *Je faisais du shopping … J'attendais un copain …* *quand un camion/une voiture/une moto/une trottinette est entré(e) en collision avec …* *un piéton/une autre voiture/un chien/une poussette/une moto/un lampadaire* *Le chauffeur était blessé. Personne n'était blessé.*	Present participles Perfect tense (revision) Imperfect tense (revision)	
Entraîne-vous: À l'oral (pp. 176–177)	Language from Modules 9 and 10		Practice for the speaking exam Presentation skills
À toi! A and B (pp. 198–199)	Language from Module 10		Reading and writing skills

The vocabulary and structures taught in Module 10 are summarised on the **Mots** pages of the Student's Book, pages 178–179.
Assessment tasks for Modules 9 and 10 combined and an end-of-course assessment are provided in the separate Assessment Pack.

MODULE 10 · LE TRANSPORT

Déjà vu

(Student's Book pages 164–167)

Main topics and objectives

- Talking about transport
- Giving directions
- Asking for information

Key language

en auto/voiture/autobus/car/métro/train/avion/
  bateau/taxi
à pied/vélo
Pour aller …?/Je vais …
  en France/Angleterre/Espagne
  au camping/collège/cinéma/château/commissariat/
  parc/marché/supermarché/syndicat d'initiative/
  restaurant/stade
  à l'hôpital
  à la banque/boulangerie/gare/piscine
Prenez la première/deuxième/troisième rue à droite/à
  gauche.
Allez/Continuez tout droit.
Montez la rue jusqu'aux feux/jusqu'au
  carrefour/rond-point.
Traversez le pont/les feux.
C'est à gauche/à droite/au coin.
C'est en face de vous.

La cathédrale/Le musée/La plage/La gare routière/
  L'auberge de jeunesse/L'hôtel …
C'est près d'ici?
Le trajet dure combien de temps?
Prenez le bus (ligne 5).
Descendez (au terminus).
Je voudrais … Avez-vous …? Est-ce-qu'il y a …?
Où est …? Est-ce qu'il faut ..?
Est-ce qu'on peut …?
… à quelle heure? … c'est combien?

Grammar

- Different ways of saying 'to'/'to the'
- Imperative – *vous* form
- Using *y*

Skills/strategies

- Using key phrases

Resources

À l'oral, page 177: Conversation 2
Cassette D side 2
Cahier d'exercices, page 74

Introduce the spread by revising means of transport. Ask the question *Comment tu vas au lycée/collège?* and allow students to give their own answer. Then introduce more complicated vocabulary by means of flashcards/icons on an OHT (e.g. plane, helicopter, boat, coach). Make sure your students know about the faux ami *le car*!

1 Describe these trips in French.

Writing (1–6). Students consolidate the oral work done at the start of the spread by correctly identifying the phrases from the key language box and writing them out.

Answers

1 Je vais au collège en car.
2 Je vais au cinéma en métro.
3 Je vais à la piscine à vélo.
4 Je vais au stade en voiture.
5 Je vais en Angleterre en avion.
6 Je vais en France en train.

Rappel

How to say 'to/to the …' with places. Remind students that there is no word-for-word equivalent for the word 'to' and that each example needs to be learned. Add this to your regular testing and revision for your students.

Before moving on to 2a, revise places and simple directions.

2a Look at the plan. Listen and note whether the directions are right (✓) or wrong (✗).

Listening (1–7). Students hear the place and follow the directions to check whether they are correct.

Tapescript

1 – *Pour aller à l'hôpital, s'il vous plaît?*
  – *Prenez la troisième rue à gauche.*
2 – *Pour aller au restaurant, s'il vous plaît?*
  – *Prenez la première rue à droite.*
3 – *Pour aller à la piscine, s'il vous plaît?*
  – *Prenez la première rue à gauche.*
4 – *S'il vous plaît – pour aller au commissariat?*
  – *Allez tout droit.*
5 – *Pour aller au syndicat d'initiative, s'il vous plaît?*
  – *Prenez la troisième rue à droite.*
6 – *Pour aller au stade, s'il vous plaît?*
  – *Prenez la deuxième rue à droite.*
7 – *Pour aller au parc, s'il vous plaît?*
  – *Prenez la deuxième rue à gauche.*

Answers

1✔	2✔	3✗	4✗	5✗	6✗	7✔

2b In pairs. Ask a question and listen to your partner's answer. Is it true or false?

Speaking. Students then replicate the activity in 2a, substituting their own destinations and directions.

188

LE TRANSPORT • MODULE MÉTRO 10

Before tackling **3a**, introduce more complex directions (see key language box on page 165). Demonstrate with a map on an OHT.

3a Read these directions and note in French where they lead to.

Reading (1–5). Students now read more complicated directions and work out where they are being directed to.

Answers

> **1** le syndicat d'initiative
> **2** le camping
> **3** le supermarché
> **4** la piscine
> **5** la banque

Le détective

The imperative. Draw students' attention to this use of the *vous* form of the imperative. They will need the information for activity **3b**.

3b Find the French for:

Reading (1–12). Students show their detailed comprehension of the texts in **3a** by identifying the correct French for the English phrases given. It will be useful for them to have a note of the French and the English phrases side by side, so ask them to write them out in both languages.

Answers

> **1** montez la rue   **2** jusqu'aux feux   **3** jusqu'au carrefour
> **4** c'est au coin   **5** aux feux   **6** traversez les feux
> **7** traversez le pont   **8** au rond-point
> **9** c'est à votre gauche   **10** continuez tout droit
> **11** c'est en face de vous
> **12** c'est juste après la deuxième rue

3c Listen to these directions. Where do they lead to?

Listening (1–5). Students now hear more complicated directions and follow them on the map in **3a** to work out where they lead to.

Tapescript

1 *Allez tout droit, et passez les feux. Continuez tout droit, et c'est un peu plus loin, à votre droite.*
2 *Tournez à droite, puis au feu rouge, tournez à gauche. Montez la rue, et c'est à votre gauche, juste avant le pont.*
3 *Tournez à droite, et au feu rouge, continuez tout droit. Alors, c'est à votre gauche, en face de la banque.*
4 *Ah, c'est très facile parce que c'est tout près. Tournez à gauche, puis montez la première rue à droite, et c'est directement en face de vous, après le rond-point.*
5 *Allez tout droit jusqu'au feu rouge, puis tournez à gauche. Prenez la prochaine rue à droite. C'est à votre droite, avant le rond-point.*

Answers

> **1** le commissariat   **2** le château   **3** la boulangerie
> **4** la piscine   **5** la pharmacie

3d In pairs. Give directions. Your partner says where they lead to.

Speaking. In pairs, students practise giving and following directions, using the key language box as support.

Student's Book pages 166–167

4a Listen to these conversations and read the text each time. Note in French the missing details for each conversation.

Listening (1-4). Students listen to four similarly structured conversations, noting the missing details for each.

Tapescript

1 – *Pardon, madame. La cathédrale, c'est près d'ici?*
 – *Ah non, c'est assez loin. C'est à trois kilomètres d'ici.*
 – *Pour y aller, s'il vous plaît?*
 – *Prenez le métro, et descendez au terminus.*
 – *Le trajet dure combien de temps?*
 – *Eh bien, cinq minutes environ.*
 – *Merci, madame. Au revoir.*
 – *Au revoir.*
2 – *Pardon, monsieur. Le musée, c'est près d'ici?*
 – *Ah non, c'est assez loin. C'est à huit kilomètres d'ici.*
 – *Pour y aller, s'il vous plaît?*
 – *Alors, vous prenez le bus ligne 5, et vous descendez à la place du marché.*
 – *Et le trajet dure combien de temps?*
 – *Mmm, oh … 20 minutes environ.*
 – *Merci, monsieur. Au revoir.*
 – *Au revoir.*
3 – *Pardon, monsieur. La plage, c'est près d'ici?*
 – *Ah non, c'est assez loin. C'est à 16 kilomètres d'ici.*
 – *Pour y aller, s'il vous plaît?*
 – *Prenez le bus numéro 120, et descendez à la plage.*
 – *Le trajet dure combien de temps?*
 – *Eh bien, 25 minutes environ.*
 – *Merci, monsieur. Au revoir.*
 – *Au revoir.*
4 – *Pardon, madame. La gare routière, c'est près d'ici?*
 – *Euh non, c'est assez loin. C'est à cinq kilomètres d'ici.*
 – *Pour y aller, s'il vous plaît?*
 – *Prenez l'autobus, ligne 8, et descendez au cinéma.*
 – *Et… le trajet dure combien de temps?*
 – *Eh bien, un quart d'heure environ.*
 – *Merci … merci, madame. Au revoir.*
 – *Au revoir.*

Answers

Answers

> **1 a** la cathédrale   **b** 3km   **c** le métro   **d** terminus
> **e** 5 minutes
> **2 a** le musée   **b** 8km   **c** le bus   **d** place du marché
> **e** 20 minutes
> **3 a** la plage   **b** 16km   **c** le bus   **d** la plage   **e** 25 minutes
> **4 a** la gare routière   **b** 5km   **c** l'autobus   **d** cinéma
> **e** 15 minutes

Le détective

y. Point out to your students that they have met this word before, in the expressions *il y a …* and *j'y vais …* Students are often unsure of the meaning of 'little words' in sentences, words which begin or link sentences, like question words and phrases, prepositions, determiners, *c'est/c'était, il y a/il y avait.* Give them a list of this 'essential vocabulary' and test them on sections of it every week.

4b In pairs. Adapt the conversation using the details below.

Speaking. In pairs, students practise changing the conversation in **4a** and inserting the details shown.

Tip box

Key phrases. Point out the phrases in the key language box at the bottom of page 166. It is essential that students know these phrases, particularly for the Speaking exam. Ask them to suggest possible endings/beginnings for each phrase. These are practised in activities **5a** and **5b**.

5a Make up sentences. The missing words are underneath.

Speaking. Students ask one another questions using the key language box at the bottom of page 166 and the words given on page 167.

Answers

> **1** Est-qu'il y … **a** un bus pour le stade?   **b** des toilettes?
> **c** une réduction pour les étudiants?
> **2** Où est … **d** le stade?   **e** ma règle?   **f** le prof?
> **3** Est-ce qu'on peut … **g** manger un chewing-gum?
> **h** avoir un nouveau cahier?   **i** prendre le bus?
> **4** Je voudrais … **j** une glace.   **k** un billet pour 'Titanic'.
> **l** être coiffeur.
> **5** Avez-vous … **m** des maillots de bain?   **n** une table
> pour deux personnes?   **o** un livre?
> **6** Est-ce qu'il faut … **p** réserver?
> **q** payer un supplément?   **r** parler français?
> **7** C'est combien, … **s** un billet?   **t** pour une nuit?
> **u** un plan de la ville?
> **8** À quelle heure est-ce que … **v** le film finit?   **w** le
> train arrive?   **x** tu te lèves?

5b Write out one version of each sentence 1–8 from **5a**.

Writing. Students consolidate the spoken activity by writing down the sentence of their choice from each group in **5a** (eight sentences in all).

> Further practice of the language and vocabulary of these spreads is provided as follows:
>
> À l'oral, page 177: Conversation 2
>
> Cahier d'exercices, page 74

1 Pardon, madame …

(Student's Book page 168–169)

Main topics and objectives

- Asking about journeys
- Discussing modes of transport

Key language

Je voudrais visiter (la France), qu'est-ce que vous me proposez?
Le vol dure combien de temps?
Et le prix?
C'est moins cher/ennuyeux.
C'est plus lent/rapide.
Ça me rend malade.
On peut discuter/jouer aux cartes.

Il y a des prix raisonnables.
Il n'y a pas assez de (parkings).
C'est bon/mauvais pour l'environnement.

Skills/Strategies

- Agreeing and disagreeing

Resources

À l'oral, page 177: Conversation 1
Cassette D side 2
Cahier d'exercices, page 75 (ex. 4)

Introduce the spread by brainstorming exotic holiday destinations, first of all in English, then ask your students to look up exotic destinations in French in the dictionary. Ensure they have looked up: China, Egypt, Japan, and cruise(liner), before starting the spread.

1a Listen to these enquiries about exotic or unusual holidays. Copy and complete the grid in English.

Listening (1–4). Students listen to complex language, but for straightforward facts. Encourage them to listen for the facts they are asked for, and not to be put off by extra details. You may wish to read the example conversation in the book, before listening.

Tapescript

1 – *Je voudrais visiter le Japon, qu'est-ce que vous me proposez?*
  – *Alors, vous pouvez visiter Tokyo et Kyoto. Vous voyagez en avion et vous passez trois jours à Tokyo et quatre jours à Kyoto.*
  – *Le vol dure combien de temps?*
  – *10 heures approximativement.*
  – *Et le prix?*
  – *1095 euros, madame.*
2 – *Je voudrais visiter la Chine, qu'est-ce que vous me proposez?*
  – *Alors, vous avez 'La Capitale Impériale' – Pékin. Vous voyagez en avion et vous passez sept jours à Pékin même, avec un car à votre disposition et des pousse-pousse bien sûr!*
  – *Le vol dure combien de temps?*
  – *Huit heures approximativement.*
  – *Et le prix?*
  – *Alors, le prix … 1057 euros, monsieur.*
3 – *Je voudrais aller à Nice le plus vite possible et le moins cher possible.*
  – *D'accord, vous avez un vol à 20h.*
  – *Oh non, je travaille jusqu'à 18 heures, je n'aurai pas le temps d'aller à l'aéroport.*
  – *Dans ce cas, il faut prendre le train de nuit, une couchette deuxième classe?*

– *Oui, d'accord. C'est combien?*
– *Euh … 82 euros.*
– *Et le trajet dure combien de temps?*
– *Vous partez à 21h47 et vous arrivez à Nice à 7h30.*
– *À peu près dix heures alors.*
– *C'est ça!*
4 – *J'aimerais aller en Égypte.*
  – *Ah, la croisière Anubis est ce qu'il vous faut. C'est intéressant comme prix. Pour 953 euros, vous avez le vol aller-retour et l'hébergement à bord d'un bateau 5 étoiles. Pendant huit jours, vous visiterez la Nécropole Thébaine, le Haut Barrage, les temples de Karnak et de Louxor …*
  – *Ah non, hors de question, j'ai le mal de mer, moi!*

Answers

	destination	transport	journey lasts	price
1	Japan	plane	10 hours	€1095
2	China	plane	8 hours	€1057
3	Nice	train	10 hours	€82
4	Egypt	boat	8 days	€953

1b In pairs. Practise the dialogue in **1a**. Change the underlined details to talk about these new holidays. Then try making up your own details!

Speaking. Students practise the dialogue in **1a** until they are happy that they can do it fluently. They then go on to adapt the conversation, according to the details in the panels on the right. Once they are comfortable with these, they can go on to invent new versions of the conversation.

2a Read the advertisements on the next page. Find the French for the following.

Reading (1–2). Students find phrases in the adverts on page 169 which they may find useful when giving the advantages and disadvantages of different forms of transport.

Answers

> **1 a** c'est rapide   **b** c'est amusant
>   **c** Préférez-vous pouvoir discuter?   **d** il n'y a qu'un choix
> **2 a** un vol rapide   **b** et surtout bon marché
>   **c** les réservations se font chez vous
>   **d** un prix raisonnable

2b What reasons do the adverts suggest for using these modes of transport?

Reading (1–2). Students now identify all the advantages and disadvantages mentioned in the adverts. Advise them of the need to find all the relevant pieces of information.

Answers

> **1** TGV: it's quick, comfortable, entertaining, you can talk, play cards, walk around, have a coffee (7)
> **2** plane: quick, cheap, you can make reservations using the Internet (3)

3a Copy these lists and add at least one item to the list of advantages and disadvantages for each type of transport. Use the phrases in the key language box.

Writing. Students show understanding and add to their personal record of vocabulary by copying and completing lists of advantages and disadvantages.

Answers

> Possible answers:
>
> | | **les avantages** | **les inconvénients** |
> |---|---|---|
> | **la voiture** | c'est moins cher | il n'y a pas assez de parkings |
> | | | ça me rend malade |
> | **le train (le TGV)** | on peut discuter | c'est long |
> | **l'avion** | c'est plus rapide | c'est ennuyeux |
> | **le vélo** | c'est moins cher | c'est lent |

3b Listen to the Soubeyran family discussing how to get to the South of France. Note how each of them wants to travel and the reason. What is their final decision?

Listening. Students take notes on the whole passage in order to answer all the questions. This requires overall comprehension as well as understanding of details.

Tapescript

– *Pour aller dans le Midi alors cette année, papa, comment est-ce qu'on va voyager?*

– *Ben, on va y aller en voiture comme tous les ans, c'est le moins cher et c'est pratique d'avoir la voiture sur place.*
– *Mais, non, j'ai horreur de ça. C'est long, qu'est-ce que c'est long et ça me rend malade en plus. On ne peut pas prendre le TGV? C'est rapide et c'est beaucoup moins ennuyeux. On peut discuter, jouer aux cartes, faire un tour dans le train. S'il te plaît papa. On ne sort pas la voiture une fois arrivés.*
– *Mais en fin de compte, on pourrait prendre l'avion, il y a des prix raisonnables à trouver sur Internet. Qu'est-ce que vous en pensez?*
– *Ben oui, si ça revient moins cher.*
– *Génial, je veux bien.*

Answers

> **M. Soubeyran:** car, cheaper and convenient
> **Sarah:** TGV, car makes her sick. TGV is faster and less boring. You can talk, play cards, walk around.
> **Mme Soubeyran:** plane, prices over the Internet are reasonable
> They decide to go by plane.

Tip box

Agreeing and disagreeing. Encourage your students to use these phrases when they are discussing.

3c In pairs. Take turns to choose a means of transport and give reasons for using it. Your partner disagrees with you and gives the disadvantages.

Speaking. Students use the (dis)agreement phrases and the (dis)advantages from **3a** to practise discursive language.

3d Choose a means of transport and write about its advantages and disadvantages. Write about 60 words.

Writing. Students now pull together all the language from this spread to write a discursive essay. Brainstorm some ideas with the class first if necessary.

> Further practice of the language and vocabulary of this spread is provided as follows:
>
> À l'oral, page 177: Conversation 1
>
> Cahier d'exercices, page 75 (ex. 4)

2 À la gare et ailleurs

(Student's Book pages 170–171)

Main topics and objectives

● Buying tickets and getting around at the station

Key language

Consigne/Sortie de secours/Réservations/Entrée/
  Buffet/Guichet/Quais/Compostage/Salle d'attente/
  Bagages/Objets trouvés
C'est où?
C'est en face/près/à côté …
  du quai numéro 3/de la sortie de secours/des
  réservations/du bar/de la grande porte.
Je voudrais un aller simple/aller-retour pour (Paris).
En première/deuxième classe, fumeurs/non-fumeurs.
Le prochain train part/arrive à quelle heure?
Quel est le numéro du quai?

Grammar

● Prepositions
● *quel(le)(s)*

Skills/Strategies

● Using IT for research

Resources

À l'oral page 177: Transaction 3
Cassette D side 2
Cahier d'exercices, pages 75–76 (exs 5–6)

Start the spread by asking how many pupils have been on a train or bought train tickets. Some may not have! Model a ticket-buying transaction with a student partner in English, giving the student the following information: class? €35, leaves at 15.17, arrives 17.19, platform 6, and ensuring you specify single/return, destination, smoking/non). Work out the French vocabulary the students will need.

1a Where would you go?

Reading (1–11). Students match the signs to the French phrases. They should match the words they already know or can guess first, and then use the word lists on pages 178–179 or a dictionary to find the rest.

Answers

1 h	2 c	3 j	4 e	5 a	6 d	7 b	8 g	9 f
10 i	11 k							

1b Listen and make notes in English.

Listening (1–6). Students listen and note firstly the place the people are looking for and then where it is. Ensure that your students recognise the prepositions in the key language box before they listen.

Tapescript

1 – *Pardon, où est le guichet, s'il vous plaît?*
  – *Le guichet? C'est en face des toilettes.*
2 – *Où est la consigne, s'il vous plaît?*
  – *Il y a une consigne automatique là-bas, près de la sortie de secours.*
3 – *Est-ce qu'il y a un buffet?*
  – *Mais oui, le buffet se trouve en face du quai numéro 5.*
4 – *Où est le bureau des objets trouvés?*
  – *C'est à côté du bar, madame.*
  – *À côté du bar?*
  – *Oui, c'est ça.*

5 – *Est-ce qu'il y a une salle d'attente dans la gare, s'il vous plaît?*
  – *Oui, vous voyez, c'est là-bas, près de la grande porte.*
6 – *Où se trouve le bureau des réservations, s'il vous plaît?*
  – *Allez tout droit, puis c'est à votre gauche.*

Answers

1 a ticket office	**b** opposite the toilets
2 a left luggage	**b** near the emergency exit
3 a café	**b** opposite platform 5
4 a lost property	**b** next to the bar
5 a waiting room	**b** near the big gate/door
6 a ticket reservations	**b** straight on then on your left

2a Complete this conversation at the ticket office, using the words in the box. Then listen to see if you were right.

Reading (a–i). Students should now be able to complete this conversation using the words from the box.

Tapescript

– *Bonjour, je peux vous aider?*
– *Oui, je voudrais un aller-retour pour Calais, s'il vous plaît.*
– *Bien sûr, en quelle classe?*
– *En deuxième classe, s'il vous plaît, et dans la section non-fumeurs. C'est combien?*
– *Voilà, ça fait €35, s'il vous plaît.*
– *Le prochain train part à quelle heure?*
– *Il y a un train toutes les trente minutes. Le prochain train part à 13h20.*
– *Merci, et il arrive à quelle heure?*
– *Il arrive à 15h40.*
– *Et quel est le numéro du quai?*
– *C'est le quai numéro 4.*

Answers

a aller-retour	**b** Calais	**c** deuxième	**d** non-fumeurs
e €35	**f** trente minutes	**g** 13h20	**h** 15h40	**i** quatre

➕ Copy the text into the students' French Work folders or ask them to copy-type the text themselves, keying in the missing words.

Le détective

quel. Point out that *quel* acts like an adjective and agrees with its noun. Remind them that they already know *quelle est ta matière préférée?, à quelle heure?*, etc.

Before moving on to **2b**, revise 24-hour clock times with your students. These are in fact easier to give and to understand than the 12-hour clock, being direct equivalents of English.

2b In pairs. Adapt the conversation from **2a**, using the details below.

Speaking. Students use the details given to ask for and to give train information. This activity, if carried out with these details but without the text book, practises both Standard Grade and Intermediate transactional language requirements.

3 Read the information about the Paris metro and answer the questions.

Reading (1–4). Students read for information and answer the questions in English. Remind them that they do not need to understand every word.

Answers

1 A booklet of 10 tickets. (1)
2 The number of the line, the colour and the direction you want to take. (3)
3 It's determined by the station at the end of the line (1)
4 No, it's simple. (1)

📝 What other cities have an underground system? Find out and write a short guide to one of them in French using the text in **3** as a model.

Students should have no difficulty finding other cities with an underground system: most major cities have one.

Further practice of the language and vocabulary of this spread is provided as follows:

À l'oral, page 177: Transaction 3

Cahier d'exercices, pages 75–76 (exs 5–6)

3 En panne

(Student's Book pages 172–173)

Main topics and objectives

● Discussing breakdowns and traffic problems

Key language

Je suis en panne.
J'ai un pneu crevé.
Pouvez-vous m'envoyer quelqu'un?
Je n'ai pas de roue de secours.
J'ai un problème avec la batterie/la roue/le volant/les freins/les phares.
Je suis sur la route nationale 10 à côté d'Auchan.
À mon avis …
Je pense qu'il y a …/il n'y a pas …/peu de …/trop de …/beaucoup de …/assez de …
embouteillages/pollution/transports en commun/ zones piétonnes/pistes cyclables/circulation

Grammar

Skills/Strategies

● Giving information
● Using a range of tenses
● Using ICT

Resources

À toi! A, page 198
Cassette D side 2
Cahier d'exercices, pages 76–77 (ex. 7)

Introduce the spread by brainstorming any car parts students may already know in French. There are not likely to be many! Then split your students into groups and get them to look up as many words for car parts as possible (particularly those which could cause problems) in five minutes. Collate the answers on an OHT.

1a Match the pictures to the phrases in the key language box.

Reading (a–j). Students match the pictures with the phrases in the key language box. They should now be able to complete this activity quickly and with confidence.

Answers

a J'ai un problème avec les phares.
b J'ai un problème avec la batterie.
c Je suis sur la route nationale 10 à côté d'Auchan.
d J'ai un problème avec les freins.
e Je n'ai pas de roue de secours.
f Je suis en panne.
g Pouvez-vous m'envoyer quelqu'un?
h J'ai un problème avec le volant.
i J'ai un problème avec la roue.
j J'ai un pneu crevé.

Tip box

Giving information. Ensure students are aware of this information before they listen to **1b**, and that they know that all makes of car are feminine (because of *la voiture*).

1b Listen. Copy and complete the grid.

Listening (1–3). Students now apply the information from the key language box to a spoken context in order to complete the grid.

Tapescript

1 – Âllo, oui, je suis tombée en panne sur la route nationale 150, au nord de Niort.
 – Quel est le problème?
 – J'ai un problème avec les freins. Pouvez-vous envoyer quelqu'un?
 – Oui. Vous avez quelle marque de voiture?
 – C'est une Renault Mégane bleu foncé.
 – Quelle est votre numéro d'immatriculation?
 – 66 87 WV 44.
 – C'est noté. Quelqu'un sera avec vous dans une heure environ.
2 – Âllo, oui, je suis tombé en panne sur la route nationale 10, à côté d'Auchan.
 – Quel est le problème?
 – J'ai un problème avec mes phares. Pouvez-vous m'aider?
 – Oui, monsieur. Vous avez quelle marque de voiture?
 – C'est une Ford Focus rouge.
 – Quelle est votre numéro d'immatriculation?
 – 41 13 RS 61.
 – C'est noté. Quelqu'un sera avec vous dans une demi-heure.
3 – Âllo, oui, je suis tombée en panne sur la route nationale 122.
 – Quel est le problème?
 – J'ai un problème avec la batterie. Pouvez-vous m'aider?
 – Oui, madame. Vous avez quelle marque de voiture?
 – C'est une Peugeot 205 grise.
 – Quelle est votre numéro d'immatriculation?
 – 72 43 PR 15.
 – C'est noté. Quelqu'un sera avec vous dans une heure et demie environ.

Answers

	road	problem	car make and colour	registration	time to wait?
1	N150	brakes	Renault Mégane dark blue	66 87 WV 44	1 hour
2	N10	headlights	Ford Focus red	41 13 RS 61	$\frac{1}{2}$ hour
3	N122	battery	Peugeot 205 grey	72 43 PR 15	$1\frac{1}{2}$ hours

1c Your car has broken down. Telephone the garage. Explain where you are and what the problem is.

Speaking. Students will need to prepare detailed notes for this activity, just as they would probably have to do in real life. They can work in pairs to prepare this. You could then ask students to read out what they have prepared to the rest of the class, who must note what the problem is.

Page 173 concentrates on traffic problems. Ask some questions to practise/introduce the key language, e.g. *Il y a beaucoup de circulation dans ta ville/ton village? Il y a des pistes cyclables? Il y a beaucoup de transports en commun?*, etc.

2a Read these postcards and make two lists: positive and negative statements.

Reading. Students read the cards and make two lists, demonstrating understanding not only of the French but also of the intent of phrases.

Answers

positive	negative
Mais il y a aussi de beaux parcs et pas mal de transports en commun pour se déplacer en mai c'est très calme et tranquille Le nord de l'Écosse est vraiment jolie, si pittoresque il n'y a pas beaucoup de circulation	avec beaucoup de circulation et de pollution En été il y a beaucoup de touristes et de voitures il n'y a pas de pistes cyclables

2b Think of your nearest big town. Are these statements true or false?

Reading (1–6). Students interact with the language by agreeing or disagreeing with the statements.

Tip box

Using tenses. This provides further tips on getting a range of tenses into writing. It cannot be stressed too often how important this is!

⟲ Write about 100 words on the traffic in your area, answering the questions below. Use the phrases in the key language box and the blue text in the postcards. Have your work checked and make on-screen corrections.

By now students should be used to the practice of drafting using ICT and making corrections, then learning a piece of accurate writing they have created themselves to give a talk. Brainstorm some ideas on the OHT/board first if they need more support.

2c Learn your corrected text to give a presentation to your group.

Speaking. Students could give an unillustrated talk to the group or could use the OHT or Powerpoint.

Further practice of the language and vocabulary of this spread is provided as follows:

À toi! A, page 198

Cahier d'exercices, pages 76–77 (ex. 7)

4 Trop de voitures?

MODULE 10 LE TRANSPORT

(Student's Book pages 174–175)

Main topics and objectives

- Talking about accidents

Key language

Hier/La semaine dernière/Lundi dernier/Hier soir
J'ai vu/eu un accident/Il y a eu un accident.
Il y avait du brouillard, etc.
La route était glissante. C'était très dangereux.
Je descendais/traversais la rue. Je roulais lentement.
Je faisais du shopping/J'attendais un copain …
  quand un camion/une voiture/une moto/un
  vélo/une trottinette est entré(e) en collision avec …
  un piéton/une autre voiture/un chien/une
  poussette/une moto/un lampadaire.
Le chauffeur était blessé.
Personne n'était blessé.

Grammar

- Present participles
- Perfect tense (revision)
- Imperfect tense (revision)

Resources

À l'oral page 177: Prepared talk
À toi! B, page199
Cassette D side 2
Cahier d'exercices, page 77 (exs 8–9)

Introduce the spread by discussing in English the causes of traffic accidents (poor weather, black ice, tiredness, alcohol, using mobiles while driving, impatience, speed, etc.) and then asking your students to look these up in French in the dictionary.

1a Read the text. Find the French for the following.

Reading (1–8). Students look in the text for the French equivalents of the given phrases. They may well have already found some of these words in the initial activity.

Answers

1 en plein centre-ville   **2** le trottoir **3** il y avait beaucoup de circulation   **4** l'heure d'affluence **5** à toute vitesse   **6** un embouteillage   **7** doubler la queue **8** grièvement blessés

1b Match the sentences to the pictures of accidents. Which is the picture of the accident in **1a**?

Reading (1–4). Students demonstrate gist comprehension by matching the pictures to the descriptions.

Answers

1 b   **2** a   **3** c   **4** d **b** is the picture of the accident in **1a**.

➕ Ask students to translate the sentences in **1b**.

Le détective

Present participle. Stress to students that this form can translate 'by hearing', 'while hearing', 'on hearing,' etc. but cannot translate the present tense form 'I am hearing' or the imperfect 'I was hearing'. Explain that potential mis-translations of this sort have meant that this structure has been left until very late in their course.

2 Listen. Copy and complete the grid in English.

Listening (1–5). Students listen and identify the correct details. Warn them not to panic if they do not understand everything. Some of the language they know, some they will know from previous contexts and some they may not understand. Point out the words in the box before they listen.

Tapescript

1 *Et sur la route il y a eu des problèmes près de Nogent sur Marne. À présent il y a un bouchon énorme sur l'autoroute A4 à cause d'un camion qui a été détourné. Ça risque de durer plusieurs heures.*

2 *Les travaux aux alentours de Paris ont été la cause de plusieurs incidents de violence aujourd'hui. Près de la porte de Bagnolet, un conducteur enragé a attaqué un chauffeur de bus. Le conducteur a été arrêté tout de suite.*

3 *Sur le pont de Normandie aujourd'hui une soudaine rafale de vent a causé un accident grave. Quatre personnes ont été blessées, dont deux grièvement.*

4 *Une inondation sur la N57 à Carny sur Moselle à 15 kilomètres de Metz a causé trois morts et des dizaines de blessés. L'autoroute sera fermée jusqu'à dimanche.*

5 *Une chute de neige a surpris les habitants d'Erckartswiller dans le parc régional des Vosges du nord. Les habitants en ont profité pour faire un peu de ski de fond.*

Answers

	problems	other details
1	big traffic jam	overturned lorry
2	roadworks	driver attacked a bus driver: the driver was arrested
3	strong gust of wind caused accident	4 people injured – 2 seriously
4	flood caused 3 deaths and 10s of injuries	motorway closed until Sunday
5	snowfall	people have been skiing

Before moving on to **3a**, introduce some further language for describing accidents (see boxes in **3b**) by describing an accident orally yourself. Write some of the key phrases on the OHT/board.

3a Read the French text. Then copy the summary and fill in the blanks.

Reading. Students demonstrate understanding by completing the summary.

Answers

1 cigarette	**2** mouth	**3** dropped	**4** burn	
5 collided	**6** slippery	**7/8** very dangerous		**9** traffic
10 injured	**11** seriously	**12** head	**13/14** left leg	
15/16 lost consciousness		**17** hospital	**18** fine	
19 certain	**20** smoke			

➕ Ask students to find specific phrases from the text which could help them describe an accident themselves, e.g. I was driving slowly, suddenly, another car collided with me.

Rappel

The imperfect tense. Revise the meanings and conjugation of the imperfect tense with students, particularly the meaning 'I was doing something when …'.

3b In pairs. Describe an accident and make notes to present your account to your group.

Speaking. Students will make their presentations more interesting if they use the connecting phrases from the tip box on page 173 and the (dis)agreement phrases from page 169.

3c Write a report of the accident, using the notes in **3b** to help you.

Writing. Students now consolidate their account in writing. Work out some possibilities with the whole class first and make sure they understand all the phrases.

Further practice of the language and vocabulary of this spread is provided as follows:

À l'oral, page 177: Prepared talk

À toi! B, page 199

Cahier d'exercices, page 77 (exs 8–9)

All the key vocabulary and structures from this module are listed on the **Mots** pages 178–179. These can be used for revision by covering up either the English or the French. Students can check here to see how much they remember from the module and use them to prepare for the assessments.

Assessment materials for Modules 9 and 10 and an end-of-course assessment are available in the separate Assessment Pack.

Further speaking and grammar practice on the whole module is provided on **Cahier d'exercices** pages 78–79.

Entraînez-vous: À l'oral

(Student's Book pages 176–177)

Speaking practice: Modules 9 & 10

These spreads give regular practice in the three types of speaking activity required for the internally assessed speaking elements of the Standard Grade and Intermediate courses: conversations, transactions and prepared talks.

The activities on the speaking pages are designed to allow students to build up their speaking skills while working with a partner independently of teacher support. They also include handy hints on how students can improve their speaking grades.

Page 176 provides speaking activities for Module 9: conversations on food and daily routine in the past tense, and a prepared talk on staying healthy.

Page 177 provides speaking activities for Module 10: a conversation on transport, transactions on asking the way and at the station, and a prepared talk on transport.

À toi! A & B

(Student's Book pages 198–199)

Self-access reading and writing at two levels

These pages are designed to give students extra practice in reading and structured writing. There are two differentiated pages relating to each chapter: A and B. Page A is at an easier level and page B more challenging. You may wish students to work on the page most appropriate to their level or work through both pages. You may feel it is useful to work with students on the activities, but it should be possible for most students to work on them independently. The most appropriate time to use each page is indicated within the relevant teaching notes.

À toi! A, page198
This page is best used after pages 172–173 of the Student's Book.

1a Read the text and answer the questions in English.
Answers

> 1 Strikes, floods, road blocks and custom problems. (4)
> 2 He is fed up with waiting and arriving at the port to find that boats or trains have been cancelled. (3)
> 3 To benefit from quick flights and reasonable prices. (2)

1b Find the French for the following phrases in the text.
Answers

> 1 désormais
> 2 j'en ai marre d'attendre
> 3 et il n'est pas seul
> 4 des centaines de voyageurs
> 5 rien d'autre qu'un rêve

2 Write a questionnaire on transport for your group. Make sure you revise how to ask questions correctly. You must find out at least the following things.

À toi! B, page 199
This page is best used after pages 174–175 of the Student's Book.

1a Match each newspaper article to the right picture.
Answers

1 b	2 a	3 e	4 f	5 c	6 d

1b Find the French for the following.
Answers

> 1 est à éviter   2 il y a un bouchon énorme
> 3 il y a eu un accident grave
> 4 un camion est entré en collision avec deux voitures
> 5 jour noir pour les automobilistes en France
> 6 les fermiers … ont arrêté la circulation
> 7 ils ne seront pas dégagés avant deux jours
> 8 la grève des douaniers
> 9 deux mille personnes ont dû attendre
> 10 avant de pouvoir regagner la Grande-Bretagne

2 You have read this advert in a newspaper. Write an article about the means of transport you prefer, using the questions on the right to help you.

Cahier d'exercices, page 74

1
Answers

a 2, 7, 6, 4, 5 **b** 2, 3, 4, 1 **c** 2, 1, 9, 8

2
Answers

Traversez le pont, descendez/marchez jusqu'aux feux.
Prenez la première rue à gauche. C'est au coin à gauche.

3
Answers

1, 3, 5

Cahier d'exercices, page 75

4
Answers

voyager – ferry – mal – l'avion – changer –
embouteillages – travaux – confortable – trottinette

5
Answers

a 7	**b** 1	**c** 9	**d** 8	**e** 1	**f** 2
g 6	**h** 3	**i** 4	**j** 5		

Cahier d'exercices, page 76

6
Answers

a ✗	b ✗	c ✗	d ✗	e ✓	f ✗
g ✓	h ✗	i ✓	j ✓		

Cahier d'exercices, page 77

7
Answers

phone call	problem	where
a	ran out of petrol	on (National) road no 5
b	breaks not working well	on (Departmental) road no 304
c	flat battery	on motorway between exits 5 & 6
d	breakdown – no lights	on main road 'Grand'route' after the hypermarket Carrefour
e	flat tyre	on the big square 'Grande Place'

8
Answers

a 2	**b** 10	**c** 5	**d** 1	**e** 8	**f** 7	**g** 3
h 4	**i** 6	**j** 9				

9 (writing task)

Cahier d'exercices, page 78

1
Answers

a J'y vais.	**b** J'y travaille.	**c** Pour y aller?
d J'y mange.	**e** J'y descends.	

2
Answers

- **a** quai = *From which platform does the train leave?*
- **b** circulation = *What traffic!*
- **c** train = *Which train are you taking?*
- **d** classe = *In which class is it?*
- **e** numéro = *What is the number of the platform?*
- **f** embouteillage = *What a traffic jam!*

3
Answers

Using *vous*:	Using *tu*:
Allez!	Va!
Prenez!	Prends!
Traversez!	Traverse!
Tournez!	Tourne!
Achetez!	Achète!

Cahier d'exercices, page 79